Thinking Difference

John D. Caputo, *series editor*

PERSPECTIVES IN
CONTINENTAL
PHILOSOPHY

JULIAN WOLFREYS

Thinking Difference
Critics in Conversation

FORDHAM UNIVERSITY PRESS
New York ■ 2004

Perspectives in Continental Philosophy Series, No. 35
ISSN 1089-3938

Library of Congress Cataloging-in-Publication Data

Thinking difference : critics in conversation / edited by Julian Wolfreys. — 1st ed.
    p. cm. — (Perspectives in continental philosophy, ISSN 1089-3938 ; no. 35)
    Includes bibliographical references and index.
    ISBN 0-8232-2307-8 (hardcover) — ISBN 0-8232-2308-6 (pbk.)
    1. Multicultural education. 2. Postmodernism and higher education. 3. Difference
(Philosophy) 4. College teachers—Interviews. I. Wolfreys, Julian, 1958– II. Series.
    LC1099.T44 2004
    370.117—dc22

                                                            2003024400

Printed in the United States of America
08 07 06 05 04   5 4 3 2 1
First edition

Contents

Acknowledgments

I would like to thank all the contributors for their willingness to be involved in the present project. I would also like to thank John Leavey, J. Hillis Miller, and Frederick Young for their thoughts and comments on the introduction.

All interviews appear here for the first time, with the exception of the Avital Ronell interview conducted by D. Diane Davis, which first appeared in the journal *JAC*. My thanks to Diane, to Lynn Worsham, editor of *JAC*, and to the journal for permission to reprint.

Preface

Thinking Difference: Critics in Conversation addresses the need to take difference seriously. Specifically, the present volume speaks of the work of difference in critical language—in the practice and theory of literary and cultural criticism in the immediate contexts of pedagogical and institutional experience. Difference has of course made possible all such experiences, all thinking in effect, even while, in the name of critical practice the motif of difference has come to function as a formidable figure for the work of reading in the rhetoric of critical language. There is then, it has to be said, a very real sense that while difference is the sign under which any distinction between theory and praxis collapses, it is this very same sign, which, while being the same and yet not the same, makes possible the thinking of such terms. If there is thinking, there—*there*—is difference. Indeed, the very title, *Thinking Difference*, says no more than what is already stated in *thinking*. Without difference, there is no thinking, no living, and, doubtless, no living on, no survival beyond mere existence as such. Nothing without difference.

While this "quasi-concept" has had variable fortunes since its earliest manifestations in critical discourse, and while it may be true that the very idea of difference now seems overworked or even exhausted from and in some quarters, it is the premise motivating these conversations — and the implicit conversations taking place between each discussion —

that, at a time in the humanities today when difference might appear normalized, as much a part of critical language and the work of teaching as, say, metaphor or identity, that this is precisely one moment in our conversations, in our teaching, when we need to reflect on what difference difference has made and what difference it continues to make. Hence the need, if not *to think* but, more actively, *for thinking;* and the idea of a certain thinking moreover in conversation, in dialogue, in debate, as that which difference makes possible concerning, in this specific, singular instance, the praxes of pedagogy in higher education. Such a necessity — and each of the conversations herein resonates with a double sense of both necessity and responsibility, of urgency and committed response — makes itself manifest in the present collection. *Thinking Difference* seeks to be open to thinking, to a thinking to come, and in its own modest fashion to open to thinking what it is we think we do when we teach, and what we no longer think about, as a result of institutional demands, at those places for example where radical praxis comes into conflict — and isn't this precisely everywhere, at every moment, when thinking comes up against business as usual? —with supposedly pragmatic concerns, requirements, demands, the signs of which are seen, known, and felt everywhere in the humanities, in what we call the humanities, today, and today, and today. Hence, in response to, and out of, this situation, *thinking difference,* the very chance of which has to be thought in each of these todays, as the promise-without-possibility (the promise of the impossible as that which arrives), tomorrow, and tomorrow, and tomorrow.

Thinking Difference was conceived just over three years ago, at a point in the humanities where there were the signs of both a domestication of theoretical reflection and, conversely, the smallest indications of a sea change. On the one hand, at the time the project first came to me, it had become commonplace to see so-called theory, so-called post-structuralism, as passé, as having no particular merit except as one more academic subject, while the "real work" was being done in the name of and in a supposed return to politics. On the other hand, it seemed from a small number of locations, from a very few voices, including a couple of the interlocutors in the present volume, that there was an effort to address in the immediately concrete conditions of teaching and the institution of higher education the problematic that "theory" both faced and was perceived as perpetuating. In a sense, of course, there was nothing new here, except that particular critics whose names were associated with the term "theory" had offered critiques from within so-called "theory" of the gleeful disparaging of theoretical discourse, which seemed all the more strange given the announcements that "theory" had had its day, that it was done, dead and buried. The sea change seemed particularly to focus, from within "theoretical" circles, on those aspects of critical endeavour usually associated with political criticism, history, and materiality.

Thus, my intention was to address, albeit indirectly, so many misperceptions, misreadings, non-readings and resistances to "theory" through the particular focus on the word and concept "difference," its operation within institutional practice and discourse, and, specifically, the possible relations between the very idea of difference and praxes and experiences of pedagogy, in order to suggest, for those who might be able to read this, that any attempted separation between *theoria* and *praxis* was artificially buoyed up by a will to misread "theory" as divorced from politics, divorced from practices. At the same time, and with the specific figure of "difference" in mind, the purpose behind the following collection of interviews was to bring back into sharp relief the very real significance of apprehending difference in all its complex manifestations and operations, rather than merely taking it as a somewhat nebulous term within those very discourses and critical schools that sought to dismiss so-called "theory."

With the exception of two critics who withdrew early on in the project, those who are gathered in conversation here are those who were first invited to take place. The critics who are here represented were invited because of a perception on the part of the editor that each had caused, repeatedly in their careers, telling, timely, cogent interventions, which in turn invited good readers to think differently, to escape habits of unthinking critical endeavour and intellectual knowingness. In short, each critic here has done much to change the way we think, the way we reflect, the ways in which—don't we wish—we read. All were invited to participate because their work was both "theoretical" and "practical" in the finest senses; they repeatedly demonstrated a care for patient acts of close reading, attentiveness to detail, rigorous faithfulness, and a commitment to the singularity and otherness of whatever subject was brought into focus.

The conversations were conducted in a number of ways. Several were conducted via e-mail, though even through this medium the format was never the same. In some cases, several questions were sent out ahead of any response. In others, question engendered response, which in turn engendered question—this potentially endless process was delimited by an agreement that only a particular number of questions could be asked. A couple of interviews took place on the telephone, and two others were conducted in person.

Introduction
"As If I Were Teaching, in Conversation"

JULIAN WOLFREYS

*with Derek Attridge, John Caputo, Mary Ann Caws, Jonathan Culler,
Werner Hamacher, Kevin Hart, Peggy Kamuf, John P. Leavey, Jr.,
J. Hillis Miller, Arkady Plotnitsky, Avital Ronell, Nicholas Royle, and
Gregory L. Ulmer*

> Every institution . . ., every relation to the institution, then calls for
> and, at any rate, implies in advance taking sides in this field . . .
> There is no neutral or natural place in teaching.
>
> —Jacques Derrida

To Begin, Being Illustrative of the Impossibility of Beginnings

No matter where one begins, one must first ascertain, as locally and
precisely as possible, just how that "where" is defined. One must also
acknowledge that any introduction, especially one to a collection of
interviews, never truly begins anything but is always a response to other
statements, to other positions. All the more so if one is seeking to talk
about and be faithful to the notion of difference, particularly difference
in the context of what might be called the "politics of pedagogy"—
and if one acknowledges, as do many of the interviewees in the present
volume, that violence has been done to difference by reducing it to
merely another concept, a theoretical tool within the machinery of teaching so-called theory. Without supposing we know what an interview is,
there is both a constant tension and an equally constant give and take
in any interview—and in that the very workings of difference.

All appearances to the contrary, difference cannot be controlled
and is what in fact makes any pedagogical encounter possible. There
is always difference at the beginning, something the very idea of an

interview brings to light. Difference makes possible the give and take of interlocutors, even if it — and, with it, the work of difference — is never recognized, or barely recognized, a feature not simply peculiar to interviews but also fundamental to any pedagogy.

Determining: The Problem

In taking difference seriously, on the one hand, and considering what takes place in the name of "an interview," on the other, should we attempt to define difference, as though it were a stable concept, as though there were no difference to difference? In so doing, should we be indifferent to difference and thus also to the differing, carefully considered responses that constitute the present volume? Should we then rush to "contain" the differences of the various contributors and the differences of which they speak? We don't believe so, for reasons we will go on to explore below. Somewhat hesitantly, we might say that "give and take," the figure by which the otherwise illegible trace of difference might be acknowledged, is one possibly appropriate provisional figure for what takes place in any introduction and why, moreover, if one is to be attentive or responsive to the effects of difference, one should hesitate before any act of definition. To reiterate what has already been stated, this "give and take" is also, it might be said, the figural embodiment of very idea of an interview, at least in principle, and perhaps also figures the principle of pedagogy, if there is any, which difference makes possible.

This introduction is wrecked therefore, even as it seeks to get under way. With respect and in response to the singularity and heterogeneity of the commentaries on which this introduction draws as being illustrative of the relation without relation of difference and pedagogy, it is not our intention to present a synthesis or summary of these and other remarks. Nor do we intend to gather together the strands that run through the various questions and responses concerning the motif of difference, as that is reflected on and articulated by the various interlocutors in their considerations of pedagogy, the university, and the humanities, from which issues this collection repeatedly gets under way, and around which the various interviews orient themselves, all the while without comfortable or comforting consensus. Such an effort to ravel up and thus "contain" — if this were even possible — the multiple differences that mark the commentaries in this volume would be neither justified nor helpful. Indeed, it would be inimical to what motivates these interviews. It would simply highlight a praxis of "containing" difference, often through appeals to difference, that pervades both the humanities and broader cultural practices, and which seeks to delimit and control the effects, particularly the political effects, of the differences among us.

What motivates both the questions and the ensuing internal polyphony of the present volume is "the difference that difference makes": what difference gives place to in the name of pedagogy, and what takes place in the name of difference within particular pedagogical and institutional situations. The differences of which being addressed here are not, at least not simply, those mimetological differences given focus within feminism, postcolonial studies, or queer theory, for example, however necessary such investigations are, and on which several of the contributors touch. The sense of difference that operates across the present collection—and which arguably comprehends, makes possible, and exceeds the local, narrowly political concept of difference—gives voice to recent (and not-so-recent) writings by Derrida and others on ethics, the university, the humanities, pedagogy, the event, advents and inventions, performativity, and what might be termed "strategic interruptions in the program." This particular sense of difference poses central questions about the idea of the institution and the praxes of teaching, reading, curricula, marginalization and hegemony, strategies of exception, and the links between technology, institutions, and whatever differences make possible and is staged in the name of "theory" and "literature." And because difference is what gets things going, there can be no introduction in the strict sense to the discussions of difference and pedagogy. What matters here is the divergent, subtle spectrum of resonant responses both to what is contained within and to what exceeds normative pedagogical practice to which a certain thinking of difference might be resistant. This, to use a somewhat awkward phrase, is "the different that difference makes": the possibility, albeit only the most minimal, of what Gil Anidjar terms a "rhetorical event" (but here we would have to open the question of what is meant by rhetoric, as Anidjar's text implies we must do, submitting that term to the most rigorous and radical investigation) in and by language effecting a destabilization of what are identified as "contexts, whether literary, historical, or cultural."[1]

The questions asked throughout *Thinking Difference*, even when they repeat themselves, whether word for word or otherwise, find themselves not themselves, but are ineradicably altered by appearing in different contexts, their emphases transformed despite themselves by the responses that arrive in their respective singular contexts. Thus, once again, there can be no true introduction to interviews, and no introduction to the idea of the interview,[2] because a motion is observed as being already under way. The movement between (the *inter-* of *interview*) opens to view both what takes place between and what determines the shifting locations of interlocution. Proleptic address or retrospective summary is therefore neither possible nor appropriate.

Interviews: "Not What One Expects"

What, then, takes place in an interview or, more pertinently perhaps, in the "name of an 'interview'"? Does an interview ever remain intact? What comes to be seen between one glance, one perspective, and another? Is not the interview, however conducted, simply an exercise in journalistic haste, having all the shimmering patina of informality as the excuse for abandoning rigor, on the one hand, while being the most formulaic and predictable, the most programmatic exercise, on the other? Are not assumptions about the nature of interviews guided by the belief that one will hear, finally, in a person's own words, what that person really thinks? We cannot pretend to answer these questions. Indeed, a direct approach to any question forgets the incommensurability of question and response. And of course, understanding this, one can always refuse the question, refuse the implied impatience of the interrogative mode, which all too often seeks to dismiss ahead of any face-to-face encounter the possibility of coming to articulate a "between" that is not simply an agreement or contract. Suspension opens other views and a concern with seeing differently, rather than merely seeing eye to eye. Moreover, every response — or nonresponse — plays with suspensive modalities and possibilities. There are any number of more or less necessary, exigent disturbances, suspensions, and thus irrevocable translation effects that derail the smooth running of the "interview," each marking a difference from every other displacement or differentiation, every difference of opinion or position. We gather around the suspension and in the suspension, which is also the "between" of the *inter*view; we gather around the interview in ruins, where response is an act of program interruption — response as nonresponse, a refusal of the question on its own terms.

On reflection, what these interviews share is perhaps their potential for exploring and engaging with the familiar and the unfamiliar at the same time. The motivating force that goes by the name of *différance* haunts any thinking, even as it makes thinking possible in the first place. Coming to terms with this force and the contrapuntal displacement it announces, the most fundamental structure or program of what is called an "interview" is dislocated from within itself; something strange and estranging can now take place. A destabilization of borders, frames, and boundaries is possible.

This should not be assumed, however. The genre and form of the "interview" (supposing for the moment that genre and form can be defined as though difference had not already ruined identities of genre or form) do not guarantee this, any more than do either the supposed challenges to "conventional" forms of writing supposedly presented by electronic, virtual, hyper- or teletechnological media or, indeed, merely conducting an exchange by e-mail, rather than conducting an interview face-to-face (which figure is of course caught in that of the *view*, suggestive not only of a sight or glimpse, but also deriving from the French verb *voir*). Moreover, to engage in discussions, conversations, dialogues, or interviews around the subjects of the university and the practice of pedagogy is doubly fraught from the outset. Posing questions and inviting discussion within the terms of the so-called institution of the university is, in a way, already a kind of neutralization. This is so, perhaps, because deviancy is tolerated and indeed given a theme park in academia. In the context of pedagogy and the university, there is a certain theatricality that reveals the inevitability of the program as "script" or text, on the one hand, but that also unveils its constitutive openness, on the other. Law, and revocation of the law.

Pedagogy and the Thinking of Difference

The various commentators in the present collection recognize the fraught, often embattled condition of teaching in the institution called the "university," especially as that institution enforces and maintains both a neutrality—which is also, in effect, a neutralization—and, therefore, a passivity (of which more in a moment). On the subject of ideological and ontological neutrality in the context of the university, Jacques Derrida has observed:

> By passing off as natural (*and therefore beyond question and transformation*) the structures of a pedagogical institution, its forms, norms, visible or invisible constraints, settings, the entire apparatus . . . one carefully conceals the forces and interests that without the slightest neutrality, dominate and master—impose themselves upon—the process of teaching from within a heterogeneous and divided agonistic field wracked with constant struggle.[3]

Doubtless, such a commentary is an *inter*view: Derrida offers an unflinchingly clear view from within and amid the place of pedagogy and what takes place in the name of "pedagogy." Such naturalization qua neutralization, occluded by the staged projection of neutrality, is inevitable because a university and, by extension, any institution "is always the construction of a philosophy."[4] It is through "what difference difference makes," to paraphrase one of the questions asked, that the present interviews address the construction of institutions and the philosophies by which they are instituted, as well as the relationship between the inevitable and endless capacity of institutions in general to "calm down difference," and the recalcitrance of difference to any calming down. Asking the question of how institutions are instituted, of the institution of institutions, is always a way of bringing out difference (and even violence, *différance* being, after all, a "war economy," as Derrida reminds us in *Dissemination*)[5] as the raison d'être of the very institutions that are dedicated to gathering in and calming that violence. What is peculiar about this kind of social system is that people at once need difference and despise it for being from somewhere else. This is a practical, everyday pedagogical situation.

It has to be said, however, that institutions are motivated by forgetting the violence that made them possible and by maintaining a degree of passivity through forgetting. In this regard, we must avoid the twin dangers of simply accepting and promoting that breakdown of remembrance, on the one hand, and of assuming that some pure disclosure of the founding violence could be either possible or desirable, on the other. The real question concerns how institutions negotiate the trace of their originary violence of difference in themselves, how they protect themselves from themselves by a sort of preemptive inoculation with that violence. The concern with such instituting violence has been questioned and challenged in much recent work by Derrida on the difference between the university without ground or condition and the university on the ground.[6] The question is as urgent as it is inescapable for, as Derrida reminds us, "if this unconditionality, in principle and de jure, constitutes the invincible force of the university, it has never been in effect."[7] And it is for this reason that Derrida names "thought" as "that which at times commands, according to a law above all laws, the *justice* of . . . resistance or . . . dissidence"[8] within and against the institutional gestures of the university in general, and the humanities in particular.

Thus it comes down to recognizing the effects of the work of difference, on the one hand, and the dangers of thinking that difference can be merely a matter of agreement, on the other. Here are the signs of the passive reception of difference as simply another keyword, another trope put to work on the pedagogical stage. Yet the "thinking of difference" does not get mobilized on or within the pedagogic scene: it *is* that scene or stage, that is, the more or less theatricalized space where difference — or perhaps more accurately, *différance* — puts in play all the differences to which we must attend in thinking. At least, if — a big *if* — this "pedagogical scene" is a space of thinking at all, then it must be, undertake, allow, call forth, and incite a "thinking of difference." Passivity of the sort that the motif of "agreement" can involve relies on the suppression and containment of difference as being in some fashion ontologically determinable, definable, and available for service as though it were just another figure, like a metaphor or zeugma. However, the passive agreement around difference indicates precisely the place where one should be the most wary, where thinking or thought might be said to come to a halt because the very notion of difference is identified in an instrumental or formalist fashion. In this sense, difference is perhaps the exemplary nonfigure for what happens, broadly speaking, in the ontological act of naming, when the name is employed to stand in the place of thinking. Judging from pedagogy and what takes place when thinking employs the name synecdochally, we should be extremely leery of the idea that we can overcome the moment of what used to be called "theory" or what might be called "deconstruction," in a propaedeutic manner, as a mere preparation for something more real and important. If, for argument's sake, "theory" is assumed to be the genus of which "difference," "deconstruction," and indeed any other such misnamed concept are the species, then the name clearly assigns a limit: to knowledge, to identity, and to the practice of teaching such apparently discernible forms as though one were on the way to a more "useful" or "practical" application.

One of the ways this manifests itself in the institution of higher education, particularly in the humanities, is in the tendency to think that the thought of difference, engaged throughout this collection, has now been absorbed and understood somehow, or that difference is just this concept, to be summarized, contained, and applied like an ointment on the troubled textual place until the difference disappears. It is sometimes assumed that we can simply go back to the academic business as usual, whether in the guise of politicism or historicism. A tireless emphasis on reading, on the other hand, might suggest the possibility of interruption or disruption of the propaedeutic program. The question of the readability of texts (in the broadest sense), which emerges as an issue only along with their more or less radical unreadability (we read because we do not know how to read: if we knew how to read, the issue would disappear into a sort of repeatable technical competence and assurance that would simply be transmitted and would involve no real teaching) seems a pedagogically indispensable way of remaining alert to difference. Raising the apparently simple issue of reading is an excellent way of holding open the question of difference, and indeed of "thinking difference" (or, to put this another way, "thinking at all"), and that it can concentrate all the motifs that Derrida has been developing in recent years about the "to come," the *arrivant,* a messianicity without messianism, and so on. There is a degree of an almost abstemious or Spartan discipline here: pedagogy involves spending much time to clear a space in which an experience of reading has a chance (albeit never more than the merest chance) of happening. From a pedagogical perspective, the difficulty is always in combining quite traditional, classical concerns (the transmission and preservation of particular knowledge, skills, and strategies of writing and reading, understanding of grammar, rhetoric and the so-called canonical texts) with the responsibility to teach what precedes, exceeds or interrupts all such concerns. This means not only that one must go through a considerable degree of scholarship, but also that one must engage in processes that may look like impudence or disrespect, with a whole range of modalities from anger to hilarity, around institutions that are always somewhere resistant to that experience, but without which they would have no chance. Different strategies can be developed to render the programmatic dimension or intention porous, permeable, and open to what it can neither anticipate nor integrate. And one can always make hyperbolic attempts, as has Avital Ronell, to secure the space of academe as a sheltering place of unconditional hospitality for dissidence and insurrection, refutation and undomesticatable explosions of thought.

In Conclusion, the Beginning

Thus, if any beginning, and specifically the beginning of learning, is troubled, this is because it always starts with a nothingness, a nothingness that is not nothing but a certain figuration of the give and take or the "between," and what might take place in this undefinable space as a result of the work of difference. Out of this "between," the question that presents itself repeatedly is the matter of address: addressing difference, the difference of address. It is a question of locating the address, in this specific context, of teaching. Whom are we addressing with teaching? What are we addressing? To whom do these interviewees believe they are speaking? These questions are also invaluable to any thinking of the interview. As Elizabeth Weber remarks, "this thinking of writing, address, and destination is also an experience of the interview, that is, of the plurality of voices."[9] To remark or respond to a plurality of voices as a provisional definition of the interview is not simply to acknowledge that there is more than one interlocutor. It is also to recognize the plurality of voices irreducible to any one tone that come to shape the contours of question, response, nonresponse, avoidance, and detour. And perhaps *plurality* is not the most appropriate word, for it seems to tremble with the suggestion of consensus or community, or with a certain finitude of voices, however many. Perhaps we should say instead "the *différance* of voices," recognizing *différance* as the gift that gives us to think, with affirmation and of resistance to any institutional norm.

Nicholas Royle
The Beginning Is Haunted: Teaching and the Uncanny

JW: Hallo? . . .

NR: Hallo . . . The beginning is haunted. That is Foucault's point when he interrupts the silence to begin his remarkable lecture "'The Order of Discourse." I wonder if it would be possible to start off with a summary of your conception of this book?

JW: Yes. Very roughly, the book has to do with difference and pedagogy, specifically the way in which the idea of difference is employed in the teaching of theory, to the extent that difference is recognized as just another concept or conceptual framework within the teaching of theory, rather than what actually mobilizes "the pedagogical scene," something Peggy Kamuf addresses (interview 3). So I have been wondering about the way in which difference is put to work in the institution of education, but also the ways in which the institution resists that, and the ways in which the institution can and does domesticate certain theoretical interests, in the name of "getting on with business"; and, to what extent those questions then become ones not of reading or thinking, but of operating a program. Those are the kinds of issues this collection aims to explore in various ways and to relate to matters pertinent to the various interviewees.

Derek Attridge (interview 2) has, for example, explored the question of alterity in terms of his own teaching experience; J. Hillis Miller (interview 12) has talked about the question of difference in relation to various areas of the discipline of literary studies, talking in part about the rise of American studies and placing English literature as very much a colonial literature in the North American university. So, while I have wanted initially to open up this issue of what is at stake for pedagogy in understanding difference, other related matters have arisen through the interviews, which take the focus away from a purely programmatic, instrumentalizing activity which takes place in the university, in order to consider this from the perspective of difference.

NR: Thank you. I'm curious, I suppose, about the ways in which the terms "institution" and "the university" are working within the framework of your questions. One of the tensions in Derrida's work in this respect has to do with the difference, disjunction or discrepancy between what he has recently evoked as the "university without condition,"[1] and the everyday reality of the contemporary university, at least in Britain. It's a question of the difference between the university without ground and the university on the ground. I subscribe without reservation to Derrida's affirmation of a "university without condition," but if one looks around, certainly in Britain, what is actually going on? At least in Britain, universities are in a terrible state. Derrida himself admits that "the image of the university [he has] cannot be embodied anywhere."[2] Perhaps paradoxically, one way of trying to countersign his affirmation might have to do with the sense that the university is in ruins. We might then try to take to heart the force of Bill Readings's book *The University in Ruins.* In this respect, I suspect that the deployment of the terms "university" or "institution," as you were just using them, functions as part of a sort of discursive regime of hallucination that serves to keep questions of reading or of what Readings calls "Thought" (with an ironic capital *T*) within an intra-institutional context. I worry about the extent to which posing questions and inviting discussion within the terms of the so-called institution or the university is, in a way, already a kind of neutralization. This is perhaps especially true in the context of the United States where, it seems to me, the "world" of universities is already more hermetic and sealed off than in Britain. In his lecture "The Future of the Profession; or, The Unconditional University," Derrida stresses the need for a "force of resistance" or of "dissidence," given the extent to which teaching and research are "directly or indirectly controlled, let us say euphemistically 'sponsored,' by commercial and industrial interests."[3] One strategy of resistance or dissidence might consist in trying to think along the polemical lines of Readings's work. What happens if we suppose that the university is, indeed, not simply in ruins but *no longer exists?* This fiction or fantasy might at least enable us to explore the potential for kinds of thinking and intellectual projects which exceed the university, which dissent or sit elsewhere. In other words, it would be a question of thinking about different kinds of address and addressee. This is one of the things I very much like about Peggy Kamuf's recent work on reading, that is to say, on reading as what goes beyond the space and discourse of the university.

JW: Can I push you to say something more about this space of reading and how you envision that?

NR: Perhaps I could try to get at this by way of the question of writing. The sort of writing pursued by those working in the humanities in British universities over the past decade or so has been massively determined by what is known as the "research assessment exercise" (RAE). Literary adjectives such as *Orwellian* or *Kafkaesque* could not do justice to the insidiousness of the RAE. While supposedly denying any coercive or manipulative role in generating, focusing, and programming research in the humanities, the RAE has given rise to a very bizarre culture of monitoring and self-monitoring. The RAE is a "repeat" exercise, happening every few years, like a medical checkup in which the condition of the patient is at once described and interfered with. On the basis of its "findings," the RAE panel of judges then gives each university department a mark out of five, grading on the basis of the supposed "national excellence" and "international excellence" of its research. Funding is then dependent on these scores. The panel thus defines and administers sickness or health (i.e. withholds or injects money). One of the obvious effects of the RAE has been a valorization and privileging of the academic monograph. A university department's "excellence in research" (Bill Readings is especially sharp on the nihilistic emptiness of this phrase) is based primarily on its production of monographs, as distinct from textbooks. This is something to which publishers in Britain have had to gear themselves. The RAE has transformed the nature and the job of publishing in Britain, so that for example (at the end of 2000, in the period just before the end of the latest "exercise") academic presses were having to take on extra staff to deal with the production of monographs, in order to meet the RAE deadline. The monograph, in this scenario, appears to be king or queen. But this is quite a laughable tyranny. The monograph is in fact being sustained on some rather peculiar life-support system, kept artificially alive — in no small part thanks to the RAE itself. As you know, what most interests publishers themselves is the production of textbooks. The RAE is effectively structured by a refusal or inability to acknowledge any difficulties with the concepts of monograph and textbook, in particular with distinctions between the two. More generally, the RAE (and what is quite risibly named "RAE culture") has sought to disavow any crisis in the concept of the book at all—I mean "the book" as what is "profoundly alien to the sense of writing," in Derrida's phrase.[4] What we should perhaps be trying to do is think about kinds of writing that break with the machinery of RAE logic, that part company with the RAE conveyor belt altogether. I hope you will forgive all this talk of hospital beds and conveyor belts: one needs a kind of mad vocabulary to respond to the madness of the RAE. What interests me, I suppose, is a sort of dissident concern to produce kinds of writing that are not simply for university consumption, if that was ever desirable or possible, and that wouldn't either be simply trying to return to some nostalgic form of the "general reader" but that open themselves up to a new conception of the "reading public." I recall coming across the figure somewhere, not too long ago, that for every thirty-seven people who do a Ph.D. in English in Britain, one gets an academic job. Within the university, within the discourse of the university, it's that one person who gets talked about, a sort of tragic but lucky statistical sprat. But what interests me is the question of the other thirty-six. Thinking about those other thirty-six means thinking about a much more highly educated, far more skeptical, gifted and articulate reading public than the one that is assumed or addressed by the everyday media. So I'm interested in a future of writing or writings that is not limited to the university and that is in some ways trying to reckon with the possibilities of a new public or indeed perhaps a "new international"; kinds of writing which will engage with those possibilities of different kinds of address, different kinds of reading that aren't academic anymore than they would be nonacademic.

JW: I think that raises a number of issues. The situation is a little different in the United States, though, perhaps surprisingly, not that much. Where the cultural difference lies perhaps, aside from the obvious absence of any nationwide quality assessment program, is in the unreadiness of the North American university as a whole, if I can put it like that, to see the demise of the monograph while not knowing what might replace it, where writing might be directed, except in the case of the work of a few people such as Peggy Kamuf; in fact, the topic of the demise of the monograph was raised at the MLA [Modern

Language Association] with a sense of horror, as though clearly business as usual were not going to continue, but without a sense of knowing where to turn. It appears that the place where monographs have been traditionally produced for a supposedly academic audience and by academic producers seems to have been unprepared for what Derrida calls the "mercenary arts," so the humanities have been ill prepared for turning their work toward the needs of a marketplace, in particular in ways that are dictated beyond their control. As to the situation of the 1-in-37, I suspect, though I don't have numbers for this, that a large number of people with Ph.D.s go into two-year institutions, into institutions with far greater teaching loads, institutions that are designated as teaching rather than research institutions, with heavier teaching loads, greater class sizes. They, in a way, occupy often very invisible spaces, and they are invisible because they're not afforded, by the nature of their work, the space or time for research or a more general space of reading and writing, which in turn seems to have become in the North American context something which has to take place on a very pragmatic level, as a way of moving those people within a purely market-driven educational form. The publisher in all of this, in between the RAE and an academic authorship, seems somehow to be caught in the face of a decline in the vitality of a market, however that might be perceived—so there's very much a sense of a system on life support, to use your metaphor, which barely maintains life, and the machinery of that support system is as troubled as the monograph itself. But, I wonder, given this highly educated readership, and given the difficulties in which specialized publishing appears to find itself as a result of market forces perhaps, do you see various forms of teletechnology occupying a greater role or taking on a greater, ever more spectral function? There are of course examples of electronic, online journals, and I wonder about these, as practical examples of spaces for forms of publication that might be, though not necessarily, places where different manifestations of reading and writing could take place.

NR: We are talking here and now on the telephone, after all. You are in the town of Gainesville, Florida, I believe, and I am in the hamlet of Widworthy, in Devon. (But of course this is also a fake telephone call, or at least a "revised" call, modified and supplemented after the event, in other words it's an undecidably artifactual or artifictional teleinterview.) I remember the last time I was in Florida, in 1995, I participated in a MOO [MUD (multiple user dialogue) object oriented], a "virtual conference" based partly in Florida but also elsewhere in the

United States and in Europe, and these were the issues being talked about then. They are obviously transforming what we do and what happens to what we do. I confess I found this MOO for the most part quite disagreeable. I was in a room at the University of South Florida, Tampa, along with twenty or more other people, clattering away at their keyboards for what seemed like, well, if not eternity, at least far too long. I have never felt comfortable in a large social group of any kind. I suppose it's one of the things about which I feel (paradoxically of course) a strong rapport with Derrida. Like him, I want to say: "Don't count me in, I don't belong." I think what most disturbed me about this MOO was a quite banal sense of the proliferation of words. It's a question of how to deal with the proliferation of text that is characteristic of "academic activity," at least in North America and Britain. (This, alas, has to do with the administration of universities as well as with the research produced by their staff, and of course it is nurtured, in Britain, by the very mechanism that one might have hoped would constrain it, viz., the RAE, once again.) I am very drawn to the notion of rarefaction. I throw this word in with an ironic ear for the resonances that Foucault brings to the term when he speaks of the "rarefaction of discourse" in "The Order of Discourse."[5] What if the RAE were to reward scholars for writing less, not more? What might one write if one were limited, say, to just a thousand words a year? Word processing, e-mail, and so forth have massively increased the ease and seductiveness of producing and proliferating text. This is something that occurs, I believe, at the level of the sentence. Teletechnology has encouraged sentential distension. I'm not pretending for a moment that I'm not guilty of participating in this myself. But I'm very attracted to the idea of writing less. I think people (and I guess I mean some people rather than others) should write less. Rarefaction will have been the law. I'm struck, in this context, by the contrast between the "rise of theory" and the later writings of Samuel Beckett. In the same period one finds an immense expansion of texts ("theory") and an extraordinary dwindling (Beckett). Suppose every critic or theorist writing in the past thirty or forty years had sought to keep pace, so to speak, with Beckett? This is something else that I think is very important here, in the context of what goes by the name of "theory" (of which there is, allegedly, always "too much"). I am thinking of the question of English as such. The growth of "theory" over the last twenty or so years has involved an immense, fascinating kind of translation effect (a sort of vast anamorphosis, if you will), whereby arguments, concepts, terms and so forth have come across primarily from

French into what is so questionably termed "Anglo-American English," and this is something that has had a very significant impact on the nature of the prose, on the nature of the kind of writing that has been produced. It seems to me that in some way this has worked to the detriment of an attentiveness to, so to speak, English itself or to the resources of English as a language in which to forge new concepts, new kinds of writing and thinking. So, I suppose there's a double focus here: I am preoccupied with the possibilities of rarefaction, with the desire (however perverse) to write less; and, at the same time, I am passionately interested in English, in the possibilities of an English that the Francophone character of "theory" has perhaps tended to elide or efface.

JW: One thing that struck me in what you were saying were two different and opposing forces, which I'd ask you to talk about. A critic who holds a particular fascination for me is Roland Barthes, who seems, in a certain way, to work very efficiently by writing less on a number of occasions, and writing less and less as he moved on, in ways which seemed very clearly not "overly complicated," so that there seem to be the effects of a different writing, a different reading also, taking place, which, because of length seems to attempt to do a number of different things. Also, in terms of this "Anglo-Americanization" or "*mondialisation*" as the destruction of an English idiom, do you think the act of writing is less also an act of affirmation and resistance?

NR: I tried to write something about this recently ["Night Writing: Deconstruction Reading Politics"], specifically about writing in English in relation to Derrida. In an essay on James Joyce ["Two Words for Joyce"], Derrida talks about the need to write "against English." In more recent work such as *The Other Heading* and *Monolingualism of the Other* as well, it is clear that his writing is at war with English. In *The Other Heading,* for instance, he talks with obvious dislike about the "dubbing" of all language into Anglo-American. I am entirely in accord with Derrida in this context but of course, like you, I can't participate in this war in the same way. For me, participation is in a sort of civil war, a war *of* the civil, within and against the civil. All of this may seem quite "underground," precarious, perhaps scarcely perceptible. It may come down only to a spectrality, to the spectrality of my feeling that what I write is not Anglo-American. My desire, in any case, is to produce kinds of text that as far as possible make themselves nonassimilable in relation to what you refer to as "*mondialisation*" or "globalatinization"—nonassimilable but of course *already within.* This is the logic of the crypt, of what I have elsewhere called "cryptaesthetic resistance" [in *Telepathy and Literature: Essays on the Reading Mind*].

JW: Certainly. I think in that process of writing there seems to be a turn back to a question of reading — doesn't there? — and a certain uncontrollable reception of what one writes, how one writes, and perhaps this directs us toward this readership you identified earlier. Would that be the case?

NR: One has to wage war, at least in Britain, but, as I was saying, this is never simply confinable to Britain. It's a global war, but one has to wage war against the most profound kinds of anti-intellectualism and indifference, a strangely disabled and disabling culture in which "reading" is equated with the forty-five words listed by the British government as constituting the basis of "literacy" (and, it doubtless follows, "citizenship"). I'm not joking. There are these forty-five officially designated words that all children must learn to read, write, and spell by the end of their first year at school: *a, the, and, of, me, my, he, she, we, you, they, it, dad, mum, at, to, on, in, up, for, am, come, go, look, see, like, went, going, play, went, get, is, was, are, can, big, said, cat, dog, yes, no, away, all, this, day.* What, I wonder, would Dickens have made of this? The rote learning of these forty-five words practically defines the lives of all four- or five-year-old children in Britain in public education. (Of course, as always, there is, at least potentially, more imaginative flexibility within the so-called private sector.) The machinery and programming of "reading" begins very early. Personally, I doubt if children should even be at school before the age of seven (which is the situation of course in various other European countries where, perhaps not by chance, so-called literacy efficiency is much higher). What is reading? What is already presupposed about the nature and concept of reading at primary school level? One has to wage war here, I believe, in the most careful, if possible good-humored, ironic and "civil" fashion. One has to keep in mind not only those other thirty-six doctoral students, in other words, but a much broader, indeed unbounded context. The question of reading is a question of war at every level: *différance* is a war economy, as Derrida long ago pointed out.[6] It involves secondary schools, people who don't go into tertiary education at all and who are absolutely crucial to the question of the addressee and the uncertainty of the addressee. So I didn't want to mislead in suggesting that I was thinking only of this "privileged" group of thirty-six. In the context of thinking about education, this is one of the things I especially like about Bill Readings's *The University in Ruins*, namely, its attention to the notion of the student as someone who does not exist: the student is to come. This is complicated, I know, but I think there is an important relation between this notion of reckoning with the "to come," with the incalculable and unprogrammable, and what might be called a "rarefaction of readers." I am thinking here, for instance, of the idea discussed by Derrida in "Biodegradables," that Kafka only has ten readers—but "what readers!"[7] There is a tension or torsion here which obviously applies in the context of Derrida's own writing. The number of readers that a text has might be very small indeed. There is this strange logic according to which something read aright or read well, read "responsibly" by a very small number of readers, can have very powerful effects, as it were, out of all proportion to this small number.

JW: I think that's right. This becomes particularly focused in specific ways. Thinking through the process of writing, considering also the small number of readers who seek to read "responsibly," there seems to me a point at which reading, in the context of the graduate seminar, what transpires on the part of some is a nervousness with regard to the act of reading in relation to the professionalization imposed on them: they want to stop reading and have a program imposed on them that gives them some form of utilitarian tool box with which they can work. Out of the sense of nervousness, or perhaps as a response to the uncanniness that reading can so often engender, they want to call a halt to reading so as to get on with a pedagogical process having little or nothing to do with reading as you or Geoffrey Bennington or Peggy Kamuf have talked about in various ways concerning reading as an open process toward a future, a "to come," as it were, not as a definable horizon but as an event of unexpected response in the powerful or "responsible" reading. I wonder if you have any thoughts on this pedagogical experience.

NR: Yes, the fear of reading is as old as reading, no doubt. As you say, the program can be reassuring: the M.A. or Ph.D. "package" becomes a kind of sedative. From a pedagogical perspective, the difficulty as always is in combining quite traditional, classical concerns (the transmission and preservation of particular knowledge, skills, and strategies of writing and reading, understanding of grammar, rhetoric, and the so-called canonical texts) with the responsibility to teach what precedes, exceeds, or interrupts all such concerns. The latter, which is precisely not reducible to the program or to the vocabulary of "learning outcomes" and so on, can doubtless be fearful, even terrifying, but it can also be the space of the greatest pleasure and even the greatest responsibility—a sort of responsible "joy of reading." No doubt, as Derrida has observed, the very identity and future of the university is at stake in every seminar or lecture: the university remains to be invented, reinvented every day. But I think it is part of the double responsibility I just mentioned that we need to consider also how this is also the case at secondary school level, as well as *outside* educational institutions of all sorts. Education at every level has to be reinvented every day, and so does the space occupied by what used to be called "the general reader." You mention "uncanniness": I think this is potentially very productive in a pedagogical context. The uncanny is a way of engaging with the familiar and the unfamiliar *at the same time.* The question of the uncanny is, for me, perhaps above all the question of literature; but it also immediately immerses us in other issues—psychoanalysis, philosophy, politics and religion. While working on "The Uncanny: An Introduction," it became increasingly clear to me how pervasive this notion of the uncanny has been in so-called contemporary thought. It's not just in Nietzsche, Heidegger, or Freud, but everywhere—in Derrida, Wittgenstein, Lacan, Kristeva, Cixous, Cavell, Zizek, and so on. Martin Jay has called it the "master trope" of contemporary thought;[8] but what is mastery and what is trope in the context or wake of the uncanny? Teaching with or through the notion of the uncanny can open up ways of thinking about radical strangeness without simply giving into terrorism. It is a way of resisting the "professionalization" you refer to and showing how it is always susceptible to the uncanny. The uncanny is, I think, essentially about the strangeness and destabilization of borders, frames and boundaries—which means that in some respects it is an especially powerful concept for questioning and keeping open the distinctions between what lies within and outside the institution or profession. The beginning is haunted, you recall.

2

Derek Attridge
Encountering the Other in the Classroom

JW: One aspect of "coming to terms with difference," if I can put it that way, can be read in the necessarily patient working through of the question of the other. This has to do with the recognition of the other, with one's relation to the other and one's responsibility *for* the other. Following on from this, as you suggest, there is acknowledged here the question of ethical obligation before any philosophical account. The phrase "human other" which you employ in the article in question is significant inasmuch as it resists reducing every other to a generalized manifestation of otherness, which occurs perhaps too often in "theoretical" discussions of "the other," "alterity," and, of course, "difference."

In attending to the "impossible demands" that you address, and recognizing the contested condition of such responsibility, how might it be possible to consider such questions in relation to the situation of pedagogy, where we encounter the "human other" constantly, and yet are placed, as teachers, within events, structures and institutions which implicitly rely on a mode of procedure antagonistic or even inimical to our sense of personal responsibility for difference and "the other"?

DA: First, a word or two about the adjective *human* since you are laying some stress on my use of it. It's a difficult word to handle, at least in some philosophical circles, because it conjures up a discourse of humanism that for many has been discredited, and because it implicitly excludes a range of nonhuman entities. The most obvious exclusion when one talks about the "human other" is the "animal other," a topic that is receiving quite a bit of attention at the moment; but the real problem is that *any* kind of limitation on otherness, or any talk of "degrees of otherness," demolishes in advance the notion of alterity — turns it, in fact, into difference (and I want to come back to your use of the two terms as if they were interchangeable). In the article you allude to, after putting forward the argument that alterity is experienced in various kinds of textual, artistic, philosophical, or scientific inventiveness, I spoke of the "human other" in order to move the discussion to what are usually regarded as ethical matters, where I believe inventiveness is crucial also. But "the other" can only be experienced as human, animal, textual, conceptual, or whatever, *as it enters into consciousness,* that is to say, in the process of *ceasing* to be other. This process is at the same time a process of change in the self under the impact of the encounter with the other; our own frameworks of understanding are reconfigured, and the other impinges upon the same. There is no way to exclude any possibility beforehand: this would be to impose a category (such as the "human") upon the other, and to set limits on the possibilities for change.

How do we encounter the other at all, you may ask, if it is wholly outside those frameworks? We do so in the gaps, tensions, and failures in the frameworks, which arise because of the exclusions on which they depend for their existence. One way of thinking of our responsibility to the other is both as sensitivity to those exclusions (and the traces they leave on our modes of understanding) and as openness to change, for it is only through such sensitivity and such openness that the other can be apprehended or, to put it better, welcomed. And in the process of change by means of which otherness is welcomed, responsibility *to* becomes responsibility *for:* although we cannot leave the other in its absolute otherness, we can sustain and cherish it. Otherness is registered in the alterations brought about by its accommodation, and those alterations don't simply produce a new mental or cultural landscape at a stroke; in a responsible response they remain active, producing further and wider change. If otherness becomes only *difference,* however, it becomes a settled part of some more general structure (premised on certain exclusions), and whatever changes it effects will continue to operate within that structure and will continue to produce the same exclusions.

I see *otherness,* in the sense in which I am using it, as inseparable from *singularity;* and this, as you say, is why I prefer the phrase "the other" to "otherness" or "alterity," though it is often hard to avoid the more general terms. What makes it impossible for the subject to grasp the other without changing in the process is the other's singularity, its resistance to the general conceptual frameworks by which we make sense of the world. This also means that "the other" is always other *to:* its otherness is not an absolute or transcendent property, but is experienced in relation to a here and now. (It's at this point that I depart most markedly from the philosopher who is the source of much of the current interest in questions of alterity, Emmanuel Levinas— who, as a religious thinker, was perfectly happy with the notion of a transcendent other.)

Your specific question about the pedagogic context implies a more general question: does this way of thinking about alterity translate into any kind of prescription or program? If the question is understood to be about the production of practical moral codes laying down appropriate behavior in given situations, the answer has to be no, since openness to the other entails a constant readiness to jettison codes. This would certainly include the codes and other institutional formalizations, which, as you say, are inimical to the kind of responsibility I am talking about. However, moral codes and programs have their place, not as absolutes, but as pragmatic guides, always subject to testing and recasting—and one way, perhaps the most important way, in which such testing and recasting happens is through encounters with the other. One has to acknowledge, too, that the other is not necessarily "good," that the changes brought about by welcoming the other may not be of the kind of which you or I, or the institutions which govern moral behavior, would approve. It's a risky business, and our moral norms provide what Derrida might call an essential guardrail.

As a teacher, I do, of course, operate on a set of principles that I believe to be appropriate in the pedagogic context, and which I would wish to be observed more generally, but it is not a set of principles that I have deduced in some mechanical fashion from a prior understanding of my responsibility to and for the other. Were I to make an attempt to spell these principles out to you, they would sound all too familiar since they were imbibed from the best of my own teachers and stem from widely influential moral and pedagogic traditions. They involve, inevitably, constant compromises: there is never enough time or energy, and there are never enough material resources, for education to happen as one would want it to. When, however, it does happen, in a stronger sense than the imparting of knowledge and skills (not that this aspect of teaching should in any way be devalued), I believe it happens as an inventive act or event (it is both) in which the student (and sometimes the teacher) experiences the other—in the manner I have described above. There can be no pedagogic method, no transferable skill, that can guarantee the occurrence of such events, so any program of teacher training must, in addition to the important task of providing such methods and skills, encourage and leave a space for the encounter with otherness, the taking of risks, which will often mean the flouting of the institutions' rules and procedures. Derrida says that when a decision that really is a decision (as opposed to a calculated action) occurs, if it ever does, it is not the subject who decides but the other, the other in (though it's hard to talk of inside and outside at this point) the subject. I would add that when teaching takes place that is more than the inculcation of knowledge and skills, or charismatic entertainment, it is the other who teaches.

JW: You speak of wanting to return to the use of difference and alterity in reply to the first question as though they were interchangeable, so let's turn to this. There is a sense in which these terms are currently assumed to be interchangeable in critical discourse. Perhaps this is an inevitable, though not necessarily desirable, side effect of the academic neutralization of those aspects or effects of radical critical thought which strive toward readings—albeit oblique or indirect readings—of the signs of alterity. What the assumption of similarity or resemblance between terms appears to do is to impose, on the one hand, a limitation of the very kind that you find "demolishes in advance the notion of alterity," while, on the other hand, it transforms it into difference, as you correctly suggest. However, the difference that is produced by the transformation is, to risk a somewhat awkward formula, an undifferentiated difference. Let me ask you therefore to address in detail for student readers the incommensurability between difference and alterity, and how one approaches articulating any discourse on the notion of alterity without limiting, determining, or demolishing the idea of alterity? Is it possible to speak of otherness at all, given the instituting violence by which language proceeds, without the effect of limitation? (You touch on this, but perhaps we can address this further.)

DA: The simple answer to your last question is no. But the better answer is yes and no because it is by a process that can be called "limiting" that we give the other a chance. To explain this, let me say a little more about alterity. The other, in the sense in which I am using the term, is not just anything (idea, entity, person, culture) hitherto unencountered; it is that which is unencounterable, given the present state of things. (Otherness is always relative to a state of things, in a certain time and place.) It is unencounterable because the modes of encounter made possible by the state of things (a state which could be described in both social and psychological terms, in the way that Saussure describes the prevailing system of language) do not allow for it. In fact, the existing frameworks of understanding and practice prohibit such an encounter because in certain specific ways they depend on the exclusion of the other for their untroubled operation. So the other is not just out there, unapprehended because no one has thought of apprehending it, or because it bears no relation whatever to existing forms of knowledge, but because to apprehend it would threaten the status quo. It might be tempting to say that the other is not just "other to" or "other than" the same (the state of things), but that it is "the other of" the same, in that it is related to the same by this necessary exclusion; this, however, would make the relation of other to same much too cozy and predictable, as though we could simply derive the other from the same. But we cannot because the occlusion of other is itself occluded. This occlusion is necessary since, if there were overt signs of the process of denial and exclusion whereby the other is made other, its otherness would from the start be compromised. Furthermore, there is no single other to any given psychosocial state, even though every other that might impinge upon that state is single. (Another way of putting this is to say that no psychosocial state is single, even though the language I have been using might suggest that such a state is possible; hence it secures its existence by a host of exclusions.)

There can be no recipe or formula whereby the other can be brought into the field of the apprehensible; this is what we mean by calling it "other." All the recipes and formulas we possess are capable only of producing further versions of the same. But we might be able to increase the possibility of encountering the other, or of the other's encountering us, by the attentive reading of what is around us. (I say "might" because there can be no certainty here; and I use the term "reading" in the sense elaborated by Geoff Bennington in response to one of your questions.) That is to say, to become aware of patterns of silence, inconsistency, overinsistence, avoidance, repetition, and so on in a cultural, textual, philosophical, or psychological field (one's own "character," for instance) might be to open oneself to excluded alterity. The classroom would be one space in which this kind of opening reading could be encouraged.

If the other comes, if an event of welcoming the other occurs, the framework of understanding the institution, the mind, the culture that has been excluding it changes in the process, and the result of this change is that the other is no longer wholly other. It cannot be wholly other if it is now apprehended. The otherness we apprehend is always, in a sense, in the past (a past, as Levinas likes to say, that was never present); what we apprehend is a trace, or perhaps it's better to say a tracing, of otherness. It is correct, therefore, to assert that otherness has to be limited to be experienced, and since there are no degrees of otherness, it is also true to suggest, as you did in your question, that it has to be demolished to be experienced. Anything less than absolute otherness is not otherness at all. However, as we've seen, there's something paradoxical about the notion of absolute otherness with which we're working: it is, in a certain way, already related to the sameness we inhabit, related via the process of exclusion I've described. (This is not, by the way, a "historical" process: it's not an exclusion that happened some time in the past; rather, it's a structural exclusion, continuously and necessarily operative, though of course it may well have had historical effects.) It's not, that is to say, a completely transcendental otherness; it's an otherness, rather, which breaches the inside-outside boundary (this is one way in which it is other to "commonsense" modes of thought). The kind of limitation it undergoes in order to be apprehended is therefore dependent on the "relation without relation" (another Levinasian phrase) that it already had with the same. In becoming part of the field of the same from which it had been excluded it transforms that field, exposing both its prior exclusion and the structural need for that exclusion; the process of limitation is therefore also a process of change. This is why I said that limiting the other (in this very particular way) is giving it its chance to affect the future.

All this is very abstract, so let me give a simple example. Imagine a class of students who possess only stereotyped prejudices about homosexuality. (This is already a necessary simplification because any such group will in fact consist of a huge variety of individuals, however homogeneous their backgrounds.) They are not consciously homophobic, but their unquestioned convictions about the world and their place in it depend on their (unconscious) exclusion of homosexuals from their sense of what is "normal." Homosexuality is an "other" (no doubt one of many) on which their secure sense of themselves depends, without their being aware of it. Suppose now they read in class, with a teacher whose comprehension of "normality" is richer than theirs, some of Shakespeare's sonnets addressed to a young man. They bring to bear on the poems their own understanding of love poetry, and perhaps they read one or two conventional accounts of the poems as the epitome of the genre. But thanks to the persistence of the teacher, and perhaps

the response of one or two students, they begin to question the ortho-
dox readings they are familiar with. Without realizing it, they are
rehearsing the centuries-old marginalization of the homoerotic, and in
rehearsing it, performing it with some self-consciousness, they are making space for a new understanding of the exclusion they have inherited. Maybe the steps toward a new comprehension of human sexual
diversity are few and slight, and maybe only a few members of the class
take these steps, but it is imaginable that for these few their lives will
be permanently changed. It would be true to say that in this process,
in being acknowledged, homosexuality ceases to be other; its otherness, however, is what has brought about the transformation. If, however, the members of the class achieve merely a reductive appropriation of the idea of homosexuality, making it conform to their existing
stereotypes, it will have been limited in a different way: it will have lost
its alterity without effecting the kind of transformation which would
preserve the trace of that alterity in the (difficult and possibly painful)
shifts in what is thought of as "normal." Not all welcoming of the other
is painful, however; the aesthetic field, for instance, provides pleasur-
able instances, and education, as the transformative welcoming of the
other, can also be an exhilarating experience.

Let me get back to your question about difference at this point. One
might say that the relation between the heterosexual and the homosex-
ual, for the students we have been imagining, has moved from one of
alterity to one of difference: the students will, from now on, be able to
regard humans as belonging to different categories they had not hitherto recognized. If this is the conclusion of the story, however, it is not
a very satisfactory one; the acceptance of difference does not go very far
toward changing the conditions that produced the exclusion in the
first place. This is more like the untransformative limitation of the other
I have been talking about. As long as the institutions and discourses in
which and by means of which we live our lives rely on the unadmitted
marginalization of homosexuals, the structural logic of alterity remains
and it remains as a potential source of power for change (which might
include change in other areas of exclusion as well, since these exclusions
are all interrelated). We can dream of a utopia in which only differences
would exist (not necessarily a pleasant state), but we live in a world in
which alterity is both the sign of injustice and the opportunity for change.

JW: A last question. You turn to what you call a "simple example"—
which is anything but simple, if by addressing that term we were to
attempt to comprehend the processes by which the "simple example"

comes to be situated or maintained "culturally," "historically," or episte-mologically — as a means to ground what we have so far been discussing. In relation to a couple of points made earlier apropos of the other, I'd like to ask you to respond to the matter of, or the idea of, the "example" as such, its role in addressing both signs of injustice and the opportu-nities which the idea of the example presents for possible change. You suggest that the other is unencounterable "given the present state of things," and this "state of things" has as much to do with modalities of apperception as it has to do with the practical experience of the constel-lation of denials and exclusions that are operative in differing ways, in many situations. You identify certain aspects, if I can put it like that, of this constellation: patterns of silences, inconsistency, overinsistence, avoidance, repetition, all of which, along with other signs and traces of effects are read as "threatening the status quo." In these interviews, sev-eral of the contributors have noted the "practical" signs of what happens when, within the institution, those traces are read as potentially disturb-ing, and resistances take effect as so many symptoms of the allergic reac-tion on the part of the institution. At the risk of pushing you to resort to other "simple examples," would you address the processes of denial and exclusion that take place in maintaining the "structurality of structure" of the institution, and would you also speak of this maintenance in specific, overdetermined cultural and historical fields—the British and the North American, for example—of the "resistance to theory" and the more recent metamorphoses that such resistance has undergone.

DA: You are right, of course: the function of the example in insti-tutions, and particularly educational institutions, is never simple. As teachers, we constantly use and ask our students to produce examples; but we rarely question the logic of exemplarity whereby a tiny instance does duty for an entire body of learning or a complex practice. Nor do we always take account of the evaluative charge the concept easily acquires. I remember being told several decades ago by an older col-league who was wedded to the lecture as a pedagogical method that its greatest value was that it presented students with an example of good critical practice they could emulate. Example as synecdoche becomes example as model.

But is the unquestioned use of examples a symptom or an example of the widespread "resistance to theory" in our educational institu-tions (and elsewhere)? Insofar as it is one aspect of a willingness to reduce teaching and learning to a mechanical process, it is; but this doesn't for a moment mean that we could do without examples. They are a product of the necessary conditions of teaching: the limitations of time, space, mental and physical energy, material resources, and so on that I've already talked about. The example is a shortcut, an economic strategy, that we all need to rely on, and it can be a brilliantly effective device in teaching—often when the very status of the example is questioned as it is put to use. My earlier example raises as many questions as it resolves, and that may not be a bad thing—except that time and space cut the discussion short.

You mention the "recent metamorphoses that the resistance to theory has undergone," and it's worth reflecting on these for a moment, perhaps to bring this all-too-short discussion to a close. The resistance which, in the 1970s, greeted the new philosophical practices emanating largely from France took the form of anger, hostility, fear, and dismissal; it was, as Paul de Man showed, not a contingent response but a necessary one, in part internal to "theory" itself. There are probably institutions where this kind of resistance still happens; they are the lucky ones. Today, in most institutions of higher education where subjects like literature and cultural studies are taught, resistance takes a more damaging form: "theory"—a blatantly inappropriate term whose referent remained obscure to those most associated with it—has become theory without quotation marks—a name for an object that everyone can point to. Introductions, guides, companions to theory have established it as something that can be learned, summarized, exemplified, and applied. (This is not to say that there are not a few exceptional introductory texts that achieve some success in resisting this form of resistance.) A significant part of the time I spend with graduate students discussing dissertation proposals is devoted to attempts to encourage work that grows out of (and often uses the terms of) the texts that have fascinated or troubled them, and to discourage the procedure that consists in looking for a suitable "theory" to apply to the "literary text."

None of this is surprising. Institutions constitutionally and constitutively look for ways to reduce all thinking that challenges the assumptions on which they are built to sets of learnable, programmable, terms. They convert the other into the same. "Theory," whatever it may refer to or be an example of, involves a questioning of such notions as teaching, learning, the example, theory. It welcomes the other, and the unforeseeable changes such welcoming brings. It need not—in fact it now probably should not—be called "theory," let alone theory without quotation marks. Whatever it gets called, it continues to operate wherever teaching and learning happen, teaching and learning in the sense that, for me, matters most—as the shared inventive opening to otherness.

3

Peggy Kamuf
Symptoms of Response

JW: The thinking of "freedom" and "responsibility" is of considerable concern in the humanities, yet the yoking together of the two in whatever formulation is not as simple as it might seem to some. Far from having an unequivocal relationship, when brought together the two terms and the concepts they invoke begin to be discerned as tracing, as well as being remarked by, various silent—yet all the more powerful for that—thresholds. It is perhaps the case that, in being brought together, the questions of "freedom" and "responsibility" give us to think a certain chiasmus, with which we must engage all the more fully.

You refer elsewhere to the "well-tended confines" of the academy (specifically, in the case of "philosophy *à l'anglaise*"). To what extent can and must we "mobilize" the thinking of difference within the pedagogic scene as, at once, initiating a discourse on the difference that operates between "freedom" and "responsibility" and perhaps also a different thinking of them (a discourse and thinking coming from some other place within these "well-tended confines") while articulating the question of difference as part of a pedagogical act that sees the threshold of thought as the very responsibility thinking of difference entails — even as it opens to questioning the institutional limits constructed in the name of "academic freedom" and "academic responsibility"?

PK:

Aphorisms of Response

(To reset the tone of the interview, aphorisms are virtually toneless, voiceless. No one speaks them, no "I" to whom their sentences can be attributed, no one to express an opinion or view in an interview. The aphorism seems to pronounce, as it were, a law from nowhere, by no one. Here it records the perplexity of the "interviewee" who has to *enchaîner*: How? Who? No one has begun to speak—yet; hence, aphorisms.)

1. The "thinking of difference" does not get mobilized *on* or *within* the pedagogic scene: it *is* that scene or stage, that is, the more or less theatricalized space where difference—*différance*—puts in play all the differences to which we must attend in thinking. At least, if—a big *if*— this "pedagogical scene" is a space of thinking at all, then it must be, undertake, allow, call forth, and incite a "thinking of difference."

2. The pedagogic scene—not the best wording, but for want of another at the moment—is essentially constituted by a division: teacher/student (these are not persons but positions on either side of the division). Saying this makes clear that the scene we are talking about is not an indefinite place where some learning or teaching may go on, in some vague or even some very specific sense. We have in mind the space of *pedagogy*'s institution, in other words, the school, the university. Even if it is adult education, pedagogy institutes the task of leading the child in a direction, educating him or her. The leader/child, teacher/student division is essential, then, to this institution. Or rather it is what is instituted as mark of division, to be repeated.

3. This division and this difference should not be read solely as a difference of power. To be sure, "teachers" can exercise considerable symbolic power over their "students," but there is all the same an element of this division that never fully submits to the power conferred by the hierarchical institution, the classification system of the classroom. Before it is a difference of power, there is division in the sense of simply more than one. Or in still other terms, before there is teacher and student, there is division, difference, right there in the face-to-face with the other, as Levinas might say. In other words, there is experience of essential otherness. In this way, the "pedagogical scene" is like every other space or place of division where essential otherness marks and makes for experience. A certain symbolic and institutional specificity of this scene is erased when it is considered—*and so it must be*— as such an experience.

4. When these institutional marks are erased or suspended, if only ever in an ideal operation of thought, what can reemerge is the condition of the face-to-face encounter as an asymmetrical division not of power, but of freedom. Because the experience of essential otherness is possible, if indeed it is possible, only on the condition of the other's essential *freedom*, which is utterly asymmetrical to whatever I think of as mine, including my freedom. For the relation in question, the so-called pedagogic relation, this means that the student-other can never be wholly and fully subject to whatever power pedagogical or educational institutions can confer on teachers or other officials of the school or university. If this were not so, then quite simply there could be no relation of the sort we are laboring to describe and to describe because it exists. The inalienable freedom of the "student" is in this sense the underlying support of the whole doctrine of academic freedom. It is the student-other's essential freedom one defends when, as one must, one defends the principle of academic freedom.

5. Erasing the pedagogic scene, with its division of power, is by no means a simple task, and it is never accomplished once and for all or at one blow. That scene is constantly reinforcing itself. It is upheld by a large network of expectations — of parents, administrators, many colleagues, and the "students" themselves — which maintains the idea of undergraduates as still "children." Hence the fiction that the university is not the real world, the ivory tower myth, and so forth, but also the sometimes discouragingly anti-intellectual environment of many university "communities," the childishness of the "social life" that characterizes so many university campuses, at least in the United States. Nevertheless, this elaborate investment in childishness can only disavow but cannot deny the reality that "students" are essentially free — emancipated from childhood — which is what makes the university a very real place, and, in that, like any other.

6. It is "real," of course, in another sense, indeed all too real. The encroachment of the so-called real world on university classrooms has made the distinction between its activities and that of other "training" programs more and more difficult to discern. Corporations are founding their own universities and universities are spawning corporations. Distance learning is being transformed by Internet technologies and these are virtualizing the "pedagogic scene." Where now does this scene take place? Where doesn't it take place? The real scene is also a virtual one, which means that the presence to each other in the face-to-face encounter of teacher/student is no longer sufficient — but it never was, in fact — to define or delimit pedagogy's scene. In other words (pace

Plato), teaching/learning has never been essentially limited to the presence to each other of teacher and student, or even to their self-presence. This now obvious fact should not just allow but also require a reformulation of the essential traits of this scene in terms that do not necessarily depend on presence and on presence as instituted in the university.

7. This reformulation of the pedagogic scene has a better chance of emerging from within the humanities' disciplines and perhaps its best chance is in departments of literature, or as it's been called elsewhere, in "the division of literature." There are at least two reasons to think so.

7a. The humanities have begun, more obviously, to play the role of the institution's *screen* — a screen for projection or for dissimulation. This screen provides the appearance, the illusion of education as presence. Within the larger economy of the university, the frivolous expense of the humanities can thus be written off against the profit there is (?) in maintaining the appearance, to the buying public, of a *university of presence*. However, the more the university of presence becomes a virtual university, then the more the humanities will have to be pressed into service in its role as screen. This condition, which has already begun to take shape within U.S. university-corporations, seems bound to produce at the very least inequities within the way the work of teaching is configured and conceived (not to mention how it is remunerated) across the different constituencies of this virtual university's real faculty. With this reconfiguration, the humanities division is at serious risk, in many institutions, of being reduced to a general-education provider, with little opportunity or responsibility for passing on to future specialists the various disciplinary skills still sheltered there, although more and more precariously. One need not spell out the consequences for the future of the humanities in the university if they cannot somehow surmount this risk. Their survival there will depend on successfully reformulating, renegotiating, and more precisely *deconstructing* the university of presence. That is one reason to believe, even if not very fervently, but still too credulously, that this necessary deconstruction has a chance to emerge first within the humanities.

7b. A second reason is that the virtuality of "distance learning" and in general the scene of nonpresence has always been the specialty of the humanities, especially of the literary disciplines. Quite simply (but, of course, there is nothing at all simple about it), it is the scene of reading some written text. Writing, the written or inscribed trace, is the originary technology of education at a distance, of virtuality, and of the nonpresence to each other of "speakers" and "listeners." Iterability (writing/reading) is the possibility of all these apparently new technologies that today seem to be replacing everything in their path, beginning with the culture of the book and the library. But reading, the practice of reading (or writing), has never been confined to the form of *books*, which have properly been called "books" for only about the last 2,000 years. The practice of reading, throughout most of its history so far (and such histories abound at present), has not depended on books. These histories remind us that the period of the book, which is now ending, has been appropriated as and by the spread of Christianity. (The period of the Good Book begins with the codex.) But just as Christianity shows no sign of giving up the ghost with the end of the book (on the contrary), no one can seriously believe that the end of reading, the end of the necessity of reading, is near. Proof is added every day that written language now saturates the world more than ever; it has spun its web around the world to a degree and in a manner that very few dreamed possible a mere fifteen years ago. Writing's trace has leaped onto a new support, which is now in the process of duplicating all the old contents of the archive but also adding to, multiplying these contents at an ever-accelerating rate. The demand made on reading and readers by all this newly supported writing has never been greater. But it is also very often now a demand that attempts to program in advance so as to appropriate the reader's activity to the general capitalization of information: its retrieval, extraction, transmission, exchange, and so forth. This programmatic concept of reading as information gathering and capitalization is nothing new, but it may now be seen to occupy a key place in the world as dreamed by information technology. Doubtless it is foolish to believe that literary, textual practices of reading can counter this concept, and yet, when so many differences have been effaced, one is perhaps left "face-to-face," once again and as ever, with (almost) bare language. Responding to (almost) bare language, to an always-only virtual language is what the reader of literature has practiced since long before the invention of the Internet. But what makes this practice of response less than or more than, other than, a program? To what does it respond? Or rather, to whom?

To whom? That's a question, perhaps, for another, less aphoristic session of this "interview."

JW: "To be chained, to chain oneself, and to move on."

The "scene of nonpresence [which] has always been the specialty of the humanities," as the last of the aphorisms has it, appears available as a commentary on the condition of this, and the other "interviews" in this collection. Shaped by these exchanges in e-mail, the idea of the interview appears to have been spirited away from itself, from the idea of an "in itself" of the idea of the interview (where at least two people come together, face-to-face). No doubt, this is too reductive as a definition of what an interview might be, and certainly this seems to be falling back on a program, but the virtual exchanges by which we are proceeding partake, necessarily, of writing/reading, and the "originary technology of education at a distance" and thereby appear, on the one hand, to have called into question the program that is called "interviewing," "the interview," while, on the other, returning to the questions of reading, writing, and education that the aphorisms address, to which they respond. But to echo what has already been asked, what makes this practice of response less or more than a program? To what — or whom — does it respond? Is it the notion of the response itself that calls into question or otherwise exceeds the program or programming?

PK: In answer to your last question: no, of course not, responses can be programmed or programmatic. It is even, no doubt, the most widespread form of "response" as experienced today: checking off a box in a questionnaire, filling in the blanks on a form, giving answers to market or political surveys, sociological studies, and so forth. Machines and all sorts of technical devices are also said to respond. But right away we also recognize that programmed response is nonresponse, if by response we mean or we *want to* mean something that interrupts and surprises any program, an event or act of response by another, some other, some other than the program. Such an event or act of response, if there can even be any, must interrupt whatever programs are running there where the act *takes place*. Response, if there is any such thing, would have to be an act of program interruption.

Of course, today, when we talk about program interruption, it is hard not to think of some sort of accident or unwanted occurrence that throws a wrench into the works of telecommunications, a small, large, or even global disaster (remember Y2K?). I used to use a backup device that, in case of a power failure or other accident, would switch you to its batteries and alert you to back up your file. I remember it kept a record of its own operations, and listed under the term of "events," by time and date, any occasions when it had been obliged to leap in to prevent the interruption of the data stream or overpower some threat to the memory banks. It is an interesting use of the term "event" to designate not an interruption but the prevention of it. What will have happened is nothing but the trace of what might have happened, if the interruption had not been prevented, which, thankfully, it was (I give the little machine a grateful pat).

Maybe all events are like that to some degree? To some degree, every event that occurs, that can be said or recorded to have occurred, is as much interruption as prevention of interruption. This would mean, to go back to the terms we began with, that every event of response would not just interrupt the program, but also prevent the interruption, save it before it was utterly lost or beyond retrieval. In any case, it's important, I think, not to make the terms "program" and "response" (or "event") into the names of forces or structures in opposition. It is clearly far more complex than that. One needs to take this complexity into account if one seeks to understand *what is happening,* the events that are happening, taking place, and taking place in virtual space, there where nothing could have happened before, at least not in precisely this way, not before, that is, not before certain events made what is happening now possible, where it is possible. We might think that it is the very structure of event, of what makes for an event, that has changed, but perhaps what has happened is that this structure's complexity has been made more manifest, and thus more unavoidable for whoever begins to reflect about these questions. But it's not just a matter for the kind of reflection we are trying at least to do here. This complexity of the event of response, of program interruption/preservation, is something more and more humans are experiencing, with or without reflecting on the precise components of the experience. Let's try an example.

Although I would be utterly clueless if I had to read the language of computer programs, I am able to use e-mail, the Internet, the Web because these programs we're talking about also allow their own translation into the more archaic or at least less efficient language of articulated words, grammar, and so forth. Or even into the more primitive, more intuitive language of icons. As a result, I need only click on the box containing a symbol for "reply" to answer using the programming language, even though I cannot write, read, or speak it. When I click that button, I want merely to put in motion a function of transmission of my message, the postal system, as it were. I hit "Reply," but I do not think of that as, in itself, the *act* of replying, answering, or responding. But of course neither is there response, in this case, unless I hit "Reply," at least unless it is *possible* for me to do so or to have done so. It is a certain *possibility* of response that is programmed as "Reply." *Response,* in the sense we were talking about it above, as that which has to interrupt the program, is also essentially dependent on the program that makes it *possible* to respond, with the program, but also *perhaps* without program or even against it. So the relation between program and response is altogether more complex than any opposition one can think of, including the face-to-face, the confrontation, the vis-à-vis, or whatever you will. A response, if it is possible, must somewhere take a path through the program that gives it its possibility. But, if it is indeed possible to respond with more than or other than a mechanical, already-programmed reply, then it is also this possibility already given by the program that has to get or be interrupted, somehow.

So, as for interrupting the program of the interview (or spiriting away its idea, as you put it), I wouldn't be so sure that merely conducting an exchange by e-mail suffices to do that.

JW: As we both agree then, the e-mail exchange doesn't necessarily interrupt or even prevent the program. In an effort to seek a response, if, as you say, this is even possible, as a path through the program, I would like to ask you how you might begin to imagine undertaking, calling forth, and inciting a "thinking of difference," as you put it in your first aphorism.

Specifically, to recall that aphorism, while it is doubtless the fact that, as you put it, "the 'thinking of difference' does not get mobilized on or within the pedagogic scene: it *is* that scene or stage," it nonetheless remains the case that, as part of the program that is named the "teaching of theory" in the university, difference is taught, is "mobilized," as though it were a definable concept, as though one could think difference ontically. How then might the calling forth of a "thinking of difference" seek to interrupt or prevent such a program?

PK: Yes, well, all of this is very difficult. And yet, you know, we should also try to remember that it's really not as difficult as all that! Recall the description in [Virginia Woolf's] *Mrs. Dalloway* when Clarissa sees the woman in the house across from hers and thinks something like: here is one room, there is another. I mean it also is just as simple as that. The curious thing is how much we tend to forget what this simplicity implies, aided in our amnesia by the illusion of a common language. But then where would we be without that illusion? I suppose *we* would be nowhere at all since it is we, the "we" who is in question there, suspended and shared out in the uncommon space of language, here *and* there, never present just here, never "present" except in some language or other, which is to say not present anywhere to itself. This shared, divided space of language always risks losing its dimensions, its spacing — here one room, there another — when sense is all gathered up in a point, when it is recognized only if given from the point of view of the subject.

One cannot bypass this strange space of multiplying rooms in order to teach "difference," as if what mattered were only a concept. There is no concept of difference that is not affected by difference from itself, by difference from self, by the other room, over there. We need to go on practicing a certain philology for there to be still room in which difference can leave a mark and be remarked. To paraphrase Heidegger: language is the room of difference.

It is old-fashioned to say so, but all the same, I'll confess that the philological approach to the thinking of difference has never, for me, been replaced or even dislodged by a more properly theoretical one. This approach alone offers or points to the justification, if there is any, for continuing to "teach" literature—that is, for continuing to require or even encourage others, "students," to read certain texts in certain ways, and principally to read texts *as written* without yet translating them into their referents, concepts, plots, characters, or, if you will, their "messages." It's the old-fashioned, now very familiar technique called "close reading." I don't suppose, however, that one can use that term in our context without brushing on the taint of New Criticism. If so, then let's substitute the name Paul de Man made available, in that finely condensed little essay titled "The Return to Philology": "mere reading." De Man writes: "Mere reading, it turns out, prior to any theory, is able to transform critical discourse in a manner that would appear deeply subversive to those who think of the teaching of literature as a substitute for the teaching of theology, ethics, psychology, or intellectual history." In the next sentence, de Man characterizes "close reading" (and here it is explicitly credited to its New Critical inventors) as that which often accomplishes the same thing as "mere reading," with the difference that it does so "in spite of itself": "Close reading accomplishes this often in spite of itself because it cannot fail to respond to structures of language which it is the more or less secret aim of literary teaching to keep hidden."[1] As the basis of Anglophone literary teaching for so long (since at least the time de Man himself was a graduate student as he recounts here), New Critical close reading will have failed to keep hidden what it wanted to keep hidden because, despite itself, it *responds* to certain structures of language. Like mere reading, it is first of all a necessity of response to something other and, in spite of itself, it "cannot fail to respond."

When I copied out just now the sentence beginning "Mere reading . . . ," I was struck by the provocation there is in calling something "*mere* reading" and then saying it, or the transformations it effects, are "deeply subversive." This is certainly not just bravado on de Man's part. "Mere reading" opens up the space where difference takes place, where transformation can occur. And, of course, to begin with, there is the transformation of the reading subjects themselves, an effect that de Man underscores by drawing here explicitly on the recollection of a pedagogic scene (to recall a phrase from the beginning of our exchange). It is the scene of the New Critical practice of close reading, which blocks or at least defers the movement from the particular to the general, from the text being read to "the general context of human experience or history." Instead of such moves beyond the text, de Man continues, students

> were to start out from the bafflement that such singular turns of tone, phrase, and figure were bound to produce in readers attentive enough to notice them and honest enough not to hide their non-understanding behind the screen of received ideas that often passes, in literary instruction, for humanistic knowledge.

> This very simple rule, surprisingly enough, had far-reaching didactic consequences. I have never known a course by which students were so transformed.[2]

It is finally a very puzzling thing, "mere reading,"[3] and that's what this passage admits when it locates the beginning of "mere reading" in bafflement and nonunderstanding. It starts there where it begins to fail to comprehend: mere reading baffles the mind.

Well, I think I'll just stop here, in bafflement.

[What follows is an e-mail letter Peggy wrote me after receiving an anonymous referee's report, whose response—or, more properly speaking, nonresponse—to the aphorisms that open the interview exhibits certain all too drearily typical symptoms. As good readers will see, the following commentary extends beyond the immediate context of the aphorisms to questions of reading and response or nonresponse taken up by the present volume. —JW]

Dear Julian,

Sorry not to have gotten back to you sooner. I've been trying to think about how to rectify the "problem" with the first answer of my interview. Now that I've been forced to consider the reader-referee's recalcitrance before its aphoristic mode (which was, I confess again, a deliberate provocation and announced as such), I find little comfort in recognizing the irony here. The reader wants me to be "more direct"! By that I understand a demand for first-person speech, in my own name, which is precisely what aphorisms exclude. And yet, the same reader also grumbles that the volume assembles all the "usual suspects for deconstruction," as if he or she is tired in advance of reading what "I" (for example) might have to say about teaching difference. Well, exactly! The aphorisms empty out the "I"'s discourse, or cut it off from the empirical, the contingent, like a phenomenological reduction (or something). But that, too, is intolerable. Maybe because it feels, to our unhappy reader, like a law being laid down and, although that's outrageously presumptuous, there's no one "there" to accuse of the presumption.

What to do? For naturally I do not wish to visit such unhappiness on any other potential readers of this interview. And yet, I believe you agree that the solution is not simply to recast the section of aphorisms into a more standard mode, even if that could possibly relieve our reader's displeasure, which I confess I doubt. (But shouldn't a volume like this also have the ambition to strain against the standard form of the interview? Or at least to invite readers to examine their expectations of that mode? Did I overstrain the limits by declining, at first, to respond as an "I"? If so, what difference does that make? Isn't that something like the overall question of this volume? Why all the anxiety when an "interview" is not what one expects? But expected by whom? And so on, and so forth.)

Nor do I want to add here explanations about why the aphoristic mode came to be imposed (by me, yes, I admit, I did it) in response to your remarks opening our exchange. Whatever I might say about that, after the fact, would have to sound self-serving. And that would not serve me or this book very well. And yet, I will also confess that I am able to see in this episode the flickering of a symptom around that thing called, in aphorism 7, the "university of presence." Because aphorisms simulate no one's presence, they are perhaps the least adapted to the illusion ordinarily sustained by the published interview. They do not pretend to reveal what some "I" thinks, believes, or feels; they contain no personal anecdotes; they don't bid to strike the chord of identification with some individual's experience; indeed, they erase altogether the person, the individual, the presence of someone speaking in answer to a question. They appear not to respond "directly," as the reader complains, and perhaps not even indirectly. When put in the place of response, in a simulated "interview," aphorisms are out of place, or they leave vacant the place of the "who" who responds.

I just said that perhaps aphorisms do not respond even indirectly in that circumstance. Perhaps. But who could say whether they do or not? Where is the "reader" who can answer, and in advance, for every other? These would ultimately be questions for university presses and scholarly journals, which must engage in such forecasting or foreclosing. It's called "refereeing publication." As invidious as this practice can sometimes be, upon it rests the very distinction between scholarly publishing and all its others, among which today we must count all the writing being "accessed"—published—on the Web. The distinction is thus more fragile and more difficult to defend than ever, as any teacher-scholar realizes after marking up students papers that cite anonymous Web sites in the their research bibliographies. But if I think one must go on yet, and for as long as possible, trying to make the distinction, I can also want to pose questions about the referee function as regards a volume like this one, which is not a collection of scholarly essays but of "interviews," however simulated they may be—or not. So, I ask: how can or should one "referee" what purport to be interviews? What standard of judgment does one apply in the absence of the putative standards of scholarship? I would willingly believe that our reader had to struggle with questions like these and would have my full sympathy in that uncomfortable task, if only it had not been abandoned or resolved in favor of *symptoms* of judgment.

But perhaps—again, perhaps—that is all there is to read here, as well, in these "interviews": symptoms. The responses are symptomatic, and that's all that one should expect of such a mode of writing or speaking. All the same, and that said, isn't this symptomization also what can be interesting about interviews and why anyone asks for them, gives them, or reads them?[4] If there is anything really of interest here to anyone (which is a genuine question), then it would have to be this relation to the symptom, which does not indulge an illusion like the relation to the other's presence in or to the interview situation, the face-to-face, and so on. The symptom is not present, above all not to me as "mine," "my symptom." To risk more aphorisms here, one might affirm: the symptom is always of non-self-presence, and the interview, if it is any good (you be the judge), seeks out this symptom. Not deliberately, doubtless not even consciously, but through the invitation to lower the guard (e.g., the scholarly apparatus), the symptom is convoked and allowed to flicker on the page. Or not.

Here, then, is my last confession, or act of contrition. The aphorisms are doubtless, like everything else said here, a symptom. Although I would be the last one to affirm what speaks there beyond what is said (as if by no one), I would not be so sure that they are a symptom of (or only of) guardedness, defensiveness, a protection from the risks of "directness." *Au contraire*, even, for one could see there, at least I could see there assertions stripped of the protection afforded the discourse of a subject who can always be excused for advancing tentatively and behind the cover of its symptomatic partiality. To risk one last aphorism, one could say, someone could say: no discourse is less guarded, less *indirect* than the aphoristic. But, by the same token I would add, no discourse is —perhaps—more symptomatic. Provided one speaks of symptom without subject, or rather with always more than one subject: interviewer and interviewee. But don't forget the others, the *readers* —provided there might also be more than one of these.

Pardon me, Julian, for this long e-mail. It occurs to me that, if you think it is apt or appropriate, we could merely insert it as a kind of foreword (or forewarning) to our interview, along with anything you might wish to add. But again, you be the judge.
As ever,
Peggy

4

Avital Ronell
(as interviewed by D. Diane Davis)
Confessions of an Anacoluthon: On Writing, Technology, Pedagogy, and Politics

DDD: You've had a great deal to say about "the writer" and "writing," and because what you've said problematizes both concepts, it'll be important for us to tease them through very carefully.[1] Do you consider yourself a "writer"?

AR: In a certain way that question might be too masculinist for me because it suggests some kind of volition, agency, control at the wheel of fortune or destiny. I would say that I have figured myself as a kind of secretary of the phantom. I take dictation. I would say also that one doesn't call oneself a writer: one is called, or one is convoked to writing in a way that remains mysterious and enigmatic for me. There was nothing that was going to determine this kind of activity or passivity — we still have to determine what writing is, of course. But sometimes I can, in a way, identify with the figures of "writing being" (*Schriftstellersein*) that Kafka threw up. For example, that of Gregor Samsa, who is this little unfigurable, monstrous fright for his family and workplace, and who has to stay in his room, kind of locked up, flying on the ceiling and attached to the desk — *there* is a figure with which I have repeatedly identified. Which is to say, there's something monstrous and a little shameful involved in writing, at least in terms of social pragmatics. This sort of logic of the parasite is probably eventually why I wrote about the drug addict and the writer as figures, often paradoxically, of social unreliability, even where their greatest detachment produces minor insurrections, political stalls, and stammers in any apparatus of social justice.

DDD: In the introductory remarks to the interview you did with Andrea Juno in *Research: Angry Women*, you are referred to as an "ivory-tower terrorist." Are you comfortable with that label? Does it seem accurate?

AR: These are questions about naming and location, and in this regard, neither term is acceptable. The ivory tower is something that I have never been embraced by, or possibly even seen; it is a phantasm. After 9/11, the term "terrorist" took an even more sinister turn than when I was associated with that word. The word has its own historicity. Kleist traces the "becoming-terrorist" of Michael Kohlhaas. Baader-Meinhof has other associations. When the word was aimed at me, I think that something like guerilla warfare might have been meant — maybe skirmishes on the premises of institutional sites. In my own private pantheon of troublemakers I would be honored to be associated with the philosopher-warrior Subcommandante Marcos — an unprecedented figure of civil warfare, theater, and poetic utterance that resists to this day appropriation by any political or theoretical discourse. It is as if he had been sprung from a Nietzschean text and the Mexican imaginary. But let's get real. When I was located in some sort of subversive pocket of the university — one of my many efforts to get a promotion at Berkeley was officially denied because I was a "subversive!" — it was for other, less recognizable, or politically sublime reasons. I am not sure how to name the place to which I was assigned. "Terrorist" seems off; it would imply a kind of being that is single-minded and fanatically set on a goal. By contrast, I would be too dispersed, self-retracting, and self-annulling in the way I work to be considered a terrorist as such. If anything, I would say that I am a counterterrorist. It is true that I have called for something like an extremist writing, particularly when I was working on ethnocide and drugs.

And also, following Derrida, I have made hyperbolic attempts to secure the space of academe as a sheltering place of unconditional hospitality for dissidence and insurrection, refutation and undomesticatable explosions of thought. To the extent that the academy is a mausoleum, it tends to expect the reverence due the dead, and my irreverent type of reverence seems to set off, in those describing what I do, some explosive language. But I would also say, in a more general and gendered sense, that very often women who have a somewhat original bent are institutionally psychoticized and isolated. They tend to be structurally positioned as dangerous creatures, so there is always a SWAT team of academic proprietors closing in on them. In this sense, I can see how the "terrorist" appellation might have grown on me or been pinned on me. But it comes from the institutional space and not from me. I was tagged.

There's also this. While I was at Berkeley, I was close friends with Kathy Acker and Andrea Juno. *Mondo 2000* declared us the "deviant boss girls of a new scene," models of subversion, and so on. That little community may have provoked some politicized assertions, marking the way the three of us would stage ourselves publicly and kick ass in a certain way. In this regard, I think one would want to look more closely at the possibility or impossibility of friendship in academia, and what it implies. Who are your friends? How does friendship set up (or subvert) a transmission system for the kind of work you do and read? One is often judged by one's public friendships. I was friends with Kathy and Andrea. And I think there was something scary about this little girl gang of troublemaker writers. Certainly, publishing with *Angry Women* did do momentary damage; it dented my career a bit — though it is laughable to offer up an imago of my career as a smooth surface to be dented. It was never not dented: one originary dent.

DDD: What kind of damage did it do?

AR: Well, I think colleagues were a little shocked to see me involved with performance artists, recontextualized and reformatted in the space of very angry, very outrageous, shit-covered, dildo-wielding, multisexual women. I think there was a gender-genre crossing that probably seemed a little excessive. If I may say something a bit strange and that comes from my studies of Schlegel, de Man, and Bataille: it is not so much that I deviated from an academic norm. Deviancy is tolerated and given a theme park in academia. It is that I superimposed a "pornographic" code, loosely speaking, on a philosophical track. What is not tolerated is this sort of imitation, which de Man writes about concerning Schlegel's bad rep as a result of the philosophical/porno graphical text *Lucinda*. This work got Schlegel into trouble with everyone, all the philosophical heavies. Even Kierkegaard and Hegel stopped fighting so that they could agree that Schlegel was a disgrace. Bataille suffered much the same fate when Sartre got at him and charged him, as Peter Connor has shown, with producing a "pornography of the cogito." Without confusing myself with these fabulous guys, I would like to think that I follow the same proud lineage of inmixation — part of a politics of contamination.

DDD: Did you have tenure yet?

AR: Yes, I did.

DDD: It's not unusual for you to refer to "rhetorical operations" in your work or to slip into your own rigorous rhetorical analysis. "Support Our Tropes" [in *Finitude's Score*], for example, offers a clever analysis of the rhetoric surrounding the Gulf War: Do you consider yourself, in any sense, a rhetorician?

AR: First of all, I recognize that this is not a stable appellation; to the extent that rhetoric is a feature of language, one is kind of overwritten by it. I don't see how one could not be inscribed in the rhetorical scene. But, of course, on a more technical and thematic level, I am very attentive to rhetorical maneuvers on different registers of articulation. I tend to try and track something like a rhetorical unconscious in a text. I am very drawn in by that which withdraws from immediate promises of transparency or meaning. For example, I am interested in "anasemia," which is a linguistic force, elaborated by post-Freudian psychoanalysis, that works against normative semantics. I am interested in tracking repressed signifiers, including the relationships between syntactical breakdowns and political decisions. I wrote an essay, for instance, about George Bush senior's inability to produce rhetorically stable utterances, an essay in which I tried to read his rhetorical machine as inexorably linked to the specific kinds of decisions he made and to the reactionary and reactive effects of his administration. Of course, every utterance is susceptible to destabilization, making the itinerary of the question considerably more complicated. In the case of President Bush senior, I looked at a repetition compulsion that was rhetorically determined. Now we are on rewind and play with the second one, also after Iraq and repetitive calls.

I have been heavily influenced by Paul de Man's work in this area, which leads me to say that one can never be detached from the rhetorical question or from the necessity of a whole politics and history of rhetorical thought, which has been largely repressed, or expulsed, or embraced, depending on where you are looking and to whom you are listening. So, indeed, if one is trying to be a rigorous and attentive reader, one has to consider oneself a rhetorician in those senses.

DDD: When it first appeared in 1989, the layout and design of *The Telephone Book* were, as far as I can tell, unprecedented in academe. The design of Jacques Derrida's *Glas* is also staggeringly unconventional, of course; but whereas the simultaneous, multivoiced columns of *Glas* challenge print's linear imperative, *The Telephone Book* seems to break more rules and to be more playfully performative on the whole. An incredibly dense theoretical work that addresses some quite somber issues (for example, Heidegger's Nazism), it also seems gleefully irreverent, taking Nietzsche's merry hammer to all kinds of conventional expectations associated with the technology of "the book." What prompted this performative text? That is, why write what wanted to be said in this particular way? What did you hope its performance would accomplish?

AR: It's important to note that *Glas* appeared much earlier and has another history of rupture and invention that still calls for analysis. We are all indebted to Derrida's exegetical energy for boosting the desire for the book and for making us interrogate the placid materiality of acts of reading. On another level of your questioning, I would like to recall that all texts are performative. But what I was trying to get at with *The Telephone Book* was the possibility of destroying the book in the Heideggerian sense of accomplishing a certain destruction of its metaphysical folds, enclosures, and assumptions. On the sheerly material level, it provided the first computer virtuoso performance in design. Every page was different, an interpretation of the text. And often I did argue with Richard Eckersley, the marvelous designer, because I felt that he was pulling away from the telephonic logic that I wanted his work to reflect and that he was becoming too autonomous — becoming a computer virtuoso. I didn't want the computer to overtake the telephonic markings that I felt needed to be continually asserted and reasserted. In a sense, we had a war of technologies — of course, over the telephone (I have never met Richard). What I wanted to effect by producing this telephonic logic that would supplant or subvert the book was to displace authorial sovereignty, to mark my place as taking calls or enacting the Heideggerian structure of the call. In other words, I wanted to recede into the place of a switchboard operator, and in that sense emphatically to mark the feminine problematic of receptivity and the place of reception. I was at the reception desk of that which we still call a "book," taking the call of the other.

What I wanted to do as well by breaking up the serene, sovereign space of an unperturbed book was to invite static and disruption and noise. I wanted to show — to the extent that one can show this — that the text emerges in a kind of violence of originary interference, a kind of primal buzz. I wanted to inscribe the kinds of wreckage to signification that aren't usually accounted for. And this could be seen as belonging to a kind of postfeminist ethics, too. There is a great logic of disturbance that rattles the text. It doesn't offer the illusion of being from that professorial space of quiet and support and cocooned sheltering. The great male professor seems to me to be served by anything from the wife function to the institutional function. But I wanted this text to be somehow reflective of women's position, of the attempt to write in an institutional war zone, and this included being rattled and taking calls that are not predictable in their arrival, that jam the master codes and jam the switchboard, ever expelling you from the safe precincts of the imagined contemplative life. When I say "great male professor," I hope you realize that I am not limiting myself to empirical qualities that might determine this entity fully. This type of professor still exists and may be distributed among so-called men and women, while others are struggling, overworked, underpaid, and so on.

When I was at Berkeley and writing *The Telephone Book*, whenever someone would ask me what I was working on, I endured a lot of mockery, so I stopped trying to present it. This book was the first theoretical or deconstructive work on technology, and the telephone seemed like an aberrant, abjected object. Why would anyone write on anything so common, absurd, banal, unliterary, or antiphilosophical? Even my colleagues who were historians thought it a preposterous project. Obviously, literary critics didn't see any point to it at all, and the philosophers I hung out with didn't necessarily get it either. There was something that had to remain stealthy and unannounceable about writing on the telephone. Derrida had laid the groundwork with his breathtaking work, *La carte postale* [*The Post Card*], a text that blew me away and took off in all sorts of directions for me. There is a woman who in one of the envois talks to him about wanting to connect to the telephone. That wasn't me, though people have wondered about the possible connection. At the time, I was presenting myself, at least to the great thinker, as Metaphysics. "I" even show up as such in the text.

What prompted the project was the surprise that I experienced when I read the interview in which Heidegger was asked to describe the nature of his relationship with National Socialism, and he said he didn't really have a relationship, all he did was take a call from the SA storm trooper. This response appeared to me to be an improbable statement—one, in fact, that might offer an access code, since Heidegger is the thinker par excellence of the call, of the difficult and necessary status of calling. And he is also the one to have pointed to the dangers of technology. He is the one—no matter what one thinks of him, and no matter how one thinks one can evaluate him, his lapses and the ways he has been disappointing (but only a very few philosophers finally haven't been). Heidegger certainly is a redneck in many ways and highly problematic as mortals go, but what interested me was this response, which is a very compelling response and nonresponse at once. If I had been the thinker of the call and had made the call on technology, warning that we live under its dominion in yet undecipherable ways, then I would be clearly codifying my response. I thought he was providing an access code to a truer reading. I went after it.

And that is what prompted me to look to the telephone and to think about its place (or nonplace) or repressed functions in thinking. My question was how you would write the history of a nonrelation, which is what Heidegger was asserting. There was a crucial nonrelation. It has a history. It's called "the telephone." It appeared to require a kind of inclination toward a subterranean history. I asked: What is this place of nondisclosure that doesn't allow for delusions of transparency or immediacy? This nondisclosure in part is why I felt that the book needed to bear the burden of that which resists signification, resists the serene certitudes of reportage or information gathering or knowledge naming that a good many academic books rely upon. I wanted it to come out with a university press because I felt that frame would rattle some cages. There are presumably many advantages to going with a trade or commercial press, but I thought that it had to reside within the university structure, that it actually would do more damage or stir up more trouble if it were to be contained by a university press. By the way, one of my motivating slogans is that a woman should be a *pain in the ass.*

DDD: Your work seems consciously to muck with genre boundaries, to operate in the face of inherited borders of thought. *Crack Wars: Literature, Addiction, Mania,* for instance, operates simultaneously as a meticulous literary analysis of *Madame Bovary,* a rigorous philosophical inquiry into the question of Being-on-drugs, and a biting cultural critique that exposes the "history of culture as a problem of *narcossism*" and America's "war on drugs" as a symptom of its refusal to take drugs seriously. But even more: the sections in *Crack Wars* called "EB on Ice," "The Doctor's Report," and "Cold Turkey; or, The Transcendental Aesthetic of the Thing Being Eaten" operate as individual literary works themselves, ranging from eye-opening futuristic fiction to sophisticated and hilarious theatrical drama. Do you set out to break up genres like this, to force them to collide? Or is it more that you ignore genre boundaries because they don't work for you?

AR: I'm keenly aware of the histories and presumptions of that with which I am breaking. Above all, I am a scholar working the German side of things. As for the stability of genres, their boundaries are not as secure as one would think. I am working within a lineage that these genres already prescribe. There is a great insecurity about their limits, and I do try to work at those limits. The history of genre is highly domesticated and meant to suppress anxiety about possible contamination and violation. I am negotiating with what genres know about themselves, which is to say that they can easily collapse, that the border patrol might be dozing off, taking a cigarette break, and then something else occurs that could not have been predicted. I will use a given genre's pretexts and inroads and histories voraciously, but then I'll also invite, in a mood of great hospitality, certain marginalized genres to participate in the "literary critical" move on a text. I work with crime story and drama, and also poetry at some point. In this sense, I am Deleuzean since Gilles Deleuze has called for writing philosophical works in the form of a crime story, zooming in on a local presence and resolving a case. In this connection, I've been very interested in the difference Freud asserts between police work and detective work. (He says sometimes you have to arrest a symptom arbitrarily just to get the analysand to advance in a certain way.) As we know from thematic reflections on the latter, very often the detective has to turn in the badge and assume a different rapport with the truth. This involves solitary tracking. Often one is outcast. Certainly, the figure of the detective is something that fascinates me. Nowadays, of course, we have lesbian detectives on the prowl, looking for some kind of disclosure or going after traces and clues—which is, after all, the position one necessarily finds oneself in when one is engaged in reading.

DDD: In the preface to *Finitude's Score*, you suggest that "electronic culture" signals for you a kind of "prosthetic *écriture*" that puts "writing under erasure"; and a few lines later, you make the rather startling statement that you're "writing for writing because it died." Would you elaborate on that a bit? Are you suggesting two different senses of "writing"?

AR: That is a very astute observation on your part. Obviously, since Plato all writing has been linked to *techne?*, so what I am getting at is a regional difference. Writing was always prosthetic and consistently viewed as a dangerous supplement, as Derrida says. But you're right because there are boundaries and differences to be accounted for. And the kind of writing, I would say, that is associated with immanence and transcendence can no longer be affirmed innocently, as if writing could be capable of true manifestation or disclosure, linked at this point to a kind of transcendental being. Writing is no longer in that kind of association with a privileged locus. The demotion of writing's claims has been thematized by so many writers and observed by so many critics that this project is not, in itself, new. What interests me, though, is the way in which writing has been, in a sense, obsolesced and divested. Of course, one has to be Nietzschean and produce at least two evaluations of that observation because there is something that, despite it all, liberates writing to another realm once its more church- and statelike responsibilities have been suspended. Something else is happening and something else is going on. There is a kind of freedom that writing still says, or tries to say, or can refuse to say. This writing is political, but according to another logic of politics that escapes simple codifications. Nonetheless, writing, in the sense that I have been outlining, with its privilege of transcendence and disclosure, I think can be safely said to have perished, died.

At the same time, what does this mean? Writing never stops dying. There is an *endless ending* of writing. Psychoanalysis has been declared dead, too, and so has deconstruction, but, as we know, the dead can be very powerful. Freud illustrates or throws this power switch in *Totem and Taboo:* when the little resentful hordes of brothers get together and kill this powerful father, what they discover is that they are left with remorse and unmanageable haunting and sadness, such that the dead father turns out to be more powerful dead than he ever was alive. He is more alive when he is dead. Thus, to declare writing dead can also, in fact, make it more haunting, more difficult and commanding. It can imply a more pressurized zone of being and a much more intense rapport with that which has died. In making this statement, I'm also aligning myself in some ways with Hölderlin's Diotima: when the philosopher Empedocles commits suicide, Diotima is left behind to read his sandals, which are all that's left of him; they are his remainder. Diotima becomes the reader of this lost foundation or footing that philosophy might have had. Diotima is one exemplary instance of the feminine figure who is left behind as the mourner par excellence and who needs to read the traces and somehow honor them commemoratively. We have this figure also, of course, in the crucifixion of one of our gods. To observe that something has died implies a complicated itinerary of finitude, and it can be an infinite finitude that becomes more and more powerful in its withdrawal, precisely *because* it withdraws.

DDD: In *Crack Wars*, you discuss what you call a "genuine writing," which you hook up with a "'feminine' writing in the sense that it is neither phallically aimed nor referentially anchored, but scattered like cinders." This genuine writer is like the addict, you suggest, inasmuch as neither is capable "of producing real value or stabilizing the truth of a real world," and inasmuch as both writing and drugging are "linked to a mode of departing, to desocialization . . . without the assurance of arriving anywhere." In your 1994 *Alt X* interview with Andrew Laurence, you suggest that this section is, to a large degree, a tribute to the work of Hélène Cixous. To what extent can this "genuine" writing be conflated with what goes by the name "*écriture féminine*"?

AR: When I use "genuine," I am already pointing toward a kind of etymological net that involves "genius" or suggests that there is something that *can't* be proper or genuine. After all, the code of genius is usually reserved for the metaphysical male subject. So I want to bear in mind the irony of "genuine," or the genitality of "genuine," because genuine has to undo itself and dismantle its premises. But what I wanted to underscore when citing this term "genuine" is akin to what I'm underscoring when I use the term "feminine" (and I put them both in quotation marks): that it is not about some recognizably feminine trait. I also use this strategy to rewrite Emma Bovary's name, "*femma*nine," with Emma enacting the femme, and of course with Flaubert being identifiable as Emma, as he himself notes in the famous utterance "Madame Bovary, c'est moi." I wanted to show that the predicament of a woman who wants to write but who has nowhere to go and little to do, and who's writing for no one, *counts* for something. I say it is the writer's common lot. The "femmanine" is already there in any kind of writing — lurking, latent, showing that all writing is exposed, unsure of its destination, unable to chart its course, unable to know if it is going anywhere but down. Deleuze has said that writing minoritizes the writer and also sets him or her into the condition, or the flow, of "becoming-woman." On some level, this phasing out of oneself is what happens to all who write, or to all who are inclined toward writing or who are written up by writing — even written *off* by writing. There is no way for you to think, really, that you know to whom you are writing, or that you are going anywhere, or that you are doing anything, in the classical sense of those terms. Emma's housewifely psychosis, her loser's sense of having no one to write to, no audience, is to be honored for its particular scenography of abjection, for its critically depressive qualities and properties.

At the same time, doesn't writing turn us all into little housewives who are sitting home all day? Maybe not with rollers on our heads, but in our little house robes and immobilizations. There is something about being under house arrest, about the solitude, the not knowing what the hell you are talking about . . . There are such moments (I hope I am not the only one outing myself here) that occur when you think, in the most expropriated sense, "What am I doing?" At just that moment, when there is nothing holding you up or bolstering your sense of who you are or what you are doing, right *then* you can maybe say that you are a "genuine" writer. So, it is according to that kind of paradoxical itinerary, or in that kind of aporetic rapport with writing, that I was trying to place Emma Bovary, who was kind of my girlfriend for a while because I really dwelled on and with her. And I got very anxious and upset that all these guys—rather prominent lit crit types—thought they controlled her or understood her and could detach from her general abjection, as though she were simply dismissible and a trash body. Of course, I tried to show to what extent she is a trash body. Through her, Flaubert invents the body of the addict. Nevertheless, there was something I wanted to show about her humbling and alienated domesticity that reflects the writer's *common* lot. And no matter how objectionable or easily judgeable she might appear to be, Emma Bovary represents what you become one day when you are a so-called genuine writer.

DDD: Your description of this "genuine" writing in *Finitude's Score* strikes me as very close to certain depictions of hypertext, itself an acclaimed offspring of electronic culture. George Landow, for example, sees hypertext as explicitly performing a kind of postfoundational writing that embraces its own value after the "death" of the author and the crisis in representation. Do you think the medium of hypertext might invite, more explicitly than print, the kind of "genuine" writing you discuss?

AR: I am not certain that it does, especially since it is so, I dare say, *masculinist* in its glee about overcoming masculinist premises about writing. So I have to view it with some suspicion. I think hypertext and many of its theories offer an overliteralized interpretation of its promise and boundaries. At some level, one has to deal with the fact it is a mere device that isn't often rigorously deployed. I don't think that what I am trying to work with is dependent on some kind of mechanical shift—and a rather *minor* mechanical shift, since one could probably demonstrate that the pre-Socratics, for example, used hypertext. I have never thought positive technologies initiate new modalities of Being or reflection. Very often these technologies, I have tried to show, respond to some sort of rupture that itself isn't even entirely new—there isn't the epistemic, clean-cut, or clear new beginning. So I think I would like to propose a far more complicated itinerary, one that couldn't be reducible to one discovery. Hypertext is more like the Wizard of Oz, right? The figure behind the special effects is hidden behind the curtains, and when we see its *ascesis* and poverty, we're a little disappointed. But it is there, and someone manages its presumed arbitrariness. One could certainly complicate what I just said, but essentially it is not so new. Of course, I am very open to discussion on this.

DDD: I agree with all you've just said, but I think that the conjunction of "writing" and the "device" is a complicated one. All texts are hypertextual, and every word is implicitly a "hot word," but I do think hypertext, when rigorously deployed as a medium, more explicitly than print technology exposes one to language's inherent hypertextuality. Your printed texts seem particularly hypertextual to me, and they seem to engage strategies designed to spotlight that hypertextuality. But print typically *requests* that the reader move in a linear fashion from one word to the next word planted there on the page. I think hypertext invites a reader, at the very least, to notice that any word could be—and so, at some level, already operates as—a hot word.

AR: I like what you're saying. It's inviting and compelling. And I do have to read my own resistance. I had a similar resistance to television, too, until I finally broke down and wrote about television. So I do feel there is a level of resistance that I need to interrogate. And that means I haven't closed the book on it, so to speak, but that there is something that is not allowing passage for me yet. I am provoked by what you said.

DDD: In "Activist Supplement: Papers on the Gulf War" [in *Finitude's Score*], you warn that the most influential proponents of virtual reality seem invested in propping up "his majesty the ego" and, to that end, describe virtual space as somehow making up for the lack of control we feel in "real life." Jaron Lanier, as you note, would like to have called virtual reality "intentional reality," since the latter indicates the sense of mastery over one's world that virtual reality simulates. But your approach to technology—from the telephone to the television to virtual reality—seems more interested in the way that *it* makes *us*, in the way that our technological creations in turn recreate who we humans are and what we can be—a process that ends up challenging the very notion of an ego in charge. Would you, then, characterize your approach to technology as posthumanist?

AR: Yes, I certainly would, though I might have to pause and explicate the meaning of "post." Still, I look to technology to affirm those aspects of posthumanism that are more liberatory and politically challenging to us. As I said, one of my concerns has been with television. Beyond the thematizations of crime, murder, and the production of corpses that don't need to be mourned, I am very interested in the way television stages and absorbs trauma, the way it puts in crisis our understanding of history and the relation of memory to experience. All of these aspects of the televisual that I have tried to read, as you indicate, presuppose a posthumanist incursion into these fields or presume that a posthumanist incursion has been made by these technological innovations (or philosophemes). On a terribly somber note, I don't see how, after Auschwitz, one can be a humanist.

My work has concerned itself with the Nazi state as the first technologically constellated polity as well as with the fact that technology is irremissible. Mary Shelley projected this view of technology with her massive, monumental, commemorative work on the technobody, which was the nameless monster. The problem with (or opening for) technology is that no one is or can stay behind the wheel, finally, and no one is in charge. And the way I have tried to route and circuit the thinking of technology—indeed, in a posthumanist frame—exposes the extent to which it belongs to the domain of testing. This view has little to do with hubristic humanist assumptions. I am interested in the difference between the real and the test, which collapses in a technological field. Every technology will be tested. Moreover, and paradoxically, that means it will not merely be a *test*. The Gulf War was a major field test; after the war, there were trade shows that announced that every weapon had been proven and tested. And so for the military, the Gulf War was a field test—and, as we know, that test cost real lives. But still you can't say someone *decided* this or that. There is something about the perpetuation of the technological that involves the figure of testing.

In any case, technology has produced different registers of being, or is reflective of different registers of being, and even our rhetoric of desire has been steadily technologized. We say we're "turned on," we're "turned off," and so on. We also say we "had a blast," which indicates a nuclear desire in desire. Nonetheless, there are different protocols of marking experience, and to arrive at some sensible reading of those protocols, one should no longer be tethered irrevocably to humanist delusions—delusions for which I have the greatest respect, of course. But humanism often functions like a drug that one really ought to get off of in order to be politically responsible. I think it is irresponsible not to be Nietzschean in this sense of risking the greatest indecency, of crossing certain boundaries that have seemed safe and comfortable and are managed at best by general consensus. Posthumanism is not necessarily popular with those who hold the moral scepter at this point. But I think it would be regressive and cowardly to proceed without rigorously interrogating humanist projections and propositions. It would be irresponsible not to go with these irreversible movements, or "revelations of being," so to speak. That sounds a little irresponsible, too, since it's a citation of Heidegger. But that's just it: one is precisely prone to stuttering and stammering as one tries to release oneself from the captivity of very comfortable and accepted types of assignments and speech. An incalculable mix of prudence and daring is called for.

DDD: Your approach to writing seems posthumanist, too. Your first book *Dictations: On Haunted Writing* explicitly examines (via the *Conversations* between Eckermann and Goethe) the possibility of writing after the "death" of the author. You redescribe writing from the angle of the possessed and suggest—let me quote you from the preface—that it "never occurs simply by our own initiative: rather, it sends us. Whether one understands oneself to be lifted by inspiration or dashed by melancholia, quietly moved, controlled by Muses, or possessed by demons, one has responded to remoter regions of being in that circumstance of nearly transcendental passivity." To a large extent, then, to write is to be a lip-syncher, to "take dictation," as you put it earlier. Writing here seems to require a kind of passivity that is not inactive but that is also not, strictly speaking, *active*. In *Crack Wars*, you note that when one writes, "[T]here are certain things that force [one's] hand," a "historical compulsion" that "co-pilots [one's] every move." So who is writing when something gets written? Or, more specifically, to what extent are you the author of the books published under the name "Avital Ronell"?

AR: To a very limited extent. As I am speaking, I don't feel contemporaneous with the one who writes because, as we discussed earlier, writing is a depropriative act; it always comes from elsewhere. One is body snatched, in a trance, haunted. Or, one is on assignment. I use that sense of being on assignment or assigned something to emphasize how I am "called" to writing. I don't know how to locate its necessity. And one doesn't know where the imperative comes from. Nevertheless, one is assigned to it, so that one is always writing at the behest of the other. At the same time, I am not trying to unload my responsibility here. it is not as though I can say that it comes from elsewhere or that I am merely a zombie of another articulation and therefore that I am in bondage absolutely. There is some of that, of course, but I must still assume the position of a signator because I become responsible to respond to this thing that I am transcribing, assigned to, haunted by. So we're talking about assuming responsibility as a signator, with a signature, but without taking credit. And that, perhaps, is the politics of writing to which I subscribe—which is not to say that I take credit for it. I am always indebted to others. I am always part of a circuitry that speaks through me, writes on me, uses me, and certainly uses my body, which has been "fragilized" and has had to endure quite a bit of suffering in order to allow me to respond to my debt: a matter of my allowance. That is the configuration in which I try at once to name my dispossession, or my possession (I am possessed by the other), and at the same time to assume responsibility—and yet not suddenly, in absolute, irresponsible contradiction to what I have been trying to say, to take credit for that which traverses me in the work.

DDD: Let me quote from the introduction of your latest book, *Stupidity:* "To write is to take a retest every day (even if, brooding, stuck, anguished, you are not empirically writing), to prepare a body, adjust your drive, check in (out of respect) with superego, put ego on sedation, unless you are a total memoir-writing-I-know-myself-and-want-to-share-my-singularity idiot." I take it that you would not call yourself an "expressivist" in the strictest sense of that term. That is, I take it that you do not think writing expresses a preexisting inner self?

AR: Only in the Bataillean sense, where there is an inner experience that somehow gets "exscribed," as Jean-Luc Nancy says. Indeed, writing has something to do with a constitutive outside, an exteriority, and cannot express but only invents and produces the fiction, if necessary and if called for, of the inside. You are outside yourself when it happens; you are beside yourself; you are pumped up as a different kind of being—or else you are deflated and defeated. In any case, it's not a constitutive thing but a performative act.

DDD: How, then, would you characterize the relationship among rhetoric's fundamental elements: the writer, the reader, and the message?

AR: Well, understanding the message as the work, I would assume that these fundamental elements are in themselves unstable, sometimes exchangeable or erasable by one another. And I would say that writing alters these elements, doesn't leave them in their place, leaves them expropriated and disfigured, unrecognizable. The work —what you are calling "the message"—in any case seems to let go of the reader and the writer. In other words, I see the work as solitary, inexhaustible, sovereign —it murmurs incessantly. But, of course, according to other hermeneutic appropriations, the reader can also produce, or be productive of the work and is inscribed in the work as its codependent, as that on which the work relies in order to be brought into being. This is one type of reading of Hölderlin: the gods —let's call them "the message" or "the work" or "the writing"—are dependent on mortals, on the poetic word, in order to be brought into time and existence. So these are different configurations in the fundamental triangulation that you set into motion. But in each case, I would say that the writing, the work, produces a type of disfigurement and distortion that requires us to rethink the place, which is never secured, of writer and reader.

DDD: *Stupidity* traces the question or problem of a kind of transcendental stupidity. Would you talk a bit about this project, both its content and its structure?

AR: It was Deleuze who named the future necessity of reading stupidity, and a transcendental stupidity, asking, what are the conditions for the possibility of stupidity? And he said that philosophy hasn't been able to think stupidity. First of all, because philosophy has been hijacked by epistemological considerations of error, error has derailed the thought of stupidity. As he says, literature has always brought the question of stupidity to the door of philosophy, which slammed that door shut, finding the theme (it is a paraconcept) somehow unworthy. Deleuze suggests that philosophy is haunted by stupidity, which, nonetheless, it won't consider. There is something about stupidity that is violently resisted by philosophy. That is where I come in: where something has been marginalized, minoritized, evicted, persecuted, left out of the picture, and of course *feminized*. Certainly, one of the impetuses for reading stupidity is promoted by a kind of postfeminist passion, protesting the way women have been called "stupid bitches" and noting what this might involve, how stupidity became an accusatory force, a devastating demolition of the other. Minorities are considered stupid, women are considered stupid, and so forth. To return to *Difference and Repetition,* Deleuze says that even the trashiest literature concerns itself with questions of stupidity. And even the most sublime literature is aware of it. In an inverted form, Henry James is very compelled by questions of stupidity and intelligence and of how one can tell them apart. Stupidity is a very slippery signifier and often turns into its other. It is not the other of thought; it is sometimes, literally, the figure of sheer reflection, proffering something like pure thought. But what interested me above all was located in the poetic act, the passivity of the poet in the extreme inclination toward surrender, the near stupor that characterizes the poetic disposition—the structure of exposure, something that poetry knows about, the extreme and secret experiences of stupidity. In this work, what I am doing, essentially, is appealing to the debilitated subject, the stupid idiot, the puerile, slow-burn destruction of ethical being, which, to my mind, can never be grounded in certitude or education or prescriptive *obéissance*. There is something about placing the question of responsibility close to the extinction of consciousness that interests me. Against the background of the ethical anxiety that has been expressed in recent years, my question tries to invoke a parallel track that is thematized in so many ways—the platitudes of dumbing down, the dumb and dumber and dumbest. What does a generalized dimwittedness, a diminished sensibility, imply for ethics?

In addition to addressing this kind of transcendental stupidity, which, of course, one needs to ponder and reflect on, I also consider other questions: for instance, who are the secret beneficiaries of stupidity's hegemony? and what are the somatizations that occur in stupidity? For Marx, for instance, stupidity is third in terms of what determines historical world power. In other words, the world is motored by economy, violence, and then stupidity. So these are some of the points I wanted to engage by mobilizing the question and problem of stupidity. In terms of micromanaging one's own history, I am also very interested in the idiot body and in our relation to our bodies when they are ill, when they collapse. How do we heal them? What do we know? Why is it that the scanners, charts, and medicalizations of the body tend to disappoint us? The rapport with the body is already something mechanical and stupid. I focus on the monthly period, which is a kind of stupid repetition to which women are routinely subjected. So there are different levels and registers of stupidity, a lot of them highly political, beginning with the only time Heidegger used the term "stupidity [*Dummheit*]": when he said his relationship to Nazism was his dumbest mistake. There I read what it means for Heidegger to say that he made a stupid mistake or I read the status of such an "excuse" for any justificatory discourse.

DDD: What about the structure? I noticed that there was a Wordsworth satellite. Are there more satellites?

AR: Yes, there is a Kant satellite, too, which is called "The Figure of the Ridiculous Philosopher; or, Why I am so Popular." I include in the book every mainstream "boss," including Christ, who is depicted by Dostoevsky as being an emanation of sacred stupidity in the figure of the idiot. I also look at the new and improved figure of stupidity sanctified by Christianity in the notion of *simplicitas*. But the Kant satellite traces or picks up signals from Kant's tortured relation to writing. Kant wrote like a pig, and he talks about it all the time. He is the first philosopher to have wanted to be an author, which is something Jean-Luc Nancy writes about in "Logodaedalus." What interested me is the way Kant does end up prescribing that a true and good philosopher will be more or less a bad writer and will not indulge in certain forms of wordplay and joyous resignification. For Kant, this decision was an agony and a renunciation. He had to renounce being a beautiful writer, a femme writer, and he becomes totally butch. He is very clear about this: he says I can't run around in pink ballet slippers, and I can't have honey—the kind you give to children to get them to drink something that they don't want to drink, like medicine or aesthetics. Real philosophy has to dispense with and renounce writing, being a beautiful writer, a true author. Of course, he also wanted to be this author that he says he renounced. So he feels he's in control of it. To the extent that he had to renounce it, it was something that he initiated. In any case, it is a tortured and charming itinerary of anxiety about not being a good writer. Henceforth, philosophy required it; it is the writing requirement for philosophy: that you be a bad writer. Anyone who writes "beautifully," so to speak, then as now, is stoned, ridiculed, and feminized. This requirement is a Kantian legacy; it's his bequest. French theory, which writes beautifully—Derrida, Barthes, Foucault are writers—finds itself judged across this legacy. Even in one of the *JAC* interviews, Chantal Mouffe responds charmingly to the first question, noting that before she got into philosophy and became a bad writer, she had wanted to *be* a writer. That is a citation of Kant about how ridiculous the philosopher has to make himself or herself in regard to writing. But this pernicious history, which I try to trace, leads to certain dismissive gestures that aren't fully contextualizable in the necessity of producing a ridiculous philosopher. This history cuts two ways: when someone says Derrida's work is ridiculous, this accusation is in itself distressing and crazy (and the person probably hasn't really read him); nonetheless, this accusation already belongs to a proud history spun out by the Kantian writing imperative.

DDD: It struck me as I read the chapters you sent me from *Stupidity* that you also take a posthumanist approach to stupidity, suggesting, in fact, alongside Roland Barthes and Gustave Flaubert, that stupidity is "prior to the formation of the subject"—which would imply that *we* are a function of *it*—and that "writing is always an immersion in stupidity." If this is the case, how would you respond to the question, why write? Is there, even still, a connection between writing and responsibility?

AR: I warn my students never to ask this kind of question. It's one of those fundamental abyss openers: Why am I writing? Why do this? Still, as we discussed earlier, there is something that forces your hand. You write maybe even *because* it is impossible. Or, maybe you write for or because of some other force that is leading you to regions you need to explore, and you don't know what kind of mapping would justify it. But, in this case, we would want to think, with Walter Benjamin, the notion of the task: *Aufgabe* in German, which includes the word *Gabe*, or gift—you are gifted—but in the double sense of poison, since the German word *Gift* means "poison." Essentially, *Aufgabe* is your task, and within it is *aufgeben*, to give up. So the task itself, your task, also enjoins you to give up the impossibility, the sublimity, and the inappropriability of it, of the task itself. It's impossible, and yet something about it is so stirring that you nonetheless find yourself moving toward it. There is always a double imperative, and I think we must all feel it when we're writing: the mania and melancholia mix, the cocktail of the extreme, inexplicable joy, and the equal sense of being demolished by its hopelessness.

One of my writing slogans has been "Who cares?" There you are, struggling in your little space of writing, and you think you have made a discovery (I am beyond that level of discovering), but nonetheless there is that "Oh, who cares?" Still, there is something about a commitment without the delusions of producing meaning or world-shattering disclosures that moves me—a commitment to writing, despite it all, despite fevers, harassment of daily tasks, the need to do other things, and so on. I also think of Beckett's response to that very question because he was considered to edge on nihilism in some ways, and he said, in French slang, "Bon qu'a ça," which translates roughly as "That's all I'm good for" or "That's all I can do" or "There's nothing else to do." And it's precisely because there is nothing else to do that you have to write. We need stories, as Bataille once said, and we need to write.

That would be the provisional response to the question, why write? It's a question, as I said, that I back away from. I don't have an answer for it. There are moments when I climb the scales of hopefulness; there are other moments when I am Hölderlinean about it, in the sense that he says writing is the most innocent of all mortal exertions. Initially, my decision to commit to writing — and it is a vow, a vow that needs to be renewed — was connected to my need to be innocent in a certain way. And I don't mean that in a naive sense. But I really felt that anything we do in our present systems of existence is highly contaminated, corporate, compromising, depressing, and so forth. And, of course, writing and publishing must have their share of this kind of conformism, but I think it is minimal, and I try to resist being a conformist in what I sign. So there was something about my commitment to writing that was not at all natural, so to speak; it was a very athletic decision, a decision to "musculate," to "work out" every day. There is nothing of a natural writer in me. I still consider it rather unnatural to be writing and desocializing. Writing, after all, is strangely allied to illness, to being an invalid. I don't know if you experience it that way, but one is cut off, one has a different rapport with time. Nonetheless, writing was the way I felt I could sustain and preserve my need for political activism in a way that wasn't perhaps as deluded as other ways. Everyone does what she or he can, I'm sure, and writing was the way I felt I could be more problematic and more of a dissident than in other ways that are currently allowed. Yet, I never had the choice, even though I say I made the choice to commit to writing. I really couldn't find a place outside the holding pen of this kind of writing. I might have wanted to work on radio or in different media or in theater — these are other forms of writing, of inscription. At any rate, precisely where there is no utility or support for writing is when I think it has to happen.

DDD: In an essay in *Birth to Presence,* Jean-Luc Nancy says that we write to respond to the call of writing itself, and that there is a constant need to keep doing it since each time you inscribe, you "exscribe" again. So one writes to attend to the call of the exscribed.

AR: Yes, but I do think there are many ways to "write." In fact, when Jean-Luc and I were in California, I had started this thing called "Radio Free Theory," and he was very encouraging. In fact, he said if he could do something besides the more conventional forms of writing, he would. I really was committed to this radio program, but it was snuffed out — too subversive, they said.

DDD: I haven't heard about Radio Free Theory.

AR: Basically, we maxed out my credit card to buy equipment, and we did some demos for a radio show that, among other things, featured post-Freudian call-ins, where we would call other people and discuss their issues in a post-Freudian rhetoric. We would call authors and critics who had bashed deconstruction and say, "You're on the air. Look, you wrote this. Did you even read this or that? What are you talking about?" Then we did little children's evening programs. They were very sadistic: stories of Dr. Schreber for your child before bedtime. And we did one thing on the Rat Man that was really beautiful and was accompanied by music. We had a correspondent in Paris, who told us what was going on there. We had correspondents all over telling us what Jameson and others were teaching. We had a lot of news — that was Derrida's idea, that I include news. Of course, it was a brilliant idea that was meant to make us indispensable. We had very creative tracks as well. It was amazing.

But it never got off the ground. It was supposed to be financed by Irvine, but they were horrified when they heard it. I don't know why. And I'm sure that sounds naive. It would have been the *Saturday Night Live* of high theory. Everything was high theory. We also had little segments that we thought altogether comforting and normal. For instance, we would offer fifteen minutes of someone giving a lecture — Adorno, Heidegger, Deleuze. You know, why not? There is an entire archive of voices on tape: Artaud, Joyce, Freud. *Freud* is on tape. We would also do radiophonic cutups that were inventive and hilarious. So a Deleuze lecture would be playing, and I would cut in as if it were a dialogue. It was very witty. And, of course, there is something very moving about hearing Freud's voice, or Adorno's, over the *radio*.

DDD: What time period was this?

AR: It was the mid-eighties. I was entirely into it. And I have to say that *everyone* cooperated. We put funny, S/M kinds of ads in journals asking for "submissions," and sure enough, countrywide, people were sending us tapes, hoping to be a segment on our show. Even Frank Zappa was going to help out because he thought it was "kewl."

DDD: If it were financed, would you consider doing this kind of "writing" again?

AR: I'd love to. That's what I wanted to do. But we couldn't get any institutional support, so the show was put out like a cigarette.

Anyway, all of that was to say that there are different types of "writing," and some kinds of very rigorous and political inscriptions do not require that you work alone. I think I would like not to have to write alone all the time.

DDD: The conjunction of writing, stupidity, and politics is an interesting one that I'd like to pursue here a bit more. In the introduction to *Stupidity*, you write, "For the writer the problem of stupidity occupies a place of deliberate latency; ever on the prowl for your moment of greatest vulnerability, it prepares another sneak attack. Unless you really know what you're doing, and then it's in your face, all over you in fact, showing no pity." What are the implications of this insight for academe for activism? Or to use your terminology, for "foolosophy" and for politics?

AR: First of all, I am writing out of an ethical concern that I articulate in the utterance, "I am stupid before the other." What happens when one humbles oneself and says, "I am stupid before the other"? I raise a question about how it is that in the unwritten history of stupidity there has always been an alterity, a nonappropriable other, that has been trashed and bashed and has received the accusatory sting of being called "stupid." So I am interested in this naming in which executive and executing decisions are made about the status of the other. And this occurs also in the testing apparatus of universities and admission policies. One interesting point in the history of testing is the invention of the word *moron* by American psychologists. This was how they filtered out immigrant children. *Moron* means "a little below average." But it allowed the immigrant children to be left back, kind of humiliated and degraded when their admissions tests were graded. These political and activist concerns have motivated and compelled me. There is a displacement, a violence in the question of who gets designated as "stupid." I need only mention "the bell curve" and other decisions that have been made about minorities. Even decisions that have been made about "clever" minorities—or shrewd or shifty minorities—are part of the same experience of stupidity: it's mechanical but upgraded to cleverness, so it is not real intelligence. I call for a kind of rewriting—rephrasing in Jean-François Lyotard's sense—according to which one would say, "I am stupid before the other." I think that would involve a surprising reformatting of what we think we know and how we think we can evaluate and judge.

I also try to show that in testing, subjects who can't respond to questions often are, so to speak, too stupid or too intelligent to offer the kind of responses that are instrumentally demanded. They might be too dialectical or not able to assimilate an accepted grid and so forth. I am interested in the humbling that occurs when one says, "I am stupid before the other," which is absolutely a taboo. You cannot imagine someone in a university saying, "I am stupid" or "I am stupid before my students." This humbling and destabilizing of the *sujet supposé savoir* — of the subject who is supposed to know or who is posed as functionary of knowing — creates minor insurrections that interest me. But, of course, one of the most stupid reflexes is to think that you know what stupidity is all about. This situation calls for another type of activism that begins with "I'm not sure I know." And you don't close the book; you don't throw the book at anyone. I fear I am simplifying the trajectory of the book right now. I hope you'll extend me some credit on this account. Suffice it to say that it would provide for a very different politics to say, "I don't know" or "I am stupid before the other," but not in the oppositional sense that stupidity is the opposite of whatever opposes it — let's say, provisionally, "intelligence."

DDD: In the "Activist Supplement," you suggest that "the opposition between passive and active proffers a deluded equation." "Take a look around you," you write, "haven't we, as a culture, been too active, too action-filled?" And you note that a "true ethics of community . . . would have to locate a passivity beyond passivity, a space of repose and reflection that would let the other come." This is not the typical view of community, which is usually posited as a product to be built and which therefore requires the active subject *building*. Would you elaborate on this ethic of community?

AR: I made these remarks on community in the context of the Gulf War with its attendant overestimation of virtual reality. This thought comes from the works of Heidegger, Freud, and Levinas — and, obviously, from Derrida as well. As Heidegger and Freud in their own ways posited, there has been too much action. When Heidegger went off track, it was under the aegis of "acting." The qualities that I am trying to describe are difficult to abbreviate, and I do not want to invite misunderstanding. The action hero, as we know — and there is no quarreling with this valorizing of the action hero — is not the thoughtful subject, though action and thought, activity and passivity, should not be easily opposed. It is much more complicated than that. Thinking is assimilable to acting. Rather than presuming and making predictable what could happen in a community, giving assigned places and determinations, if one opened up a space of radical passivity, one might see what comes, what arrives. Rousseau, for example, called for a mode of being that is in recession — he calls it "the *far niente*," the nondoing that opens you up to a disclosive dimension of being. From there, one might be able to hear the call; or, the call might be put out in a way that is entirely surprising, perhaps unrecognizable, and perhaps irreducible to codified meaning. Something would occur on the level of absolute and unconditional hospitality to being, to the other. These are the kinds of considerations that have prompted me. Rather than think we know in advance what community is, or what we are building, as if it were ours to build, we might *allow it to come*. To allow and allow and allow is the experiment that I would want to conduct.

DDD: Eduardo Cadava suggests that your writing compels us to rethink our assumptions about "language and subjectivity, encounter and relation, responsibility and decision." And he emphasizes the latter, even suggesting that your works "are nothing but the very trial of the concepts of responsibility and decision." If those concepts tend to be soaked, even marinated, in humanist presumptions about intentionality and autonomy, your work seems consistently invested in tracing out an ethics of decision (of "responsible responsiveness," as you have called it) that takes off from a posthumanist perspective — from the "presupposition that we are always, in advance, under the influence of others." But some would ask what this responsibility, this ethics of decision, would be based on if not on the intentionality and autonomy of the subject who acts.

AR: This question is a difficult one. Eduardo is discussing here a trial of decision. Everything has to pass through the crucible of undecidability. There is a trial, and, as Derrida has pointed out in "Force of Law," it is not the subject who makes a decision. In fact, if decision is called for, it has to encounter undecidability. If we knew, then we wouldn't have to decide, but there is a moment of madness, where a cut, a decision, an incision is made. And that madness shatters the contours of the subject. What I have in mind here is a more Levinasian inflection. In other words, ethical responsibility for the other is prior to subjectivity. It's only through this ethical relationship that a subject can emerge, according to Levinas. There is something like originary liability: you are liable prior to any empirical evidence of guilt. That is, prior to any subjective coagulation, or sealing process, there is something like a liability that hovers between guilt and owing and innocence. You are already marked by this being-for-the-other — that is, you are indebted, kind of guilty, kind of ready to assume responsibility prior to anything else. And this would be the first moment of being taken hostage in the experience of radical passivity. The status of "autonomy" cannot be stabilized in this subject who acts. In *Stupidity*, I try to read the Enlightenment values of sovereignty and autonomy and how they are dented and undermined by so many currents and considerations.

One issue that I have tried to grapple with, because it is not clear, is where responsibility begins. In "Trauma TV," I began by citing a psychoanalyst who made the assertion, concerning World War II, that one was made responsible by dint of having *seen*, having *witnessed*. So there is already a testimonial quality to responsibility. What this means is that the boundaries are really moving in on you because it displaces the categories of doing to *seeing*—you are responsible even for what you have *seen*. Responsibility is monstrous. As Derrida has observed, once you say, "Well, I have acquitted myself; I have acted responsibly," that is your moment of irresponsibility. In the very moment that doubt is removed and you feel you have accomplished your ethical task, you have relinquished it. It is in this context that decision, then, needs to be placed and understood, but not as a preemptive strike or with the assumption that judgment has been made, conclusively, definitively, and in a way that we could consider it to close the case. There is a temporality of decision that has to be scrupulously considered.

DDD: In *Finitude's Score* and in *Stupidity*, you note that writing, for you, is a "nonplace" in which "one can abandon oneself to abandonment" and discover an "ectopia of all 'proper' places." Whereas for Aristotle, "good" writing takes off from common places—topoi—you're interested instead in a kind of atopical writing. Would you elaborate on that a bit?

AR: I am interested in that which obliterates the originariness of site, which is haunted and difficult to condense into material qualities. But I would have to ask you how you are construing Aristotle? Do you want to say something about Aristotle before we continue?

DDD: In the most general terms, he lays out the topoi, and in the fields of rhetoric and writing studies, it is generally taken for granted that "good writing" begins from common places, from conceptual starting places that are familiar to both of us. So we begin together and can then take a new course together or run down an old one. The point is that the connection is made across common places.

AR: You know, in this regard, I'm sure I could be taken to task because I do, in fact, begin with common places. I think I remain in many ways Aristotelian. What could be more common than drugs, the telephone, secretarial relations in writing, stupid mistakes, housewife psychosis, and so forth? In that regard, I think I do follow the prescriptive pad. So the odd thing is that there are moments when you can trace a lineage. Those who might consider my work outrageous, or completely unfathomable in terms of a secured contextual milieu, might consider precisely such moments in which I answer the ancient call to begin with common places. But, of course, when one *philosophizes*, the common place becomes dislocated from its locus. I also situate myself within the German lineage of ironizing, subverting, and displacing certain horizons of expectation. After all, to be in a tradition, I feel you also, in this apparent paradox of absolute loyalty, have to show a moment of disidentification and departure. You split. Extreme loyalty to a tradition might force you to be entirely untraditional if you are attuned to the historicity of what you're doing, where you're coming from, where you are going. Obviously, you can't know these things absolutely, but you can endeavor to be attuned. It doesn't mean that one is enslaved by mere replication but that one effects repetition with difference. One could be upholding tradition precisely by masking its many figures and identities.

DDD: You suggested in your interview with Andrea Juno that because of your irreverent writing style, your refusal to censor the play of language—in fact, because of the pleasure you take in its play—you "tend to be associated with a writing which is considered 'morally wanting.'" Why do you think there is such a resistance to wordplay in academe? What investment is bolstered by declaring it "irresponsible"?

AR: Well, in the first place I house an unusually cruel and sadistic superego: there is always censorship and reprisal. I am, however, willing to say that I affirm irresponsibility in the Nietzschean sense. Nietzsche says we have to be rigorously irresponsible—that is, we must be nonconformist; we must not kiss up or suck up to the powers that determine whether or not we get a grant or get approval. With the exception of an early Alexander von Humboldt grant (before I started publishing), my work has not been funded. At this point, one might have expected some support—I don't know why one would have such an expectation, but perhaps because those working in similar and contiguous areas are supported. What I am saying is that the urge to chastise someone for being irresponsible—which, I assume, is not being said in the Nietzschean spirit of trying to be a free spirit, so to speak, with all the reservations and preambles that he appends to that—is also antiwoman. Women are irresponsible; they are not responsible enough to the phallic hold of the academic ideology unless they are servants who accept and name their servitude and who practice the strictly coded politics of gratitude. And that practice could include turning yourself into the authority of women's studies, or ghettos of feminism, instead of fanning out, disseminating, making trouble, kicking ass in all the "wrong places" and in ways that are barely recognizable according to the determinations that govern what are acceptable and responsible forms of objection. Being "responsible" in this negative sense means, precisely, not inciting highly problematic incursions into the domesticity and peaceful home fronts of the university. There is a lot to be said for this appellation.

But, again, being "responsible" in that sense—where you are not necessarily courageously pitted as one against the multitude, or doing something that is not recognizable, or not very appreciated—being responsible in this "negative" sense means keeping things clean, bordered, serious, *manly*. To be irresponsible implies a feminization, the double entendre, the double meaning, so there's this slippery feminine kind of masking and masquerading and makeup that's going on: she is "making it up," she's "faking" and "making," and so on. And, in literary history, that kind of notion of wordplay and fooling around with language and sedimented levels of signification always got linked to forms of anality—such as Shakespeare's Bottom, who is the great punster, an obsessional neurotic, or the Rat Man, who is Freud's case study of obsessional neurosis. There is always some sort of reversion to anality that is implied in wordplay or word disfigurement and distortion, so that the anal retentive hegemony of the academic stronghold is, I am sure, upset by this kind of thing. But to call someone "irresponsible" is, in the first place, a gesture that doesn't read the political implications of undermining monolithic meaning, doesn't read what it means to refuse to underwrite the notion that there is just the sanctioned dimension of accepted meaning. Language is arbitrary, radically arbitrary, which means that to a certain extent I am being extremely faithful to the rhetorical imperative, the imperative to understand the artifice and affirm the disjunctive nature of linguistic positing.

As I indicated earlier, there are institutional repercussions for this kind of linguistic misbehavior. I have many writing selves, many personae. I'm also the very *responsible* chair of a department, for instance, and a prudent professor, if I may say so. We have to understand that I am producing effects on different fronts here, and *affronts*. But if I were to situate one of these "posthumanist" selves, I would want do so in terms of the buffo in romantic literature — the one that de Man, Schlegel, Hegel, and others discuss. The buffo breaks into fixed narrative structure or theater and performs feats of ironic destruction and performs like the Greek chorus that would interrupt the narrative. The buffo is the interrupter par excellence. You wouldn't know if it comes from the inside or the outside, whether it's an *in*vasion of the narrative line or an *out*burst. The buffo releases an expression of rage. I would want to be seen as a relative of this buffo, who is also related to Nietzsche's staging of the buffoon — the one who really destabilizes and is unassimilable, carrying with her or him the mark of interruption. Rhetorically speaking, the buffoon is an anacoluthon — or, that which interrupts the smooth logic of accepted meaning or signification.

I take responsibility for those kinds of feats of ironic destruction and for producing certain disjunctions within the academic text. For Schlegel, the buffo becomes an important figure leading up to his great essay on unintelligibility. Very often the curse of irresponsibility quickly slides into a demand for intelligibility, which I think is a reactionary demand. And that would be the lie, this intelligibility. Schlegel says we would all collectively freak if intelligibility held sway over our affairs. It would destroy our families; it would destroy everything. He was beginning to trace out and map a notion of the unconscious. There's something unfathomable, and therefore potentially destructive of smooth and totalizing narratives, when unintelligibility is allowed to surface — unintelligibility being the condition for possible meaning and intelligibility.

DDD: Would you say that your dedication to wordplay, textual performance, and genre busting is in any way associated with your devotion to tracing out an/other ethics of responsibility and decision? That is to say, do you consider your writing style political in any sense of that term?

AR: To interrogate meaning is a political gesture that forces one to interpret community and sociality in its possibility. In that regard, yes, it has to be viewed as such. Traditionally, communication and community involve gathering around stabilized meanings. So by taking risks — and it is not I who is taking risks but rather language is risk taking and risk making — by *surrendering* to the risks that linguistic positing inevitably demands of one means, at least at some level, to hear and heed the call to break with the oppressive dragnet of reactionary significations. There is a class struggle in my texts: there's the girl gang speaking, the little gangster, the hoodlum; there's the high philosophical graduate student who studied at the Hermeneutics Institute in

Berlin; and there's the more sophisticated Parisian, and so forth. There are different voices, compulsions, denials, and relations that emerge in the texts. But there is the continuity of the more "prolo," proletariat, and very often wiseass girl who is watching this stuff happening and commenting on it—again, like the chorus or the buffo—who's ironic and whose narcissism involves a kind of sarcastic, biting, metacritique of what is going on but without ever becoming anti-intellectual. That's important. I never embrace the anti-intellectual tendencies of the American academy. But, then, my boundaries for what is intellectual are very, very generous, I think. A lot belongs to that space.

Indeed, I am always questioning what is proper to meaning and what is propertied by our estates of meaning, of teaching, and so on. It is not that I am playing with meaning but that meaning is playing me, and playing through me, on me, and against me all the time. I am inscribed in that disjunctive flow of meaning's regimen. Again, I want to note that I don't sit there as the pilot in the great *Star Trek* fantasy, with fabulous equipment and such. Actually, even in *Star Trek*, they got lost in space a lot. I don't decide; it decides me, it plays me, and I surrender and listen to it or take it down, as would a secretary taking shorthand. I suppose I don't repress it or call in the police to clean up the scene of the crime.

DDD: You don't censor it. You let it play.

AR: To a certain extent, I let it perform itself. Of course, there's also the part of me that's impish, a troublemaker, and that kind of dares and counterbullies what I consider to be these gigantic "bosses." In a traditional sense, I don't censor it, and I don't censor myself. But at the same time, it's rigorous; it is not stream of consciousness. There are strategic and tactical maneuvers that I do, of course, decide on and work with. It *is* work.

DDD: When you said earlier that you do indeed start with "common places"—how much more common and comfortable can you get than the telephone?—that made a lot of sense. But I have to say that it just doesn't jibe with the *experience* I have when I read your work. Your telephone, after all, turns out to be something completely unfamiliar, not really a "common" place at all. That experience sort of fakes the reader out. Your texts are *jarring* in this way; they are in no sense comfortable or comforting; they jerk the reader around a bit. It is difficult to name exactly what's going on, but even at the level of the sentence, or of the phrase, your work delivers a kind of disorienting smack.

AR: That is interesting because it's familiar. A very long time ago, at the beginning of my career, when I wasn't getting any jobs and I was completely destitute and desperate, I told my friend Larry Rickels, who became the chair of German at the University of California at Santa Barbara, that I didn't understand why this was happening. And he said, "You are going to have to become aware of the sheer radicality of your work, which is in sum an outrage." And that was the first I had heard of it. There's this little girl in me who just doesn't get it, who thinks she's really handing in the right assignment. Of course, we know from Freud and then Lacan that everything you hand in is your own *caca*. And you are *so proud* of it. Still, there is this little retarded or naive parasite being in me who doesn't know this yet, who doesn't realize it, who thinks she is so loving, who sees herself opening up to everyone, and who thinks, "Why are they mean?"

I don't know what this absurd anxiety is about, this desire to be able to say, "Have a nice text." It could be an effect of having been severely undermined. De Man said that I was a "professionally battered woman" before this term came into the public domain. I was beaten to a pulp by all sorts of institutional experiences; for example, I was fired illegally. There is still that part of me, the abused child of academia, who wants to be accredited and who wants to be told, "This is highly responsible work; we see you in the tradition of the Romantics and Hannah Arendt; you're in touch with the necessary mutations of your historicity." That part of me appears to persist.

When *The Telephone Book* first came out, I was greatly distressed. I felt exposed, that I wasn't one of "the boys." When I saw *The Telephone Book*, it came to me that I had broken with recognizable norms, and this prompted a narcissistic blowout. I really had a very bad depressive reaction because I felt it wasn't recuperable as typical scholarly work. I guess there is a double compulsion: part of me wants to please and to be institutionally recognized, patted on my back (or ass), but another part of me would feel molested by that kind of recognition. It's actually kind of a class warfare. There is the little bourgeoise who thinks, "Well isn't it time that I got some comfort here?"; and the other street girl who says, "Nah!" So you're right. When you say that this work "jerked [you] around" or was "jarring," violent maybe, that surprises me, and yet, of course, I was there when it happened.

DDD: Well, it jerked me around in the most wonderful way. In *Crack Wars*, you cite Flaubert: "The worth of a book can be judged by the strength of the punches it gives and the length of time it takes you to recover from them." Your books pack major punches. In "The *Dif-ferend* of Man" [in *Finitude's Score*], you discuss Lyotard's notion of the *differend* but offer another version of it, one that "talks and negotiates" — you call it the "affirmative *differend*." This version says, "let's talk," and you say this implies listening, a "talking as listening" that strains past oppositional logic. And yet, in *Crack Wars*, you note that to say "I understand" is to cease "suspending judgment over the chasm of the real." Is this listening and straining not aimed at understanding? Does it perhaps suggest that there are affirmative ways to *embrace* the withdrawal of understanding that the *differend* indicates?

AR: Yes. In *Stupidity*, there is a section called "The Rhetoric of Testing," which is on de Man and the irony of understanding. Citing de Man's elaboration of the problematic, I say that there would never be a moment where one could say, "This has been understood." I often appeal to Nietzsche's ever resonating and recurring utterance, "Have I been understood?" He sends it out in a sci-fi way, and I still hear it signaling to me, "Have I been understood?" It is a big question, a big interrogatory challenge. The irony of understanding is that the only knowledge we could have is that we have *not* understood, not fully understood. This irony, I think, does produce, in part, the articulation for a kind of political commitment. At the same time, it doesn't mean that we have not understood terror, genocide, misogyny, racism in a certain way. Still, having registered injustice doesn't obliterate the necessity of our incessant reading and questioning. The place from which such decisions as ethnocide, genocide, or murder are made is a place that thinks it has understood and can act on the basis of a certain understanding that doesn't doubt or question itself. I think that to presume that one has understood is often murderous.

DDD: In your essay "The *Sujet Suppositaire*" [in *Finitude's Score*], you suggest that "a question regarding the transmission of sexual marks as a condition of knowledge can be posed under the name 'Oedipedagogy.'" Rumor has it that you have also taught a graduate seminar called Oedipedagogy. Would you unpack that term for us and tell us a bit about the seminar?

AR: "Rumor has it" — this strikes me as funny. I have written on rumorological paranoia and other channels of transmission that occur everywhere — on the job, off the job, on the streets — and how rumor is this parasitical utterance that Rousseau was invested in, of course. But what I mean by "Oedipedagogy," briefly, is the way pedagogy is linked to desire but also to the structures of parricidal writing or overcoming your teachers. This intentional dimension abides in the teaching relation where all sorts of aberrant transferential or countertransferential structures can be observed. At the same time, you never entirely overcome the teachers that you are killing. This situation is something I try to read with and against the grain of something like the anxiety of influence, upping the amps on parricidal engagement or on such tropes as jealousy and appropriative rage. In the introduction to *Stupidity*, I speak of graduate students "packing heat." When you publish something, you're putting yourself before this tribunal that is going to judge and evaluate what you've done. And there were so many graduate students, especially at Berkeley, who were intensely competitive and jealous with one another or of me. Some were loving and wonderful; but, obviously, the site of learning and teaching is a highly charged atmosphere, and I wanted to bring to the fore the impossibility of teaching *while* I was teaching and also to scan the virginal space of the student body that lets itself be filled by the professorial phallus. Of course, these were quite controversial ways of considering our profession, but they're also canonical discursive formations around the fact of learning that I don't want to exclude.

In the seminar, I wanted to explore the more phantasmatic dimensions of acts of teaching, beginning with Socrates and his affairs of the heart and the phallus. We read Lacan on transference, Derrida's *La carte postale*, and *Frankenstein*, which is an allegory of teaching and learning, self-education, and the relationship of the master to the creator. (At one point the monster says, "You may be my creator, but I am your master.") We also read Blanchot on the difference between a teacher and a master teacher, which is very compelling. In the Rat Man, especially, the parameters of the relationship between the analyst and the analysand were very interesting to explore. And with all the difficulty and disjunction of translation, I wanted to see what could be retained of that relationship in the scene of teaching. What are the differences between Lacan as analyst, as teacher, as writer? What's the relationship between Plato and Socrates, as analyzed by Derrida in *La carte postale?* What's the relation between the mentor and student—between Arendt and Heidegger, Goethe and Eckermann, Batman and Robin? We also looked at the new laws legislating against sexual combinations in the classroom or in the university. When they first were proposed, Foucault, who was at the time at Berkeley, said it was absurd to try to legislate desire out of the scene of teaching. But what interested me especially was the hidden phantasm of sodomy as the groundless ground of the transmission of knowledge, and how its ghostly echoes still sit in on sem(e/i)nars — the etymological roots of seminar, seminal works, and other offshoots of the seed of knowledge.

DDD: Pedagogy-pedarasty.

AR: Voilà. The relationship reversed, or arse upwards, so to speak. Plato and Socrates, for example, as read by Derrida. And certainly in the case of Freud's Rat Man, the obsessional neurotic, where the Rat Man is exemplarily *coached* by Freud. The Rat Man was unable to name his symptom or disease, so Freud, filling precisely the space of learning, decides to guess in order to help him. In German, to guess is *erraten*, so that's the first "rat" insertion: he is going to "*rat* him out." Freud says the Rat Man, trying to explain, stammers, "and then . . . and then . . . and then," which is followed by ellipses and a dash, and then Freud writes, "Into his anus, I helped him out." This, for me, became the paradigm of learning: let me help you out — "Into his anus, I helped him out." There's this kind of moment of violence, of sticking it to you that true teaching has to enact. Of course, I am symbolizing highly here; no one should think we're solely pursuing a dildological pedagogy. But the question is where teaching arrives. When? Is it a trauma? Is learning a trauma, as Werner Hamacher once suggested? If so, does it come to us at night? When does the promissory note that you give to each class (you are promising that they will have understood) come due? Will they understand five years from now? In a dream? In the space of the so-called unconscious?

It's also a question of locating the address of teaching. Whom are we addressing with teaching? What are we addressing? How does the question of address determine the essential quality and possibility of teaching? In the Rat Man case, the patient calls Freud "Captain" after the Captain who scared him with the story of penetrating rats. The analysis starts taking hold when Freud is addressed as the Captain — the sadistic, cruel, inserting, penetrating Captain. Whom are we addressing in the pedagogical scene, or what are we addressing, and how is that structured? These are some of the questions that emerged from the texts we looked to, including the *Reveries of the Solitary Walker* written by Rousseau, who at the end of his work names his debt to the woman he lived with, an older woman, and he turns everything around. He reverses the charges. She becomes the *origin* of all of his work. Turning around, he feminizes himself, so to speak. We also read Nietzsche on higher education; he says that even when we think we are taking notes freely, we are attached like a Bic pen to the paternal belly of the state. We interrogated questions of academic freedom, too, and

Samuel Weber's text on institution and interpretation. The final text was Deleuze's *Masochism: Coldness and Cruelty,* on the kind of contract you sign when you enter the scene of pedagogy. In Deleuze, the sadist abhors instruction, whereas the masochist signs on with a teacher, and instruction takes place. The final phase of the course was on our interrupted relation to law, which constitutes the scene of pedagogy.

DDD: Now that you've completed *Stupidity,* what's next for you?

AR: I have a few things happening, but I think the title of my next work will be *The Test Drive,* which is about the extent to which we depend on testing in our modernity. It's connected to what I tried to show in my article on the Gulf War: that, figuratively, our whole country, our national body went through an HIV test and scored HIV negative. The argument was bolstered by the relentless rhetoric of a bloodless and safe war. You could see the collapse of AIDS hysteria with the diction of warfare. *The Test Drive* was motivated as a project by Nietzsche's thought on the experimental disposition — among other things, an antiracist position that he took. And another work that I shelved for a while, *Politesse,* involves the intersection of ethics, politics, and aesthestics — and also the question of politeness. I had the privilege of talking to Levinas about it at one point, and he said that *politesse* is the space where God still resides. This project is something that I have worked on for quite a while that I may unfreeze.

A good part of me wants to venture elsewhere, though. I want to do theater or performance. These books are heavy burdens for me. I feel excessively obligated to them, and I don't entirely understand the nature of that obligation, that call. You caught me in one of the few times in my life when I'm between books. So first of all, I am trying to recover. I'm on a recovery program from writing. I've been clean for about a month. Of course, I get very anxious when I am not writing (not writing means I'm not under the command of a book — there are articles, reports, tenure reviews, letters). At the same time, I am kind of drawn to other ways of performing the inscription. And rather than just continue to do as I have, I want to think about what other ways might be possible. But still, these unfinished books are yelling at me, screaming for my attention. There is something very tormenting about unfinished books. And they each take years. I would like to get to the point where I "finish" these unfinished books and then could go elsewhere and do other things. But my health problems have kept me at home, too. So I don't see myself staying up till four in the morning preparing off-off-Broadway productions of Eckermann's relation to Goethe, or whatever. But other types of inscription, nonetheless, would be a real temptation.

DDD: Obviously, your work has been enormously controversial. Are there particular misreadings or misunderstandings that you'd like to address or respond to here?

AR: You know, I am touched by this question, and I am very sensitive to the kind of rescue mission it entails. At the same time, though, I feel deeply that it is not my place to assume the posture of authority, or to place myself in the control tower that lands the right reading, the right understanding, and sees to it that certain calamities don't occur. I feel that the work is not mine to correct. When a misunderstanding does come to me in a way that I find intelligible, I try to address it in the next work. Since I question the closure of interpretation, I can't allow myself to slip into the place that would prescribe how texts are meant to be read. I have to rigorously affirm their having been sent and having gone out to do whatever it is they have to do. A text's got to do what a text's got to do. Even if it brings shame upon my name.

The only thing I might signal—and this cannot be corrected, and I can't provide a correctional facility for such critical behavior—is that often, especially coming from England, there will be reviews of my work, in which the *guy* will say that I should be beaten for the way I write, or that I should be smacked for this or that. These reviews, that is, involve a supplement of physical abuse. In the early part of my career, I was pushed off podiums and stages; I was interrupted and just largely reviled in the most Ivy Leagued places, the big leagues. Somehow, I provoked violent responses. And this response is just a dimension of my work that probably should not be left out of the picture. These critics and colleagues may want to learn to read their own symptoms, may want to consider why it is that a little girl's work can provoke such reactionary responses. The level of rage that prescribes physical correction and censorship is interesting to note. That's all I'll say. The misunderstandings are probably necessary, and the calls for violence are symptomatic and real. One thread of my narrative entails the continuing saga of a manhandled woman, psychoticized by institutional forms of undermining that do occur. I am fortunate in many ways, though. At times, I feel like a cartoon character. I have survived so many batterings, and I am up again and running— at a slower pace, but after this explosion and that removal of ground, I'm back on the scene. I feel very welcome here in New York, so that's wonderful. But perhaps some readers/critics would like to reflect on the recurring shift to violence, the desire to do violence, to violate this textual body.

5

Arkady Plotnitsky
Difference beyon∂ Difference

JW: This project concerns questions of difference, as this figure is "mobilized" or, as is more likely, contained, neutralized, or domesticated within pedagogical processes and institutional structures. In what ways does the institution we name "the humanities" effect this and for what reasons?

AP: Even were one to think in terms of the last thirty years or so, properly responding to your question would require a massive endeavor—a historical-conceptual investigation on the scale of Foucault's projects. For so much depends on a great variety of particular and sometimes unique junctures or, when they are possible, specific links between or within such junctures. It is through such junctures and links that both processes, indeed (since there are further stratifications) both *types* of processes that you mention and the interactions — the "or" of your sentence — between them play themselves out. Even the basic parameters of such an answer, or of the ways of asking such a question, would require a massive *mobilization* of resources and arguments (and figures of difference) well beyond my limits here. Accordingly, I can only sketch a few such parameters, which appear to me especially germane to the working of "the institution we name 'the humanities,'" or the academy and culture at large at this point.

The (disjunctive) conjunction *or*, appearing in your first sentence, is itself an important figure of difference or the interplay between affinity and difference, proximity and distance, connection and disjuncture since, as with *either or*, it may mean both "either one or the other" and "both." I do not think that one could rigorously use the "or" of "either or," here and bypass a more Derridean (not the same as Gödel's!) undecidability just invoked.[1] "Or" joins the two signifiers *o* and *r*; read, for example, as *zero* (the opposite of *or*), nothing, and reality (everything?) or zero and real numbers (collectively designated as *r*, which of course include zero) in mathematics. The *or* of Stephanie Mealworm's *Or* involves and branches into these elements through what Derrida calls "dissemination." Dissemination is, of course, yet another figure of difference introduced (in part by coupling it to both *difference* and undecidability) via Derrida's reading of Mallarmé in "The Double Session" in *Dissemination*. Logic would try to contain this dissemination of "or," and in certain cases, such as that of mathematical logic, would offer a sufficiently rigorous and workable space of such containment, but not without certain unexpected complications, such as those of Gödel's theorems, either. By contrast, reflecting and reflecting on the disseminating possibilities or inevitabilities of "or," key radical philosophical approaches to "difference" analytically expose and strategically deploy both this particular dissemination and the more general complexity found in the functioning of "or" — the complexity we can give to *or* through which we construct this functioning. Indeed, the very proliferation of "or" in my commentary here is itself irreducible, but also enabling. The same type of "or," I argue, also governs the relationships between mobilization and containment — mobilization *or* containment — of, in turn interactively, difference and (*or*) the figures of difference in, to return to your careful formulation, "the institution *we name* the humanities." (It also appears to echo Derrida's "the strange institution named literature," on which I shall comment below.)

I do agree that *containment* and *not mobilization* of difference, often through an appeal to difference, tends to dominate the humanities and a significant part of our culture, especially at this point of history, although this may be inevitable in more general terms. I shall, for the sake of economy, speak primarily of containment, although its satellites, such as those you invoke, must be kept in mind, as must, conversely, various satellites of mobilization. I shall also primarily speak of difference, while in turn keeping in mind its equally important satellites, such as exteriority, alterity, or otherness, on one hand, and multiplicity or plurality, on the other. After several decades of circulation and overcirculation of the figure or figures of difference, at this point one sometimes needs to give more space to, to *mobilize* the figures of, similarity and commonality (or repetition, for example, via Deleuze's analysis), and to *contain* some of our figures of difference. Indeed, this is necessary in order to give a proper rigor to our understanding of the workings of difference and the figure or figures of difference, to begin with. For, how different are most, perhaps all, different things, or how different can they possible be? It can certainly be, and has been, argued that no *"absolute* difference" is ever sufficiently different. That is, absolute difference is never a sufficient figure of difference, anymore than any absolute, or at least any *absolute* absolute, positive or negative.

In any event, it appears difficult to disentangle the two types of processes you speak of: those mobilizing the figures of difference and those containing such figures, or difference itself, as difference and figures of difference are interlinked in turn. Some of these figures help and enhance the workings of difference or certain differences, as differences are in turn different, and are thus better understood in terms of different figures. (Any invocation of difference is bound to appeal to a figure of difference, however unspecified such a figure may be by such an appeal and however unpredictable a potential response to this appeal may be.) Other such figures help to contain these workings and are in fact, or in effect, figures of containment of difference; it is not always easy, and sometimes impossible, to decide which are which. As the work of containment appears to be more powerful and pervasive, we may even deploy certain figures of difference in order to contain the effects of differences, let us say, the political effects of differences, upon us. Thus, different forms and different figures of difference are always in a complex interplay of mobilization and containment, often entangled and sometimes undecidable as to which is which. The history of the humanities during the last thirty years shows an enormous range of this interplay. Certain terms indicate and generate sites of this interplay, or else are *mobilized* by an analysis of this interplay itself. It is certainly difficult and, it appears, rigorously impossible to guarantee a decidable calculation of the spectrum of effects, including those of mobilization or containment, a given enactment of a given form of difference, or a given engagement with a given figure of difference, can produce. Where such an enactment or engagement itself belongs on this spectrum already poses this problem.

The more radical among the available theories of "difference" pursue this type of acausal and arealist dynamics. That is, such dynamics are productive, efficacious of certain effects, those of difference among them, while disallowing any description of their ultimate workings in terms of difference (especially as *absolute* difference, alterity, exteriority). (I discuss these conceptions under the general rubric of "nonclassical thinking" in a recent study, *The Knowable and the Unknowable*.) I shall, however, continue to speak provisionally of such dynamics in terms of figures of difference or, one might say, "difference beyond difference." First, these conceptions appear to be germane to your question, and, second, the figure or figures of difference are fundamental to the development and deployment—*mobilization*—of these difference-beyond-difference conceptions. The ideas of Nietzsche, Bataille, Blanchot, Lacan, Althusser, Levinas, Lyotard, Deleuze, Derrida, Irigaray, and de Man, or, in science, those of Darwin in biology and Heisenberg and Bohr in quantum theory could serve as primary references here. As will be seen, one can also invoke a number of literary figures over a much longer history, although this history may be extended in philosophy and mathematics and science as well. Naturally, we must grant differences between these conceptions and the different degrees of radicality of each, or, especially in the case of literary figures, of a given interpretation of each. Also, and more crucially, none of these theories precludes "calculations" of various effects in question, that is, either analysis or predictions of certain effects. Despite and by virtue of the limitations at the ultimate efficacious level and by virtue of the incalculable undecidability of certain effects, these theories make such calculations possible where they were previously impossible, and often enable better calculations throughout. They do so in part by rigorously engaging with the incalculable and the undecidable, just as Gödel's famous theorems do in mathematical logic. To miss the incalculable and the undecidable means not to be sufficiently rigorous. In other words, our theories (or figures) and practices of difference, and our readings of such theories and figures, must confront this undecidability, beginning with our "decision" in any given case as to what in fact constitutes a mobilization or a containment, and of what.

This view is not in conflict; quite the contrary:

1. Certain of these texts and concepts have been decisive, even uniquely decisive, in mobilizing the figure of difference in perhaps its most radical aspects and implications, especially in the humanities.

2. It does follow, however, that we must consider equally irreducible and more persistent forces, for example: psychological (possibly even physiological and biological), intellectual, cultural, political, or other forces that compel us toward containment, crude or subtle, of both difference and the figure or figures of difference, and of the interplay of difference and its figures.

3. In short, we encounter, on the one hand, the *more or less irruptive emergence* and mobilization of the figures of, and emphasis on and practices of, difference or differences and, on the other, the *more or less continuous containment* of them.

These three propositions provide a short answer to your question, *my* short answer. But then, there are no other answers, no "*the* answers," and no "*the* questions," as Nietzsche was first to understand in full measure, thus also announcing arguably the most radical figure of political difference still found. "'This is *my* way; where is yours?'—thus I answered those who asked me 'the way.' For *the* way—that does not exist."[2] Obviously, as short and particular in its perspective as it is, this answer requires still further qualifications, which I shall offer below.

First, then, as concerns mobilization, my view is as follows. The humanities *primarily* mobilize such figures by engaging, at *certain* moments and at *certain* points or junctures, with *certain particular* types of concepts and texts, which appear to make such a mobilization more rigorously necessary, more urgent and demanding, in engaging with them. The humanities, or at least again *certain* humanities, at *certain* points and at *certain* junctures, appear to allow for or even compel such engagement more readily or more permissively, at least again at *certain* points, than other academic institutions, say, "the institution we name science."

The last differentiation needs immediate qualification, however, since there are moments where the figures of difference, sometimes in the most radical form, become crucial in mathematics and science as well, usually the moments of crisis, such as those that accompanied the emergence of modern biology, quantum theory, or Gödel's works on incompleteness and undecidability in mathematical logic.

I should further qualify that, in referring to these particular conceptions, I do indeed see them as figures of difference, or "difference beyond difference," and they find their conceptual and epistemological correlative in key philosophical figures of "difference beyond difference," invoked here, such as those of Bataille, Blanchot, Lacan, Derrida, and de Man. That is, I do not only mean the emergence of certain philosophical problematics (of whatever kind) at such crisis points in mathematics and science, in the manner of Kuhn's "paradigm shifts," although the latter is important, and would in turn apply to the work of the philosophical figures just mentioned. Beyond itself enacting a "paradigm shift," Kuhn's figure is of course itself a figure of difference and of difference beyond difference, significantly indebted to both Darwin's ideas and the epistemology of quantum physics. It is also makes us more attentive to the workings of difference, especially in the history and philosophy of science. As I have indicated, the emergence of most figures of radical difference, difference beyond difference, tends to be irruptive, paradigm changing. Their containment is, by contrast, more continuous and persistent. We must in turn interrupt it.

Now, in the workings of such irruption and interruption in the humanities, one might, to some degree, single out the role of literary texts sometimes coupled to certain philosophical texts or readings, such as Derrida's reading of Mallarmé. This deployment may take place in and through readings of older texts, previously read otherwise than in terms of the figure or figures of difference. Derrida's reading of Mallarmé is a particularly powerful example of such a rereading. Of course, this type of rereading also takes place in Derrida's and others' readings of philosophical texts, such as those of Heidegger and de Man, especially in their rereading of both Kant and Hegel, or of Nietzsche. Literary works, however, are decisive for all these authors. I am not, at the moment, strictly referring to a particular role of literary studies in this respect, especially Anglo-American literary studies, and specifically in juxtaposition to "the institution we name philosophy," although the case is indeed germane here. For one thing, a philosophical engagement with a literary text could take place outside literary studies, however the latter might subsequently use this engagement. Such was indeed the case in, among others, Derrida's readings (at least up to a point), Heidegger's readings of Hölderlin and Rilke, or Deleuze's more conceptual *mobilization* of literary texts. I would also like stress the qualified nature of this appeal to literary texts on my part, since, in my view, while this type of coupling with literature is common and effective, it is not indispensably essential. The deployment of texts and concepts here in question may be more independent, wherever in the humanities it takes place. Certainly, the rereadings of philosophical texts just mentioned are equally crucial in the present context, including in literary studies. Nevertheless, a certain singling out of literature is justified in the present context.

Bataille, Blanchot, Lacan, Lyotard, Deleuze, Derrida, and de Man: all have emphasized and exemplified this role of literature on many occasions. Some of them have even defined literature, at least a certain model literature, in terms of such a mobilization of difference and its figures, especially Blanchot and de Man, and, in a more qualified and ambivalent way, Derrida. Derrida often stresses the significance of literature in his work and, hence, of its role in the mobilization of certain figures of difference and of difference beyond difference there.

While I want to focus for the moment on literature itself, this is not, let me add, to neglect the significance of other arts and the disciplines that study them in this context. It may, nevertheless, be cautiously argued that, as far as the mobilization of differences and figures of difference, and especially of "difference beyond difference," is concerned, both literature and literary studies have played a leading role, sometimes even a leading philosophical role, in recent history.

Indeed, it may be argued that literature, "the strange institution named literature," and, hence, a certain literary register open to texts whose classification is more complex may be even more permissive than literary studies as concerns a mobilization of difference and figures of difference, or, once again, of difference beyond difference. One can connect Derrida's earlier view of "literature" in conceptual-epistemological terms of figures of difference and difference beyond difference, as in Mallarmé, and his more recent view of "the strange institution named literature," seen in political-judicial terms as an "authorization to say everything" ("anything" may be more accurate). I refer in particular to "The Strange Institution Named Literature" in *Acts of Literature* and "Passions: An Oblique Offering" in *On the Name,* but other later texts may be cited. These connections are complex, and it is of course not merely a question of literature's special authorization to engage with figures of difference and difference beyond difference by virtue of its authorization to say anything.

But then, would not literature itself be the part of the institution we name the humanities, and in what sense, for example, given the pervasiveness of M.F.A. (Master of Fine Arts), writer-in-residence, and related programs across the United States? Admittedly, these may, at least at the moment, not be the places where figures of difference have most appeal or which contribute to the mobilization of these figures, but they may become such places, as happened with John Barth's work at Johns Hopkins in the late 1960s. In teaching critical theory and philosophy to current M.F.A. students myself, I can certainly see such possibilities. The case of philosophy or of the institution we name "philosophy" entails yet another set of complexities, assuming, again, that there is one institution of philosophy, or of literature. This assumption *or* the assumption of the impossibility thereof is equally germane to the institution or institutions we name "humanities." This makes me persistently qualify here, referring to *certain* moments, *certain* points and junctures within and without the academic humanities, and to many in-betweens, many locations and interactions between the academic humanities and their many others, within and without. For the academic humanities are themselves intramurally heterogeneous, while being interactive. On the other hand, in thinking this interactive heterogeneity, or heterogeneous interactivity—this radical, and yet reciprocal, exteriorization of the inside and the interiorization of the outside—placing an "or" between them helps and enables the emergence and mobilization of difference and differences, or difference beyond difference, and their figures.

This emergence, I'm arguing, tends to be irruptive and often singular in nature, and the mobilization difficult and often short-lived, continuously resisted and often defeated, by the continuity of containment, far more widespread and persistent. The reasons, as I said, range from very general epistemological and psychological (possibly even biological), to broadly cultural-political, to specific institutional reasons; and the interactions between these forces are decisive throughout. Most of the authors here invoked address and emphasize these multiple dynamics. I will restrict myself to a few key points.

Derrida's crucial early elaboration sketches this problematic in a broad and powerful outline:

> What always threatens this [precarious] balance [of the representation of the *anthropos* linked to the manual-visual script of audio-phonetic writing] is confused with the very thing that broaches the *linearity* of the symbol. We have seen that the traditional concepts of time, an entire organization of the world and of language, was bound up with it. Writing in the narrow [pre-Derridean] sense—and phonetic writing above all—is rooted in the past of nonlinear [Derridean] writing [that] had to be defeated, and here one can speak, if one wishes, of technical success; it assured a greater security and greater possibilities of capitalization in a dangerous and anguishing world. But that was not done *one single time.* A war was declared, and a suppression of all that resisted linearization was installed.[3]

Derrida's (rightly) emphasized qualification and the "war" (rather than "battle") metaphor are crucial. Your own language of "mobilization" (now on both sides) is not irrelevant either. Deleuze and Guattari would invoke conflicting "war machines," such as nomadic machines mobilizing difference vs. state machines trying to repress, contain, or fight difference and the figure or figures of difference. These figures indicate the continuous history of the emergence, mobilization, and containment of, interactively, both difference and the figure or figures of difference, and especially those of "difference beyond difference."

These figures or unfigures, again, refer to the "processes" that may be ultimately inaccessible, whether now or in the future, in any terms (such as "process") and by any means, but without them nonlinear writing and its other radical effects would be impossible.

De Man would link the rupture of the linearity and continuity of the symbol, invoked by Derrida, with the *discontinuity* of allegory and still more radically irony (a discontinuity beyond discontinuity, especially beyond absolute discontinuity). These are tropes belonging to, in de Man's famous essay title, "the rhetoric of temporality."[4] To cite his later, equally famous, invocation of a figure of "difference beyond difference" in "Shelley Disfigured:" "[Shelley's] *The Triumph of Life* warns us that nothing, whether deed, word, thought or text, ever happens in relation, positive or negative, to anything that preceded, follows, or exists elsewhere, but only as a random event whose power, like the power of death, is due to the randomness of its occurrence."[5] De Man proceeds, as does Derrida, from this point to the interactive dynamics of irruption, mobilization, and containment, now more specifically in the context of literary studies and, by implication, in humanistic historical and aesthetic studies and ideologies in general. Literature helps the irruptive emergence and success, however short-lived, of difference and difference beyond difference, and their figures or unfigures. De Man writes:

> If it is true and unavoidable that any reading is a monumentalization of sorts, the way in which Rousseau is read and disfigured in *The Triumph of Life* puts Shelley among the few readers who 'guessed whose statue those fragments had composed.' Reading as disfiguration, to the very extent that it resists historicism [or aestheticism] turns out to be historically more reliable than the products of historical archeology [or aesthetic ideology]. To monumentalize this observation into a *method* of reading would be to regress from the rigor exhibited by Shelley which is exemplary because it refuses to be generalized into a system.[6]

A number of passages from Deleuze, or Deleuze and Guattari, could be cited here as well, despite —and sometimes because of—a greater hope for difference and its figures expressed throughout their work, especially from Deleuze's *Difference and Repetition* on. (A similar argument can be made in the case of Irigaray.) Also, Foucault's investigations, in his earlier but especially in his later work, in terms of "power," his (often misunderstood) name for his own conception of "difference beyond difference" and its effects might be called into question here.

Such questions may not be altogether resolved at the theoretical level in Deleuze and Guattari's work, or in that of Foucault, and some of their arguments may be questioned. But they are posed and lead to many specific analyses and examples of psychological, political, and cultural forces involved, and of their richly interactive relationships. But then, these are perhaps the only "solutions" possible here.

Obviously, Freud's work and psychoanalysis (however, one approaches them) bear heavily on this problematic. These connections would, however, require a separate discussion. Here I would like, first, to reiterate that the work of Nietzsche, arguably still the greatest thinker of difference, has been decisive and indeed indispensable to our understanding of the problematics here addressed, and to the work of virtually all authors mentioned. The very circulation of Nietzsche's work during recent decades has been crucial, more so perhaps than that of Heidegger (for whom Nietzsche was in turn a decisive figure), significant as Heidegger's work was. Second, I would like to invoke Hegel, "the last philosopher of the book and the first thinker of writing," as Derrida calls him in *Of Grammatology*,[7] and especially *The Phenomenology of Spirit*. All passages and elaborations dealing with the dynamics here considered may be seen as rewritings, however radically (a complex question), of the key elaborations of Hegel's great work.

But then, to paraphrase Shelley, if Hegel comes, can Kant be far behind? We are still inside this great "Bermuda triangle" of Kant, Hegel, and Nietzsche, the great names of problems, great figures of difference and difference beyond difference. We are still subject to their winds and storms. I shall have occasion to return to these weather figures and Shelley later. Is "weather" itself not a figure of difference, perhaps even an archetypal, primordial figure, if there could be one, and certainly naming the difference that, as chaos theory has taught us, we cannot ultimately predict or control? This is not to leave Descartes, Spinoza, and Leibniz, among others, out of the picture, and all figures of difference in turn. And, I am afraid, Plato and Aristotle are closer than we think, not to speak of Heraclitus and his *diapherein*, or literature from Homer on.

Tracing your question to what is arguably its earliest known history in the Heraclitean *diapherein* and Homer, or my invocation of weather, each would be a fitting ending point for my answer. There is, however, yet another set of dimensions to your question that one should not bypass here — its political dimensions. They are, to be sure, manifest and implicit throughout my comments so far. One could argue, however, that, especially during the recent decades, political forces were critically significant in, and even primarily responsible for, mobilizing the workings of difference and figures of difference (and its key correlatives, such as alterity and otherness) both in the humanities and the contemporary culture, or geopolitical world at large. This is in considerable measure true. One need only mention the most prominent recent developments in the humanities to illustrate this point—gender studies, gay and lesbian studies, postcolonial studies, or still more recently studies of "globalization." (The latter is a peculiarly nondifferential term, prompting Derrida to speak of "mondialisation," which is not altogether effective either.) The significance of these developments in the present context is momentous, and it has been the subject of many investigations. Rather than pursue this subject in detail, which would be difficult to do here, I would like to relate it to the preceding discussion in two key ways.

First, at least insofar as these developments help and enable the mobilization of *figures* of difference, they are not independent from the mobilization of such figures through concepts, texts, or readings, as here addressed. While admittedly a more complex question, the mobilization of difference itself is part of this dependence or, better, the interaction between conceptual-textual and political mobilization of difference and figures of difference. One could demonstrate how the developments just mentioned, especially in literary studies, borrow from the authors, conceptions, and texts addressed here. I would like, however, to stress instead the reciprocity, a mutual engagement, which may well be more decisive, especially at this point.

Second, along the lines of containment of difference and its figures, this containment, while common and inevitable in general, has been distressingly pervasive and persistent, sometimes to the point of the emergence of near reactionary agendas (at least intellectually), in these otherwise progressive and liberating developments. One of the main reasons for this may well be that what is most difficult to grasp and accept, and what is most resisted, is what I call here "difference beyond difference" and its figures or the impossibility of figures it entails. The workings of this "difference" and its unfigures make, I would argue, containment of difference and figures of difference, including those of a more manifest character (rather than only difference beyond difference), especially difficult.

This point is inherent in, as well as exemplified by, Derrida's comment, cited above, on the continual technical success of such containment in the war against nonlinear writing and its difference beyond difference. Here, however, I would like to cite de Man's critique of

Schiller's program of aesthetic education. Paradigmatic ever since Schiller and widespread throughout the contemporary humanities, this program may be shown to define, by its repression or its incapacity to grasp, the actual workings, effects, and unfigures of difference beyond difference. De Man sees in Schiller and his (mis)reading of Kant, the figures shaping this misreading—or his aesthetical-political ideology and pedagogy in general—as those of the containment of difference and the figures of difference, even if in the name of "difference and freedom," a containment resulting from this repression of difference beyond difference. By contrast, de Man's readings of Kant and especially of Kleist or Shelley pursue these authors' radical deployments of conceptions and unfigures of, or disfigurations into, difference beyond difference and beyond figures. One of Schiller's main problems is reading Kant in terms of figures or tropes and tropological systems.[8] As de Man points out, however: "Aesthetic education by no means fails; it succeeds all too well, to the point of hiding the violence that makes it possible."[9] This, I think, is what persistently happens throughout the humanities as much now as it has always done since Schiller and the Enlightenment.

But aesthetic education does fail sometimes, as do other forces of containment, however rarely. The Enlightenment itself, or at least the culture with which we associate it, is defined by the possibility and the actualities of such failures, as is indeed clear from de Man's juxtaposition of Schiller with his contemporaries just mentioned (along with Kant, Rousseau, and Hegel; and several others might be added to this list). This observation may even be seen as one of de Man's points of departure.[10]

Now, we—at least some of us—also live in these uneasy transformations. The point concerns what one wants and is able to resist, and to what extent. I would still, at least for the moment, bet on "difference" and "difference beyond difference," and on trying to mobilize and advance (in either sense) it maximally, with the qualifications given earlier.

These qualifications are also part of an advancement, this advancement of knowledge *or*, inevitably, the unknowable (again, using "or" in the above sense), including some of the figures, proper names and concepts or figures (or unconcepts and unfigures), which have been mentioned here and that define the recent history of the mobilization of the figures of difference. I think that a maximally *critical* attitude toward and, to use Nietzsche's more "scientific" view, a persistent and thorough testing of these theories is as decisive as there is in the case of traditional or classical theories. This is of course what Nietzsche urged in the latter case. We must now test these new theories in turn. But this testing also entails maximally *rigorous* investigation, which, so far, has been uncommon in criticism of such new theories.

I have argued elsewhere that twentieth-century mathematics and science or technology may confront us with such tests and may well require more radical theories and figures and unfigures. Nietzsche at one point said, "And this is why: Long live physics! And even more so that which forces us to turn to it—our integrity! [Und darum: Hoch die Physik! Und höher noch das, was uns zu ihr zwingt, —unsere Redlichkeit!]"[11] Nature and (biological) life have been a major source and resource of such surprises. Shelley's great "final" question, closing or opening his last and (forever) unfinished poem, *The Triumph of Life*, "Then, what is Life?,", is still our question. I have little doubt that it requires yet unheard-of figures and unfigures, and the dead matter of modern physics hardly requires less. But then to ask what is life is also to ask what is mind, whether human or animal. And here, too, new figures and unfigures are inevitable, for example (to take only one such example) after Gödel's theorems, which showed the formally uncontainable richness even of mathematics, considered as apparently so formal. But of course there are other fields, in politics or yet again in literature and art, old and new, which are bound to take us in new directions.

Success is not assured, whether against the containment of difference, or of some as-yet other, perhaps more radical and effective "difference," or even of some other figure that one might ultimately prefer to advance or mobilize. This type of qualification is important since some containment appears inevitable and indeed necessary, once a mobilization is under way. (These quasi-military metaphors are not altogether satisfying and I would like to contain rather than mobilize them.) We cannot be decidedly certain as to whether we advance even in the short run. We must, in our decision, which has to be taken, take risks in this respect as well. There are many other risks we take. It is, if one still prefers a military metaphor, a minefield. Under the conditions of difference beyond difference, which we cannot circumvent, nothing is *ultimately* assured, but successes are not impossible either. This is perhaps why Nietzsche liked to speak of both the uncertainty of the future (and of his love of it) and of the necessity of a philosophy of the future, a creation of something new, perhaps even something lastingly new, almost forever new. I do not think we can and want to do without "almost" here.

JW: Can we effect change within the educational process through reading, writing, and teaching students to be attentive to difference and alterity?

AP: I am tempted to put a "then" into your question ("Can we, *then,* effect change . . ."), given where I ended my previous answer, especially given the seemingly perpetual success of Schillerean ideology and programs of education it shapes in various fields. One can, again, think in terms of more general "technical successes" in the war against difference (or alterity), invoked by Derrida, or in terms of several other theories invoked earlier. Following your question, I shall, however, speak primarily for the moment in more pedagogical terms of the humanities and its institutions, such as literary studies, where de Man's analysis is especially useful. (Philosophy may also be considered from this perspective, since, for example, Schillerian readings dominate the studies of Kant, directly or indirectly through Schiller, or through parallel tracks.) The successes of such ideologies and programs are undeniable and undeniably persistent. As I have argued earlier, however, these successes are only seemingly perpetual and continuous, even in those especially persistent and ubiquitous ways in which these ideologies and programs tend to enter and take over the more irruptive events of the emergence of difference and figures of difference, especially in their radical forms, such as that of difference beyond difference.

In this work of resistance to the containment of difference by mobilizing radical difference, reading must play an indispensable role, albeit not a unique one. "Effecting change within the educational process through reading" and, it follows, "writing and teaching students to be attentive to difference and alterity" through reading, as you put it, is not only possible, although sometimes difficult, but necessary and even inevitable. I cannot see how this could be avoided, even leaving aside the fact that figures of difference have been put to work in recent history in the humanities and especially literary studies primarily through reading of literary and philosophical (or psychoanalytic and linguistic) texts. One can especially think of the work of Derrida and de Man, and their followers, but this landscape of reading is much broader. Gender studies or postcolonial and other minority studies have opened immense new areas of the problematics of difference through reading. Naturally, I am speaking not only of published works but also of the massive pedagogical efforts of readings (and readings of readings) in the classroom, through conferences and lectures, with faculty and student audiences.

The effects of readings, even though sometimes contained (in either sense), have been and are bound to continue to be extraordinary — those of, among many others, de Man's readings of Shelley and Kleist; Derrida's reading of Mallarmé, cited above, again, one of a great many on his part; Irigaray's readings of Sophocles; Cixous's reading of Joyce and Kleist; and Deleuze and Guattari's reading of Kafka are obvious and perhaps especially pertinent cases. But there are a great many others. Admittedly, this history (and a longer history of literary studies) was more centered on reading than hitherto. First, it reshaped the concepts (and figures or unfigures) of and practices of reading by centering them on reading itself and its figures or unfigures, including in literary and philosophical texts (read as "allegories of reading"). Second, and correlatively, it reshaped them by centering both our reading and our thinking on the problematic of radical difference (or alterity), difference beyond difference, alterity beyond alterity. This history, however, also, in part by this new emphasis, both more sharply focused the more general significance of reading in intellectual history, especially in the humanities, but also elsewhere, and this significance certainly extends well beyond that of reading literature. As I said, the reading of philosophical and other texts, on their own or coupled to literary ones, has been just as decisive.

This argument extends well beyond deliberate or overt cases of reading, whatever is read. It is impossible to *read* Hegel rigorously other than as a reading of Kant, however explicit our reading of Kant while reading Hegel may be or however much reading of Kant we engage in our reading of Hegel, whether in our scholarly work or in the classroom. The point is not simply the significance of certain inevitable Kant effects in Hegel's text, but that a rigorous reading of Hegel's text inevitably brings out these effects. Such readings of Kant's texts have been and will continue to be crucial in effecting the changes you have in mind, in large measure by virtue of these texts' engagements with questions and figures of difference, alterity, exteriority, and so forth. In other words, it would be difficult, if not impossible, to enact an agenda to your question, to make our students and ourselves "attentive" (perhaps too weak a word here) to difference and alterity, without reading.

I am aware that I am thus reiterating part of my answer to your first question, but this *re*iteration (it has its difference) is important. Reading is a crucial, irreducible part of this mobilization or emergence of the figures of difference in the humanities at the very least. Even nonreaders, such as, say, Nietzsche, are still readers, and it is difficult enough to read Nietzsche, let alone to be Nietzsche. One might add, however, that the subject of Nietzsche as a reader and reading Nietzsche as a reader are crucial subjects only sporadically addressed so far.

It may be shown that reading is indispensable not only in the humanities but also (albeit differently) in mathematics and science as well. Permit me on this point to refer to my recent article "Reading Bohr," published, it may be added, in a technical volume on quantum theory and addressing scientists. I argue that, in an encounter with Bohr's work and in this work itself, reading and the emergence of figures or unfigures of difference beyond difference and beyond figures (which, I also argue, define quantum mechanical epistemology) are fundamentally linked together. Physics is also reading. Paul Dirac, one of the great physicists of this century, famously referred to reading as "a waste of time," having read Dostoyevsky's *Crime and Punishment* only at Einstein's urging. (Einstein was a great reader of Dostoyevsky, which is not irrelevant here.) And yet, as Dirac acknowledges, some of his (as well as Bohr's) greatest work in quantum mechanics came from a *reading* of Heisenberg's great paper introducing quantum mechanics rather than merely familiarizing himself with its findings in mathematical terms. It is also worth noting that Heisenberg has arrived at his findings, conceptually at least, through rather remarkable figures of difference and of difference beyond difference, and thus established the rigorous foundations for the radical epistemology of quantum mechanics.

Naturally, pursuing the agenda or agendas of practices and strategies of readings suggested by your question requires great flexibility, from selecting particular texts and connections between them to coupling our readings to conceptual work, and to political arguments and discussions as well. It may well be the choice of such couplings—the texts and junctures that they define or that define them—that determines the effectiveness of reading in pursuing these agendas at this particular point. Above all, however, this pursuit requires renouncing any dogmatism and, conversely, promoting skeptical attitudes. Indeed, most of these works urge this attitude. All the texts, but especially Nietzsche's, teach us not to follow them, not only in the sense of not following them blindly, but also in the sense of moving in new directions. Zarathustra sends his disciples away with the following: "The man of knowledge must only love his enemies, but he must also be able to hate his friends. . . . One repays a teacher badly if one is always nothing but a pupil."[12] This is a great lesson for ourselves and our students alike, a lesson helped by reading.

JW: Considering the temporality of the pedagogical act as a series of so many "heres" and so many "nows" that simultaneously mark both continuity and discontinuity (the "series" that is the course or lecture series, and, conversely, the possibility that some event in the classroom might take place that no prescription can take into account or account for) as, in Werner Hamacher's words, the movement "between the repetition and its interruption, between the connexion and its break,"[13] in what ways does the performance of the pedagogical "here" of the *hic et nunc* depend on the simultaneous effect of difference and on the momentary blindness to difference that allows the expression of every "here" as the acknowledgment and experience of the present, of presence *as such?*

AP: First of all, we must indeed *acknowledge* the experience of presence, even analytically, rather than only performatively, as here through our "blindness" to difference (or perhaps in this case we must both perform and acknowledge it analytically). As I have indicated, deconstruction (of the metaphysics of presence) is also an understanding (prepared by, among others, Nietzsche and Freud), a very effective understanding of why presence is inevitable, of how it arises (specifically in and through the play of differences), and how it works. The second part of your question reflects the dynamics, both macro (a series of lectures or a course) and micro (a more local event or effects within a single class, or even a shorter interval), of the same type that I have outlined earlier. This understanding, reflected, via, I think, both Derrida and de Man, in Hamacher's remark, is shaped by a figure of difference and indeed that of difference beyond difference, alterity beyond alterity. The reason for this is that, as discussed earlier, while the effects of various continuous and discontinuous types, or those of chance (a form of discontinuity), are produced, the ultimate underlying dynamics responsible for these effects is not subject to description in their terms, or in any other terms, "dynamics" included. Indeed, it is this (difference-beyond-difference) character of this dynamics that is responsible for the radical effects of chance or other disruptive, singular effects considered here.

This view locates the workings of difference and difference beyond difference, and exposes their significance and the significance of their effects in all pedagogy, however one may aim to resist or contain difference in one's pedagogical practice or, however one tries, conversely, to mobilize difference and its figures. No one can avoid it and we all depend on it because *both* mobilization and containment of difference and its figures invade and split whatever we aim to pursue, whether in terms of mobilization *or* containment, or a given combination of both. There may, however, be differences in the balance of mobilization and containment in one's assessment or one's performance of this dynamics, differences that depend on the agenda one pursues. Accordingly, one can deploy, including in the classroom, different strategies and tactics, both of moving between different effects (repetition and interruption, continuity or connection and break, chance and necessity, and so forth) and of handling the impossibility of fully controlling such transitions.

The cases with which I am primarily concerned here are those of mobilizing differences and figures of difference, which require strategies and tactics of great complexity and flexibility. Those of their containment may, however, deploy very complex strategies and tactics as well. We need to master them in turn since we cannot mobilize difference and its figures without some containment, including the containment of some differences and some figures of difference. (Some of these strategies and tactics are of course the same to begin with.) However, insofar as we want to mobilize difference and its figures, especially in their radical form, we might want, to whatever degree possible, to deploy and play out more continuously figures of difference and reflect upon the character of the situations in which, and of the processes through which, we do so. We can do this, first of all, by commenting on these situations and on the particular play of mobilization and containment of difference that shapes each (there may be commonalities between them, too, and both commonalities and particularities may be reflected upon here as well). In particular, we might want to reflect on the institutional structures that differentiate readings pursued in pedagogical contexts versus those pursued outside them, or on the interplay of both types of reading, since, especially in the case of literature, we cannot always unequivocally separate them. Second, again, one might pursue texts and readings that themselves explore this dynamics, either overtly or allegorically. Here, I would think, reading Deleuze and Guattari on philosophy as a pedagogy of concepts in *What Is Philosophy?* in a course offered in literature departments could be especially effective. (I have taught this work in this way on several occasions.) We can even do both, read such texts and reflect on the situation of reading them, as they themselves reflect on such situations of reading. Certain particularities or even singularities of our acts of reading are bound to interrupt such *dedoublements*, and sometimes "double-bind" them more radically; and we might want to explore these situations, too.

JW: In our acts as critics and teachers and, indeed, in our acts of reading and writing, can one articulate the figural work of the "between" as that which places us —in the very figure of *interest* —as subject to difference, in the place and the taking place of the "between"? Does tracing such a figuration involve a comprehension of spatiotemporal relationships that cannot be reduced to the hermeneutic simplicity of either a final meaning or an absolute structure? And, if this is the case, how do we bring this knowledge to bear not only in our analyses but also in the pedagogical process, in the face of structural, institutional imposition? How do we maintain difference —supposing this to be possible —in the process of teaching students to be attentive to the effects of thinking otherwise as they take place in the pedagogical encounter?

AP: The figure of the "between," while significant, does not altogether satisfy me as the figure of difference (much depends on your quotation marks, however), especially in dealing with difference beyond difference or alterity beyond alterity, as we've been discussing. These figures, to reiterate, reflect that which produces effects of difference and its avatars or of their opposites and interactions, or various forms of in-between-ness, without itself being the subject of any figuration or even disfiguration in these terms or any other terms. This type of alterity-efficacity seems to be more decisive and more rigorously pertinent in the set of contexts at stake here. It also produces spatial and temporal, and spatiotemporal effects, and their multiple articulations, sometimes in terms of each other (i.e., spatial articulations of time or temporal articulations of space), without, again, itself being subject to any such articulation. Accordingly, while I agree with you on the impossibility of reducing this dynamics to "the hermeneutical simplicity of either a final meaning or an absolute structure," I would be reluctant to speak of spatiotemporal relationships at the efficacious levels, as opposed to certain effects of a spatiotemporal type. One might argue for a similar situation even in physics, especially in quantum theory and ultimately even in relativity, a prototypical spatiotemporal theory. Perhaps you have something similar in mind here, and your quotation marks around "between" imply something along these lines. I have reasons for this suspicion, which will appear momentarily.

Can one articulate the *figural* work (to the degree, again, this phrase applies) of such an alterity? Why, of course! That is, we can and we cannot, *or* (in the above sense) undecidably both. This would have to sound, rightly, familiar. This is why Derrida asks:

What am I to do in order to speak about the *a* of *différance?* It goes without saying that it cannot be *exposed.* One can expose only that which at a certain moment can become *present,* manifest, that which can be shown, presented as something present, a being-present in its truth, in the truth of a present or the presence of the present. Now if *différance* [is] (and I also cross out the ["is"]) what makes possible the presentation of the being-present, it is never presented as such. It is never offered to the present. Or to anyone. Reserving itself, not exposing itself, in regular fashion it exceeds the order of truth at a certain precise point, but without dissimulating itself as something, as a mysterious being, in the occult of a nonknowledge or in a hole with indeterminable borders (for example, in a topology of castration). In every exposition it would be exposed to disappearing as disappearance. It would risk appearing: disappearing.[14]

Indeed (this is the reason for my suspicion), your question may be read as an ingenious and cogent gloss on Derrida's "presentation" of *différance* in "Différance," also giving this gloss a well-taken pedagogical twist. How does one present something like this, something beyond all possible presentation or indeed conception, all conceivable unrepresentability and inconceivability included? More accurately, we must refer to what makes us speak even of *différance,* or—inescapably, always already—*write* it (both in the narrow sense and in Derrida's). Besides, *différance* is only one of an interminable series or network of terms, an irreducibly multiple and disseminating ensemble of Derrida's, which are "neither terms nor concepts."

But then, it is not only Derrida's matrix that pursues this type of alterity, but also those of Nietzsche, Bataille, Levinas, Blanchot, Lacan, Foucault, and de Man, or those of Heisenberg and Bohr in their quantum mechanical epistemology. And there are also the works of a number of literary figures, whose work shaped that of some of the figures just mentioned. Indeed, they do so in very similar terms, even though, again, one must grant the difference between them and the different degree of radicality of each.

Hence, my reply above that we can and cannot articulate the (un)figural of radical alterity *or* both at once; as we have seen, Derrida's matrix deploys this undecidability specifically in this context. More rigorously, we can articulate certain particular effects and certain configurations of effects, through which and only through which this type of alterity (alterity beyond alterity) can manifest itself, and which indeed make this alterity analytically unavoidable. That is, it is made **analytically** unavoidable given the nature of these effects and their configurations. However, we can never articulate the ultimate alterities-efficacities (each time different, even while each time unknowable) that give rise to these effects and these configurations of effects. This view implies a new form of epistemology, that of knowable effects on the one hand, and, on the other, of the irreducible unknowable and inconceivable efficacities of these effects, ultimately unknowable even as unknowable, especially as absolutely unknowable (all these are still merely "figures").

We have been pursuing this type of articulation and this type of knowledge (which disallows the ultimate articulation and the ultimate knowledge alike) in our critical readings and in our teaching of the texts in question for decades, naturally, with various degrees of success. At least some of us have done so. (This type and level of understanding of this conceptuality and epistemology are not altogether common even now). This pursuit has, for some of us, radically **and**, to some degree, irrevocably changed some of our pedagogical practices. These changes took place despite and because of the enormous resistance to these theories and practices, or of the complexities of the overall intellectual and political dynamics considered earlier, the dynamics themselves considered and defined by these theories. Now, this indeed being the case, how, you ask, do we bring this knowledge to bear not only in our analyses but also in the pedagogical process, in the face of structural, institutional imposition? It seems to me that properly—carefully and rigorously—reading such texts and teaching such theories form a necessary form of imposition. At the same time, this imposition, as any involved in pedagogy, may and, in my view, must be tempered by some of the conceptions of alterity in question, for example, those of Levinasian ethics or of Deleuzean or Derridean politics, or by what Derrida calls "democracy to come." Indeed, I would argue that these conceptions allow us to do so much better as far as the ethics of pedagogy or any intellectual and cultural exchanges are concerned than traditional forms of enactment of difference and alterity, that is to say, of the containment of more radical forms of both. This is also "how we maintain difference in the process of teaching students to be attentive to the effects of thinking otherwise as they take place in the pedagogical encounter," or at least this is one way of doing so. For, to return to Nietzsche and Zarathustra, as "for *the* way—that does not exist."

I would like, however, to end on a figure of "between" after all, and a literary and a reading *note* (also in its musical sense), and a literary version of "democracy to come," one of Shelley's dreams. I want to end here on yet another great closing or opening question of Shelley's poetry, perhaps (perhaps!) not quite as dark as "Then, what is Life?" in *The Triumph of Life*, on the final question of "Ode to West Wind," Shelley's perhaps most famous and most "in-between" question: "If Winter comes can Spring be far behind?" It is peculiar that Nietzsche, also in Italy (in Genoa rather than in Florence, where Shelley writes his poem), speaks of *The Gay Science* in the language of Shelley's poem, which he perhaps knew. He says: "It seems to be written in the language of the wind that thaws ice and snow: high spirits, unrest, contradiction, and April weather are present in it, and one is instantly reminded no less of the proximity of winter than of the triumph over the winter that is coming, must come, and perhaps has already come."[15] Rather than referring only to a seasonal change, Shelley's question may also be shown to relate to a local moment, moment between moments, even between times (*zwischen den Zeiten*) either in the Autumn and in the Spring, as in Nietzsche's April. At such a moment the wind and the weather can move in either direction, toward winter or toward spring. However, it can be further argued (I do not believe it has been so far) that the ultimate power (Shelley's word, but it needs a Foucaultian sense here) or the ultimate efficacious dynamics of the movement is irreducibly beyond all our knowledge. (So I cannot end on a "between" after all.) Shelley's poetic physics is closer to quantum mechanics than to classical physics or even chaos theory, which defines the weather. In this more skeptical and darker reading, "If Winter comes can Spring be far behind?" is indeed a question and not an anticipatory celebration of Spring. Nietzsche does not forget his "perhaps" in April either. Can, then, Spring be far behind, if Winter comes? Yes, it can, sometimes even in April, over which Winter can still hold in its power, or to which it can return. But it does not have to be far behind. It may or may not be far behind, it may be almost and even inevitably here at any point. But then, Spring is not always a happy time either, while Autumn and even Winter sometimes may be. This chance is still governed by Shelley's darker question, now my own final question: "Then, what is Life?" Over life, that is, over death, we cannot triumph; it always triumphs over us.

6

John P. Leavey, Jr.
Q & A: Whims, Whim-Whams, Whimsies, and the "Responsiveble" Interview

JW: What difference does difference make?

JPL: You have provided me with the luxury of a single question, which becomes, in a sense, an examination. But that question has multiple intonations and tunings, and I shall attempt to work with those which appear without much difference, almost the value of the comma in the intonation systems, that unhearable difference which disquiets the ear.

Quodlibet 1

One might expect in a quodlibet, which is a mixed medley of texts or songs — in addition to the thesis for disputation or the disputation itself — the place of the desire or citation, but for our purposes here, I leave aside the sound track or the citation mostly for the disputation or the fanciful. A quodlibetary. Somehow this here recalls, the more I proceed, a text that Derrida often leaves aside, a pedagogical one concerned with philosophical style, with the frivolity of a stone statue awakening, an archeology of the frivolous. The form of this interview, because of the singular question, is then singular too: a written excursion whose layout might itself indicate a difference — a whimsical interview on a whimsical question — the whim-wham quodlibetarian.

What is the rubato of a question? Is it the rubato of tempo or dynamics? Could what follows be designated as a "School of Translation," analogous to Czerny's "School of Velocity?" And is difference a part of the analogy and/or of (the) translation? How is each of the terms of the phrase of your question to be translated? For many, that would mean, how is each of the terms to be read? And if the terms are terms of a relation, how should I indicate the relation and the difference across the face of each term?

Quodlibet 2

The rules of this interview place another context around this question. Not only is the question a question, it is a means to address the pedagogical. My answers, my conversation, my interlocution with you are to recall themselves continually to that occasion, that situation, that is, to the pedagogical. They could perhaps render a pedagogical moment or be a discursive moment concerning the pedagogical. The difference of these two, and more, will always be in question. Too often that difference is reduced to the performativity of a piece or a phrase. In music, we could say its execution, which then leads us to consider the instrument, its structure, and its science, which refer back then to how that instrument is tuned and played, and how the player plays that instrument. In voice, the difference I am discussing might be considered closest to the problem, because the execution is one's own. And the performativity is not only on the instrument but also of the instrument. This would be to begin to rethink the status of the instrument and of performance. Nonetheless, this technological condition I am considering is more fundamental still, with this difference between the instance and the discourse caught in the grain of the voice, the windpipe, the breathing. An unheard difference even if recorded or written.

I wanted to begin with a series of journal entries, dated several days after your first (and last) question of more than a year ago.

Quodlibet 3

A journal entry dates, differentiates, even within the quotidian and everydayness of the calendar. The journal carefully marks out the calendar, the spatialization of the taxonomic sameness, perhaps seriousness or sadness.

The first entry was simple. Thinking, processing, certainly not ready to answer this question encompassing a whole series of questions, I considered the question. I was struck by the problems of music and discourse enfolded within your question, which brought to mind the following musical references: the Pythagorean comma, just intonation, the intonation systems, tunings for various keyboards, perfect pitch, the inability to differentiate certain tones, musical dictation. For me, musical dictation in a music theory class was much like *dictée* in a French class, a total disaster of the personal pedagogical moment; how does one learn what one cannot hear? Or then teach it, even if all this is a matter of memory of the contextual scale of tuning, for which, then, what difference difference makes is to deny the concept of perfect pitch. And your question brought to mind perversities of the pedagogical: the certain danger and trust regarding the child, the ways in which American society idealizes the child to the detriment of its education, the ways in which education could be argued to be society's writing on the body of the child, the written, subjected body of the child idealized as untouchable, even by another child. I use the impersonal "its" in relation to the child to mark just how much the body of the child gets removed from its "engendering."

The second journal entry might be considered gestural. The only acceptable position is to refuse the question. The question would have to be a joke, like the supposed call from or a drink to a certain Martin(i) Heidegger in "Envois." Either there is too much difference or too little, and either way the difference of difference is not without difference, even if only the unpronounceable French letter *a*, now read or said here in the United States with a French accent. What was said in French without difference becomes the Inspector Clouseau moment on this side of the Atlantic, in all the serious halls of academic discourse. Or the difference of difference, to take up a different medium, is like the Pythagorean comma in intonation, which evens out the tonal difference of the well-tempered system. *The Well-Tempered Clavichord* is to be heard and played then as one answer to what difference difference makes. And so I could say, as part of the gesture of refusing this question, that the difference of difference is pedagogical and bourgeois too, with the keyboard instrument, particularly the piano, being the instrument of the middle class and the translation of the well-tempered clavichord in the history of instruments.

Third entry. What is the place of form in an interview? One can always refuse the question, as stated above, the rhetoric of refusal (of not enough time to consider the intricate details, etc.) being a recognition of the occasionality of an interview, as if to say: "No, no, the question overruns this venue, this forum. I must speak more informally, as if I were teaching, in conversation."

Teaching, even when lecturing, is not a lecture — how is this term to be said, between English and French, here in this context of the instability in voice or eye — is not the slow work of reading. Perhaps I should answer that what the difference of difference makes, rather than unpronounceable, hence unheard, is illegible. It can't be read any more than heard.

Quodlibet 4

Isn't the quodlibet also a set of examples? As a medley, quodlibet appears to confirm this. What of the disputation? Is the disputation a form of argumentative medley? The status of the pedagogical moment that mixes these many genres of the quodlibet: disputation, example, whimsy, appears then to be more akin to the interview. How are all these — the interview, the pedagogical, and the genres of the quodlibet — related? Do the relations reduce to the desire of/for knowledge in the pedagogical, which would then appear to make any interview and the genres pedagogical moments?

Let me take up an example, one that mixes translation and difference in a certain phrasing. How is one to hear the difference, in this example, through this example, of the question you pose? The example is taken from Whitman's *Leaves of Grass:* "I too am untranslatable." To put it bluntly, this statement is possible only in rubato, in the rubato between the one that speaks and the attribute of untranslatability, and let us leave aside the hawk and the I, possible narrators and speakers, which would complicate this hearing and writing, even of the difference as the "barbaric yawp" of either. If the I is untranslatable to itself, then the I cannot say I except in the rubato of the attribute of untranslatability, in the difference that such a difference makes, the ever so small difference of the tautology of I to I (technically, grammatically, in the declension of the pronoun, of *I* to *me*): "You will hardly know who I am or what I mean." The "hardly" of this knowledge limns the difference that difference makes.

I realize that I am not responding, just yet, to your question. Or possibly, I am stealing the time and the concepts to rethink your question. And it probably appears that I am quite some distance from the overt concerns of such a question, which might be more properly concerned with the history and philosophy of "difference." I agree, to be sure. But if teaching is some kind of translative space, some space that registers the differences within its own space even as a hospitality of the other, then there is the problem of rubato, a musical term that does not apply to composition but to performance, to interpretation, and perhaps, through performance and interpretation, back to the composition.

Rubato steals without recompense or gives recompense only with difficulty: how does one repay the value of rhythm or accent? How does one give back what was taken in time and tone? Translation balances these kinds of accounts all the time, without time, in the time of the coming about of its payment: the translation itself, which is always already considered peremptorily out of date. The status of the "out of date" is also that of teaching. I can never keep pace as a teacher or a translator. Either ahead or behind, I can never be "on the mark." And the effects of that encounter, in the classroom and in the translation, cannot just be assessed then and there. The educational institution should be the one social space that recognizes and is antagonistic to being right there, on time, transparent in its statement, missions, and service. Leadership in education cannot be to provide the payoff that a certain rhetoric adopts as it tries to prove the worth of education, which I would want to argue should be, in a certain sense, worthless. I recognize the dangers of such a statement, one that equates value with a particular translation of value (worthwhile, worthless), but I hope the context of my remarks makes clear the diremption of that particular translation that wants to forget its status as a particular translation for the benefit of a universalization of value.

Quodlibet 5

Arresting time. From time to time, like the difference of difference, the time of time is ideal, regrettably for reading, to the very time of the question. Such an arrest in that very time is responsible to the very question it arrests. Hence teaching is to be irresponsible at that "moment" of time. At that moment, translation, supposedly made possible in the arrest, is executed and compensated, hence illegible. I am not trying to say that there is a secret, invisible ink with which translation writes (there is, but that is not my point). Its invisibility occurs in the very moment that the translation is considered transparent or is forgotten for its sense. To go to, say, the ideality of sense, of a sense in order to translate something from one language to another (which I have to do all the time) is too often to arrest time on both a micro and macro level of consideration. Translation, according to Venuti, wants and is wanted to disappear, to be invisible. But the illegibility of translation is not its disappearance. It is its occasionality, the fact that it occurs here and now, as if the execution and compensation could occur without rubato or as if the rubato could be forgotten, if not unheard, unremembered. In one sense, I am speaking badly about a complex process of rhythm, which appears to be measured, hence meter (and there is a complex body of differentiation of meter and rhythm in numerous fields, music, prosody, poetics, for example), but which in another sense overturns any differentiation of space and time, or rhythm and meter. I am trying to mark out the relation here of the "is" and the "make" that underlie your question.

And yet, you will rightly say, I am not answering your question. Both a bad interviewee and a bad pedagogue. Even with all the drifting and being adrift that an interview implies, there are banks and shorelines to be navigated, avoided at times, and at other times to be sought for refuge. And there are questions to be answered or not. But if the status of the question is what I am stealing (from), the rubato of the question itself in an interview, then what remains, with or without the question? In the hardly knowable stealing or difficult recompense?

A direct approach to any question forgets the impossibility of not being able to pay, of the incommensurability of question and response. Q & A is "always" a relation of whimsy. The citation (its laws, its rules of payment, repayment; the contexts never repaired, and so on) might indicate this as well. But we need to see about that.

Perhaps—the modal of all responsibility, the contextuality of the pedagogical event—structures the difference of difference as the precision of the ma(r)king of difference, like the ma(r)king of truth. The question itself, as a question in English/American, to speak a translated medium, if one can speak one or the other, posits that the making of difference is crucial for that difference. In other words, the question is not, what's the difference?—a question that can eliminate the question as question. That is, the rhetorical question points out the problem by eliminating its difference. In another language, the problem would be the tautology of the question. How can one steal from a tautology? Is there a pedagogy for such an event or desire? And what would be the politics of such a question? I realize quite fully that we could, perhaps should, also reread de Man's allegories here according to a different rubato: the *allegory of reading* as reading politics.

To make a difference by means of difference, rather than to be a difference by means of difference. The question you ask assumes the difference of difference, which could be read in the following way: The necessity of an ideality that is in fact lacking is what defines difference. In other words, difference's presumed lack of ideality for the solution it proposes by the assumption of *the* difference, of the *different* difference, is what defines the difference of difference. The teaching I would propose, in other words, irresponsible teaching, does not teach (from) that *recompensed* ideality. Nor does translation. The difference always marks time without ideal difference, even if, of course, we hardly know that difference. But it always makes a difference, which in "our" language indicates that the difference is worthwhile, has some importance or significance. And yet then the terms of difference and making are translated ever so slightly from what can be compensated even in this value system. Against the time of ideality, there is the time of teaching and translating. And only in a situation of rubato, never on time or in tune.

I am, of course, leaving aside all the previous answers to this question, even if those answers never stated the question as such or in this way. The question of difference, one could say, has a very long history. It came into existence at some point. It was enunciated in any number of ways that would translate this question, but not the question itself. Derrida and Deleuze, to take the two obvious examples.

Derrida gathers together the bundle of chances that makes the question "relevant" today, hence yesterday (January 27, 1968). And Deleuze systematizes that history philosophically in *Difference and Repetition* (1968). Here is neither the place nor the space to review their actions, to observe the inversion of Platonist ideas as one of the steps on the multiple immaculate conceptions of reading that Deleuze performs *a tergo*. Or the *a tergo* relation of Plato and Socrates in the fortune-telling difference of the beginning, also illegible in the I's of the dialogues in "their" writing signed Plato, in the multiply grained voices back from the beginning of philosophy, if we were to read Derrida's *La carte postale*.

Quodlibet 6

"Difference and Repetition" could be an answer to your question. Certainly the basis for it. It points to the noological level of the question and examines the image of thought as difference. What a citation sound track that would be. Like Leibniz's in the last chapter of The Archaeology of the Frivolous, *Deleuze's text would be a long footnote printed below this interview as its double, barely readable in its fine print.*

What difference do those differences make, to translate the question just a bit? The immaculate conception (that is how Deleuze designated his work in the history and reading of philosophy) is always from behind, *a tergo*, from the voices back from the beginning, from the difference of the difference, from the birth of the virgin mother necessary for the virgin birth of the child, both different, hence the same, yet always different. Also in the ear, philosophy's ear.

The attempt to make the different slide into the same is always tempting. In fact, the totally different, the monster, is always domesticated and becomes the pet monster, like the writerly text of Roland Barthes (*S/Z* is always "mis"read by avoiding the difference of reading). The writerly, according to Barthes, is that everything but the text is read, and it is, unfortunately, so often read, hence domesticated, as readerly, as a special type of reading, rather than as the end of reading, of the absolute difference from reading, hence never written. The writerly is always in rubato to what is read, and only in that noncoincidence is it writerly but not written.

And so what difference does difference make?

How am I to understand and translate this turn from *esse* to *facere*, from "is" to "make," from being to making, being made, being on the make. Like the truth made by Augustine, that is, contrary to what one would expect of the truth, the essence of truth is fabulation — like that fabulation of the truth, the making of difference isn't difference, it is precisely what the difference of difference makes, makes in the sense of does, fabulates, acts, constructs. Without that move from "is" to "make," without the turn from "difference is" to "difference is made, makes, is on the make," there is no reading. But also, even with that move, there is no reading. Only in that difference between the two, in their translation, is there reading, a politics of reading. The fabulation of the politics of reading recognizes the space between the impossible being and the impossible ma(r)king of rubato. If there were a beat, then to rob that beat cannot be made up. The time has already past. But in that being past, which cannot be made up, there is still the time to make up, both in the sense of deficit and in the sense to catch up (and to love as well). Politics recognizes that fundamental disconnect as the possibility of its discourse and its action.

So a perhaps essentialist question or even rhetorical question gives way to a political question according to the whimsy of my reading of your question.

And so I fabulate with a series of examples that respond to the quodlibetical.

Deleuze's idiot is Dostoevsky's man from underground. *Notes from Underground* is a political text, written under the censor and after the prison experience and deferred sentence of execution. Political in its weak rejection of the political for the supposed religious. And yet, after the censor, after the possibility of restoration, Dostoevsky recompenses nothing. A certain note to the reader establishes a rubato of voices that the author is not the narrator, and so on, a difference that constitutes the quodlibet of the idiot in its various poses. A known solution, Christianity, desired, is stolen, and the political poorly compensated in its theft. And yet, that recompense, in its very poverty, makes the difference whose difference is the political. What difference difference makes is always answered by the political. How to teach this without reducing it to a transcendental condition of the political? This difference of difference then is always consequential for reading, teaching, translating.

But the political, even in its rubato of the transcendental, is bureaucratic. Teaching, not only the institutions in which it takes place, but its times, its syllabi, even in its sociology of its structure, is bureaucratic. The bureaucratic, for me, returns to Kafka, to someone who knows the bureaucratic, the rooms, the monsters, the multiple snags of the paper that only dreams of becoming paperless. The paper machine, the bureaucratic machine, is like the court: everywhere, nowhere, without effect, on paper but undocumented, destroyed, legible but never read, or illegible and always read (as in *The Penal Colony*) or like the legendary actual acquittal in *The Trial*, not published and never read, as Titorelli, the painter, explains: "'The final verdicts for the court are not published, and not even the judges have access to them; thus only legends remain about ancient court cases.'" Adapting the words of both the painter and the priest, we could say that "'Everything belongs to'" paper, which "'receives you when you come and dismisses you when you go.'"[1] All of this, of course, on paper.

Quodlibet 7

And so the difference of difference and the difference it makes are bureaucratic and paper differences, which, to my mind, does not belittle them but in fact courts those differences as pedagogical, as the recompense that translates rather than remunerates the difference. Unless the transcendental is under rubato, hence political, there is no difference. Unless difference is under rubato, there is no difference. Unless there is the quodlibet, hence difference and whimsy, there is no interview and no teaching.

7

Mary Ann Caws
Thinking about This . . .

JW: Although this project concerns questions of difference, particularly difference within pedagogical processes and institutional structures, and whether change can be effected within the educational process
through reading, writing and teaching students to be attentive to difference and alterity, I want to begin at something of a tangent. In the
introduction to *City Images*, you initiate your project by commenting
that "[k]nowing any real city, and still more so, knowing what it is to
know a city, may be as much about passive as about active experience."
The provisional acknowledgment of the significance of allowing oneself to know, and coming to recognize this process, as opposed to actively
seeking out, in this case, the experience of the city, but also, in the context that concerns us here, the "acquisition of knowledge" is perhaps
one of the most urgent and necessary of questions for those of us engaged
in what is loosely termed "theory." Which gives rise to several, interrelated questions. To what extent can we work with our students so as
to encourage them to explore the potential for an affirmative passivity while, within the limits of the academy, we open our own roles to
another manifestation of affirmative passivity, which can both teach
and learn from our students, serving as a form of "affirmative resistance" to the quantitative demands of the educational structure and
experience? In what ways might we do so? And in what ways might
we begin to imagine passivity as a difference within thought that opens
both us and our students to the experience of pedagogy?

MAC: "I inhabit wildly a *cabanon* in the Vaucluse [J'habite sauvage-ment un cabanon dans le Vaucluse]." —André Breton. He didn't, but I do sometimes.

Attentiveness to difference and to sameness has to be developed or then, better, has to be given a chance to develop. In my view, this is equivalent to a kind of passive learning, to be actively encouraged. Encouraged everywhere: in a cityscape, in a countryside, in a text: I think of it as an open field, and would invoke, if I had it before my eyes, a magnificent piece of writing and thinking by the British Marxist nov-elist and art critic, John Berger, also an artist, called simply "Field."

Let me leave that piece, that field, implicit then, and in its place — remembering, however, how open a field it is — offer a word on pas-sive learning, and teaching it: anyone familiar with those moments of sudden recognition we think of as Proustian moments is no doubt con-scious of the way an openness to such experiences works, or more appropriately, plays on the mind. The essential, it seems to me, is to make certain to remain in one of two states, which perhaps are nearer than might be at first assumed.

The first would be a mental situation close to a Zen conscious-ness, in which you are open to the world, and notice everything on the same level. An ant crossing the table will seem — will *be* — as large in your mind as an elephant crossing a bridge or a camel a desert. Table, bridge, and desert, ant, elephant, and camel make the same difference. Everything and nothing.

The second would be what the surrealists call "a state of readi-ness" — *un état de disponibilité* — in which you are ceaselessly aware. Aware, but not necessarily active in your awareness. This is defined in the same way, as objective chance: an answer in the outside world to a question you did not know you had. I did not know I had a ques-tion about passive learning, but now notice also it might be the same as an answer.

Mary Ann Caws
Nôtre-Dame-des-Anges, Vaucluse, France, June 2000
or then
New York, New York.

JW: The matter of the open field that you leave as implicit, this gesture appears to place me, and perhaps whoever reads this, at the limit of that field. Ready to enter, I nonetheless find myself paused. I want to respond in as open a manner so as to encourage a response without directing that answer (that is to say, without implying the ghost of an answer that I imagine I would like to hear or believe I might discern in the opening your answer makes possible). How does one begin to encourage actively — to direct perhaps without directing — the passivity that one desires, without imposing another kind of control or limit? How, for example, might you encourage an awareness of what seems to be at work in the dislocations in the signature effect which you offer in your response?

MAC:

Dear Julian,

If I understand your pause at the opening of the open field that is my present answer to your question, I would say this to start one's wandering in it. As a prelude to the path, then, I would think poetically inclined readers might investigate open field poetry, artistically inclined ones might start on that path armed with the memory of various open field paintings. The point would be to open as many paths as possible: the possibilizing of imagination. Our own as teachers — writers, readers, and our encouragement of that in others — as opposed, for example, to one method of reading *passe-partout*.

It calls above all, perhaps, for energetic redoing. A specific example in the field that most interests me: in poetry and the translation of it, I find rereading, retranslation, rethinking of it more valuable for students and for us at the moment than the endless poring over what has already been done, thought, translated. This is of course the surrealist point of view, but it has proved intensely valuable for undoing that which has gotten stuck in its unimaginative closing off of possibilities, and setting it free in that open field I would like to encourage all of us to wander in.

P.S. Ah, what about those not ready to strike out on their own, in an openness they hadn't wanted to envisage quite yet (or ever)? What about some other path, a guided tour of the place? Before you ask, let me field that question, and admit I had forgotten that side of things, imbued as I am with the spirit of come-what-may-ness inculcated in me and, I presume, other adepts of the surrealist mentality.

Perhaps we could get there through the signature problem you hint at, namely, that the learners of primarily passive paths (the pathologically oriented readers, if you like, needing orientation or even, to begin with, "occidentation") will go on elsewhere after a first trial. They might, in a stronger moment maybe, proceed on to actively passive and perhaps even eventually active thought or wandering in and outside of paths already set up, take up one signature after another? Signatures of different genders, views, physiques, and the equivalent. That is, they might adopt one system of reading/learning/inquiring, and then a second, third, ad infinitum or boredom? The latter would presumably aid a breaking out into a new part of the field, if not a newly opened one. Here's, then, to boredom.

JW: Your last response appears to raise at least the ghost of a question on sexual difference, on the politics of sexual difference as a matter of what you call the "signature problem." At the same time, it seems to me that the question of sexual difference as a signature effect, if you will, of institutionalization has become, in certain ways, the signature of path building across different fields, even though there the institutional maintenance of path building implies the constant erection of signs saying, "Keep off the grass." So that the very premise of "teaching difference" seems a matter of instituting indifference.

Now critics such as Jacqueline Rose have argued that a Derridean thinking of "*différance*," for example, involves itself in a reading of subjectivity that overextends its own political potential. I'd like to ask you to address this overextension as the necessary work of difference in relation to and in excess of the matter of institutional indifference as a pedagogical norm. Does *différance* thus comprehended make a difference to the indifferent pedagogy of difference now conventionally situated, and is this fundamental to a political reading of the subject and of sexuality?

MAC: Well, Julian, it seems to me that my now responding to this question in April of 2001 is presumably and evidently destined to be different from any previous consideration we might have undertaken together. That is, the bounds of institutionality and of definitions of "*différance*" as well as of "difference" are constantly changing, thank goodness. The grass we have to keep off or make a path across is not the same as that in front of King's College when I was at Cambridge in 1986, when you had to (1) be a fellow or (2) be accompanied by a fellow to cross it. Which wasn't the same as the library Virginia Woolf couldn't read in, or the dreary meal she ate, being different. Difference itself gets deferred, doesn't it? So my having *lost* the question you posed means my answer now is not the same. Nor is the institution, nor our politics, nor our subject, nor—perhaps—our sexuality, who is to say?

So much for the constancy part of the "constant erection of signs saying, 'Keep off the grass,'" you mention: it verges, let us hope, on inconstancy. So much, too, for the command: it changes also. Now, if you permit, I'll just leave some of those terms in their original being-ness, okay? Especially the nouns, and mention only the verbs of "saying" and the "keep off." Don't we *say* differently, just as we *see* differently, according to the seasons of the asking and the response? Yup. Which leaves me with the "keeping off": what a wonderful term. It causes me to reflect on the idea of what I want to keep off me, not just what I am summoned to keep off. In short, about politics, institutions, verbiage, and sexuality: their very shifting character leads to a shifty answer, swiftly wishing itself adaptable to now, say, April, or then, say, November. I am heartily against "indifference," because it feels like the lack of feeling I would think we would want to cling to, not keep off of. It would not be part of any sign system I could or would participate in.

8

Jonathan Culler
Resisting Resistance

JW: As we have witnessed in the humanities certain turns to obviously political criticism and to cultural studies, so there has been a noticeable rejection in certain quarters of "theoretical" discourse, which is to say most crudely, "poststructuralism" or "deconstruction," in favor of a sometimes explicit, sometimes highly encoded return to what Geoffrey Bennington has recently called "thinly veiled pretheoretical habits." One secondary or indirect effect of this development has been a naive "resistance to theory" on the part of both undergraduate and graduate students, students who've not read, not been given the chance to read, or who've encountered negative, journalistic commentaries from some academics or read only hasty, thirdhand summaries and critiques.

Given the relatively recent self-opening of so-called deconstruction to questions of political, ethical, and pedagogical responsibility, how do we maintain the question of difference, even as we teach students the significance of difference, of reading for difference? How do we make sure that our students grasp the question of "reading difference" as crucial to understanding their role in the academic institution, the educational process, and the pedagogical experience?

JC: I would say, first, that if we are talking about students and educational processes, we have to resist the temptation to talk about teaching monolithically. It has been my experience in recent years that undergraduates, though they may have had some limited exposure to theory bashing in the media, have really not paid very much attention, so that if they sign up for a course involving a certain amount of theory, they are very likely to find themselves interested, excited by the enterprise of thinking in different ways. In other words, they have not learned anything so well that it is a serious obstacle to trying out a different style of thought, whether it is Derrida, Foucault, or Judith Butler. On the other hand, one certainly cannot predict or ensure that these students, with their varied interests and willingness to engage in serious intellectual struggles, will be attracted to deconstructive readings — some will and some won't. In recent years, I have found them more responsive to the form it takes in Judith Butler's work on performative notions of identity than to any other, so for me that would be one concrete way to encourage a thinking of difference or alterity.

The case of graduate students is rather different. I see a lot of graduate students from other fields who do not have settled opinions about theory — for instance, graduate students in Asian studies may be above all curious about how to work on literary texts and what theory can offer them for this enterprise they may just be beginning (since learning the languages has taken so long). Graduate students in English and comparative literature, however, have chosen a certain identity in deciding to engage professionally in this field, so they are likely to start with firm beliefs about what sorts of enterprises are politically progressive and what are politically dubious. Often, of course, they have not actually read the texts whose political valency they think they know, so assigning some of these texts is a useful step. But I think that there is a lot of deconstructive work in feminist theory and queer theory that can help to put some of these presuppositions in question, and there are even essays in postcolonial theory (I've used some short essays by Stuart Hall and some pieces by Anthony Appiah) that engage in deconstructive moves and help to promote the idea that this may be a productive way to think about difference.

I am talking here about what I do in general theory courses. I expect that others who teach more specialized seminars in literary theory would operate quite differently, addressing a self-selected audience of those prepared to engage the more elaborate deconstructive engagements with political and ethical questions. But aside from an occasional seminar on Derrida, I haven't had time for that sort of teaching in recent years.

JW: Let me address a couple of points you make. Taking the experience of teaching undergraduates first of all: one aspect of "teaching theory" is that it becomes compartmentalized institutionally, and rationalizations are either implicitly or explicitly put in place about the location of the general theory course, which appear quite reasonable—and therefore all the more difficult to resist. There is always the argument about the difficulty of particular material—you mention a greater degree of responsiveness on the part of students to the work of Judith Butler, and the performative notion of identity is certainly one way to approach the question of difference in a specific manner. However, while undergraduates may not have paid that much attention to the resistance to theory, either within or without the university, a different manifestation of resistance can emerge in the face of difficulty among those who are not those you describe as a "self-selected audience." One manifestation of this resistance emerges in questions such as why do critics have to write in such a complicated or technical fashion about literature? Another, different manifestation of resistance expresses itself in questions such as if the ways in which we've been reading in other classes have been all right, why should we need to learn different ways of reading? These admittedly very basic questions are of the kind that many, if not all, the contributors to this volume have encountered in various forms. Drawing on your own experience, would you explain how your own teaching manages to move through such resistances to difference toward what you describe as "a more productive way to think about difference"?

JC: I have a divided response to the sorts of resistance to theory that you mention. On the one hand, I am certainly aware of it as an important phenomenon among students, and, more important, among other academics and the public at large, who expect that work in the humanities should be immediately accessible to anyone with a modicum of interest in the subject. While I resist that idea in principle— we ought to be able to write for specialized audiences, as people in other academic fields do, without being accused of immorality or obscurantism—I have devoted a good deal of time and effort to writing about literary theory and "theory" in general as clearly as possible, in books on structuralism, semiotics, and deconstruction, in books on Saussure and on Roland Barthes, and most recently in *Literary Theory: A Very Short Introduction*. I don't believe that in writing in an accessible manner I am betraying literary theory, or selling out, or eliminating the radical character of theoretical reflection. (If I have misunderstood or misrepresented some particular aspect of the theoretical enterprise, I am eager to know about this, but generally complaints about my work have borne not on some particular mistake or misrepresentation but on the enterprise of popularization itself, at which people permit themselves to sneer.) To defend the making accessible of recent work in theory is not to claim that someone reading my *Very Short Introduction* will be immediately installed at the most radical cutting edge of the subject, but I contest the view that theory is corrupted or denatured if it is made accessible. A good deal of my teaching of literary theory takes the form of explication of difficult theoretical writings, and one of the exercises I use requires students to reconstruct the argument of some difficult piece of critical argument.

On the other hand, when students or others express dissatisfaction either with difficult critical writing or with the idea that they should learn about theory and expose themselves to other ways of reading, I don't see it as my job to overcome this resistance. Freud reportedly told H.D. when she was his analysand that when others criticized psychoanalysis, she should under no circumstances defend him, for that would only deepen the resistance. I would not go this far, and I would generally defend the theoretical enterprise if it were attacked in my presence, but I am content to allow people who wish to remain uninformed to do so. I have no interest in the idea of a required theory course, for instance. It seems to me crucial to the dynamic of teaching that the students who are there want to be there. And, indeed, I begin my general theory course with Roland Barthes's *S/Z*, which is notoriously difficult to read. The beginning takes a great deal for granted, sets up obscure oppositions and generally rebuffs a reader who is not willing to give it the benefit of the doubt. And the fragmentation of the text makes it something one cannot easily read in normal sequential fashion, noting the high points as one proceeds. One has to struggle and make choices about what to reflect on and what to ignore. I begin with this text so that students who are temperamentally unsuited to the theoretical enterprise can escape from the course before they are committed. I want to avoid a situation in which they are seduced into a course and then find that they can't handle the sorts of difficulties they will encounter in Lacan, Derrida, Judith Butler, and Jacqueline Rose, for instance.

Having said that, let me add a couple of remarks about theory and the resistance to it. Despite complaints about jargon, it is my experience that students actually enjoy acquiring technical terms. One needs to be willing to explain them and to avoid taking them too seriously. There is a ludic dimension to the creation and deployment of a theoretical language, whether it takes the form of the positing of a technical metalanguage or the transformation, as in Derrida, of words from the text into terms with a theoretical resonance. You can even invite students to create their own terms—a hard thing to do, but certainly relevant to the idea of a theoretical enterprise. Finally, though, the answer to resistance to theory, to the question of why one might need to plunge into this arena if one is content with one's ways of reading, is the simple and time-tested one. You already have theories and just don't know what they are; it is through implicit theories that you have become a reader, so if you are interested in understanding your own practices, you need to study theory.

JW: In what ways does your pedagogic practice remain attentive to difference?

JC: For years now, I have taught a course called "Literature and Theory," which begins with Roland Barthes's *S/Z*—because in it students can discover the worst right away and drop the course if they can't bear this sort of writing, because they can learn a lot about how literature operates from the varied reflections of this decentered book, and because it poses the problem of reading from the outset and makes sufficiently outrageous and unfamiliar claims about reading and literature so that the students have to start thinking about what they have taken for granted. *S/Z* starts with difference: the opening page tells us that constructing a model of narrative structure for narratives would make the text "lose its difference. This difference is not, obviously, some complete, irreducible quality; it is not what designates the individuality of each text, what names, signs, or finishes off each work with a flourish; on the contrary, it is a difference which does not stop and which is articulated upon the infinity of texts, of languages, of systems, a difference of which each text is the return."

And shortly thereafter, still on the first page, Barthes writes, in what I explain is a translation that to my mind effaces a crucial aspect of the difference of the text, of a choice that must be made: either to relate each text to the model or else "to restore each text not to its individuality but to its function, making it cohere, before we even talk about it, by the infinite paradigm of difference [remettre chaque texte, non dans son individualité mais dans son jeu, le faire recueillir, avant même d'en parler, par le paradigme infini de la différence]."[1] "Jeu" here is not well translated as "function" but would be better glossed as "difference when not interpreted as individuality but as differing." I think that, to make sense of the odd formulation of "making it cohere . . . by the infinite paradigm of difference [le faire recueillir . . . par le paradigme infini de la différence]," one might think of a microphone that picks up sounds. One needs a particular sort of sensing device — here the open-ended idea of difference — to pick up the features or the play of texts that interest those who choose this option rather than the reductive science, the straw man that is set up against this idea of difference.

So explication of possible ideas of difference is the pedagogical point of departure. Then I move to Barbara Johnson's superb essay "The Critical Difference: BartheS/BalZac,"[2] with its explication of this difference, which Barthes speaks of as "self-difference," and its later explanation that differences "between" are likely to be a projection of differences "within."

Since I also teach Saussure early in this course, and emphasize the chapter on linguistic value, where we learn that "in the linguistic system there are only differences, without positive terms,"[3] one could say that difference is the connecting motif, the underlying theme of my teaching of literary theory, and one of the topics that students are likely to choose to write about in their final exam (for, yes, I do believe in exams, which compel the students to compare and synthesize rather than to write a paper about a single critic or work of criticism).

In the course of this study of difference, though, I inevitably find myself struggling against the idea of difference Barthes took pains to distance himself from: difference as an identitarian essence. Most of my students believe, so deeply that they often don't even realize that they believe this, that each of us is different from the other and that difference is a powerful explanatory principle. People read differently from one another because they are different, each one unique (though they share this belief in their uniqueness). Even though they eagerly take to Judith Butler's account of the performative nature of sexual identity, for instance, even if they become avid social constructionists, they still believe at some level in the uniqueness of each individual, a uniqueness that is simply a given. For me, this conviction of uniqueness is the most convincing proof of the power of ideology to produce sameness.

I thus find myself in the odd position of championing difference of one sort — self-difference — and fighting against the most current interpretation of difference, as a quintessential feature of identity, something my students possess by virtue of their status as Americans. The students and I circle uneasily around the differences associated with group identities, for they generally are uneasy with differences that would make all members of a group the same (they are more receptive to the idea that women are all different from each other than to the idea that women necessarily share a difference, by differing from men, however much I try to stress that positional or diacritical difference is not essential difference).

In sum, then, my teaching is certainly attentive to difference, to the problem of difference, not because it celebrates the inherent differences of individuals, or even because it focuses on the differences of people who are differently situated or have different histories, but because it grapples with the problem of *différance:* difference, differing, self-difference.

9

Kevin Hart
Going to University with Socrates

JW: In what ways and to what extent can the notion or motif of difference disrupt students' expectations of pedagogy while also encouraging in them the beginnings of processes of thinking otherwise?

KH: Individual cases differ too much and are too interesting for a general response to be appropriate. Asking a first-year English or comparative literature student to think about difference is not the same as asking a second- or third-year student, who may well have come across the notion before, let alone asking an honors student who should know something of the complex heritage of the notion and be aware of its institutional stakes. And of course the issues resituate themselves at other levels with graduate and postgraduate students: some might have a deepened, ramified sense of difference; others might treat it as routinely as people a generation or two earlier treated a word like *paradox* or *ambiguity;* and still others might see it as something to rebel against. A first-year literature student is best introduced to difference, I think, by being invited to read a poem or a story very slowly. That is invariably surprising, even shocking, to a student coming to university. "You mean we don't have to cover all the poem in the tutorial?" their faces sometimes say. Or maybe, a little later, their faces ask, "You mean there is no one, single message that we should carry away from the poem?" That second thought can be very worrying for students coming to tertiary studies, although it can be a productive worry. If one does not learn to read well, one will never get to "think otherwise," as you put it. In the last instance, though, reading well cannot be taught. Even the very best teacher can only help students on their paths to being vigilant readers. One can show how important it is to slow down, to attend to figural language, to the sensuousness of what is written, to slips and slides of meaning, to loose threads in the text, and so on. (I like to recite to my students Nietzsche's fine words in *Daybreak:* "to read slowly, deeply, looking cautiously before and aft, with reservations, with doors left open, with delicate eyes and fingers.") To read well is something that we must partly teach ourselves by reading and rereading poems and stories and essays that matter to us. A good deal of what counts in the academy as "reading well" these days is applying a grid to a text, and even if that grid is the very best understanding of difference, it can be little more than the expression of a new consensus. Of course, hardly anyone in a university, or outside the university, will ever learn to "think difference" in a serious and effective way. Only a handful of people each century do that.

JW: What is your own institutional or pedagogical experience of working with the motif of difference? Does it produce suspicion or resistance in students?

KH: No matter whose work I am teaching — Shelley's, Schelling's, or Schleiermacher's — I ensure that my students have a text before them, and I require them to have read it closely before coming to class. I usually set readings about the poem, novel, or passage that alert the students to conflicting views about the text in question. Often a class proceeds by following that conflict, so that different assumptions about the text emerge and, sometimes more interestingly, different *sorts* of assumptions about a text come to light. It is by no means trivial that some literary texts develop from philosophical, political, or theological assumptions, or that some theological texts make important, if undisclosed, literary assumptions . . . In some classes questions come up about different ways of moving through a text, why this text has been chosen for study, and so on. For a while, my most pedagogically effective class (in a doctoral course centered on Maurice Blanchot) turned on putting Robert Antelme's *L'espèce humaine* alongside Marguerite Duras's *La douleur.* For two or three years, I found each time that particular seminar came up the discussion of those two texts made students question their assumptions about writing and ethics. In the weeks to come, they became far better readers, at least in some respects. They asked new, quite demanding questions of themselves, and that became apparent in the discussions each seminar.

With undergraduates, one of my most productive classes has been when I have come into a tutorial with parallel passages from the Gospels. My favorite text for this sort of class is the parable of the mustard seed as told in the synoptics. I begin by simply asking everyone to read the different versions of the text and to say if there is something curious, odd, strange, or noteworthy in any of them. The pious and the impious turn out to be equally resistant readers of the different versions of the parable. For both groups the very fact that the text before them is registered as "Scripture" makes them inadequate readers. So it can take them a while before they see how peculiar it is that a mustard shrub becomes a tree, or that all of the birds of the air can find a place to sit on as modest a plant as a mustard shrub. If the class works, though, students ask what is missing in that parable; and perhaps a member of the seminar will remind everyone of the association of the Messiah with the cedars of Lebanon. What is Jesus doing with that messianic figure? And is "Jesus" the same in these versions of the parable? Some students begin to see that Luke and Matthew, for example, set up the parable in quite different ways, and so they take their first step in redaction criticism. A little transmission analysis can be of great help to literature students, I find, even if they're not at all interested in editing. For one thing, it can make them more watchful with respect to the distinction between the sacred and the secular.

JW: In what ways do you see the institution that we name the university as being reliant on, and yet inimical to, the work of difference?

KH: The very word *university* asks us to imagine a unity of knowledge, a community of scholars, and it bespeaks a time when that was possible. As recently as the early 1970s, when I was an undergraduate there were events that could make you more or less believe in it. As a student of philosophy, I was told that philosophy was *the* ground of all knowledge, although it turned out when you looked closely that all sorts of folk were not able to stand up straight on that ground. All a lecturer in philosophy had to do was mount a course on the philosophy of history to show that those tweedy chaps in the Department of History didn't have the faintest idea what "history" was. You see, I went to university with Socrates.

Philosophy presented itself to me as an undergraduate in two ways. On the one hand, it was an endless, introspective meditation on its own concerns—epistemology, logic, metaphysics, and (it was the 1970s, remember) the philosophy of language—and there the focus was on making ever more subtle distinctions. On the other hand, philosophy was an aggressive attempt to get (as we were taught to think) hopelessly confused people to think clearly. Or was it an attempt to take over the entire university, to claim it as really belonging to philosophy? Hence those courses on the philosophy of religion, the philosophy of economics, the philosophy of art, the philosophy of science, the philosophy of mathematics, and so on. By the time I was a third- or fourth-year student, it was expected that we think that only philosophers occupied the ground of knowledge. The only competitors worth taking seriously were pure mathematicians and scientists of the harder sort. The real competitors, everyone knew, were folk close to home, those who argued that only formal logic supplied a solid ground. (We knew too that the logicians argued among themselves. And I know because for a while I passed for one of them: my best undergraduate work was an essay that clarified Saint Anselm's version of the ontological argument by casting it in polished logic and then putting some questions to it from the perspective of possible world theory.)

I'm telling you a story about my undergraduate years: maybe I'm generalizing a little, and I realize that I'm not saying anything about the cult of cleverness that departments of analytic philosophy can generate. That sort of cult is as destructive in a university as the cult of personality. All the same, I think my story illuminates the modern university as it was supposed to be. That exemplary modern institution, the University of Berlin, was founded with philosophy having a lead role to play. About ten years ago, I taught an M.A. course entitled "University Discourse" that looked at various discourses on the idea of the university—those of Kant, Fichte, Newman, Heidegger, and Derrida, as well as all sorts of government reports—and it became clear how fragile the unity of "the university" was. If it is a community, it is one that allows for different aims; it must allow for knowledge to be transmitted, for that knowledge to be criticized, and for new concepts to be invented. At any one time, those activities will seem not to converge, even on a distant horizon.

It was in the late 1990s, long after I had taught the seminar on academic discourse, that the Australian Federal Government started to make deep cuts in tertiary funding. What was revealed, when the knives had hardly been displayed, was not unity but division among academics. I was surprised to find how many of my colleagues now seemed to believe that universities, even faculties of arts and science, should be vocational, not oriented to a quest for the truth. They were struck by a cultural fatalism; they appealed to vague notions like "change" and "economic trends" without much desire to investigate how those words were being used and abused by government. By 1998, when the damage to tertiary education in Australia had become catastrophic and irreversible, at least in my lifetime, the only unity the university had was supplied by the central administration. And that was merely formal, since "the university" had meanwhile declared itself a legal entity quite distinct from academics and students. We teachers and students found ourselves suddenly outside the university, while people who neither taught nor studied had deemed themselves "the university." Now *that* is difference! No surprise that when that split appeared teachers and students became subject to a thoroughgoing program of homogenization. The most effective way an administration can eliminate difference, I've found, is by lowering standards. If the general understanding in the corridors is that no one is expected to be challenged, if students are merely clients paying for a product, then classes are a gray muddle. In a country like Australia where anti-intellectualism has become government policy, difference and homogeneity can easily get along in a university.

JW: In what ways does an attentiveness to difference help to maintain both a resistance to a fall into generalization and an affirmation of singularity?

KH: I find that undergraduates are generally quite happy to recognize that there are differences between texts but are less easy about identifying differences within texts. The former view fits very comfortably into an ideology of individualism that, if unchecked, can converge very quickly with systematic social injustice. The latter requires people to read well and to think critically; and critical thinking can lead one, now and then, to identify with a common good and so, to some extent, to diminish the significance of oneself as an individual. In the terms in which you pose your question, I would hope that students could be led to investigate the differences between "individualism" and "singularity," and to see that "singularity" does not, and cannot, imply a self-enclosed world. This has clear political implications, but I do not engage directly — urge first-order positions about current events — with either politics or religion in the classroom. If students wish to hear me talk about such things they can always come to one of my talks outside class. I think it is good that students can know their teachers' first-order views about politics and religion, but those views need not enter decisively into a seminar on Samuel Johnson or Elizabeth Bishop or Gregory of Nyssa.

JW: If difference is one name for a mode of radical alterity irreducible to an identity, as you suggest in *The Trespass of the Sign,* would it be possible — and this is admittedly a risky gesture — to see the name of God as the articulation of difference in other words?

KH: Your question raises so many pressing concerns I could not begin to address them in the detail they require. Let me restrict myself to just one point: the name of God in the Christian faith fits neither into talk of identity nor into talk of difference. The Christian claim is that there is one God, but that God is and always has been an affirmation of difference. Father, Son, and Spirit are one God but have always and already differed from each other: not as distinct subjects, not as modes of being, but in a manner that is strictly mysterious. In a theology of the economic trinity we can talk with apparent assurance about the economy of salvation occurring in a movement from the Father to the Son though the Spirit. Yet in a theology of the immanent trinity, were it to be anything more than silent adoration, we would have to call into question the very words "Father" and "Son" which make no sense from the perspective of eternity, were it to have a perspective. But I won't open the fat dossier marked "Negative Theology" today. We would be here forever, not because of me, but because of it. And I won't broach the complicated debates that separate Latin and Greek Christianity on these points. Should one begin the doctrine of God by talking of the divine unity, as the Latin tradition has it? Or should one begin by talking of the divine trinity, as the Greek tradition does? How should one hold together the economic and the immanent trinities? Karl Rahner's theorem that the economic trinity *is* the immanent trinity strikes me as a partial truth. Although we should not think that there is a God beyond God, a superdeity who transcends even the revelation of divine love, we should be wary of reducing the deity to history. One thing is clear: the doctrine of God as triune renders doubtful the claim urged by some deconstructionists that God is the very model of simple unity. I differ from many people marked by reading Derrida in that I don't think that theology, in each and every case, can be assimilated to what Heidegger called "onto-theology." And I wish that those writers who convict theology of adhering to presence and unity and a firm ground would read a bit more theology before rushing into print on the subject. The issues are complex, and their complexity should be respected.

JW: In your experience, how do students respond to the counter-intuitive questioning of theology that the work of Derrida articulates?

KH: Even though Derrida is a hedgehog rather than a fox, he is a very foxy hedgehog. He has the one big idea—let's call it *"la différance"*—but he is a remarkably good reader of all sorts of texts, and so he can keep showing us in surprising ways how the thought of *"la différance"* is fecund, important and productive. So when he turns to issues in philosophical theology, he has lots to teach students of theology, not because of any theology he proposes but because he makes us look twice and thrice at texts we thought we knew rather well. Speaking very generally, and with qualifications in mind, I would say that Derrida approaches theology from within a horizon whose vanishing points are philosophy and literature. He does not think theology in a theological manner, and for a very good reason: he is not at home there. Theology can be done only within the dimension of faith; outside that, one is doing something else, or running the risk of doing very bad theology. Derrida's God is a philosopher's God for the most part, and that limits the interest his remarks on God can have for a theologian: there will always be premature reductions, nuances of doctrines that he misses, and so forth. And when he writes about Augustine, well, he often has interests at heart that are close to his experience and his idiom, though that doesn't stop him from saying some very interesting things about the nature of confession. When he attends closely to praise or prayer he can unsettle, in useful ways, the assumptions of any student of theology. And were he to read a passage from one of the Gospels or the Epistles, as I hope he will do one day, I don't doubt that he would make us read that text more closely than we have done before.

Is Derrida's questioning of theology "counterintuitive"? I wonder what an "intuitive" questioning of theology would be? Perhaps Barth and Jüngel would be intuitive questioners of theology, because they approach the subject theologically. From their perspective, Tillich and von Balthasar would be counterintuitive. Goodness, a distinction that puts Tillich and von Balthasar on the one side! Now *that* is intriguing! Seriously, von Balthasar would have to be on that side of the line since he wishes to present theology under the sign of the third transcendental, beauty, and the history of theology tells us that his decision is counterintuitive. And thinking of the history of theology, what about Henri de Lubac? Does his *Surnaturel* put intuitive or counterintuitive questions to theology? To answer that question, we would need to think about the relations between systematic theology and the history of theology. I think such a discussion is needed today, not just with de Lubac in mind, but in order to put pressure on the undeclared assumption in many theology departments that systematic theology is, de facto, the history of theology with a little dab of speculative theology on top.

For Derrida, the question takes hold at various levels. Perhaps questions of writing and transmission, Derrida's signature questions, strike many theologians as counterintuitive. I fear, though, that many theologians are not as familiar with the history of theology as they should be: a little transmission analysis carried over from their New Testament studies would be to the good. Yet I think that systematic theologians could learn a good deal from Derrida's remarks on revealability and revelation. Those comments are intuitive with respect to the debate between, say, Barth and Brunner (or, if you like, Barth and Bultmann). It seems to be very suggestive to say that revealability and revelation arrange themselves in the form of an aporia. An aporia is a "negative form," Derrida says, and the formulation gives rise to a new style of negative theology, one not readily related to that practiced by the Pseudo-Denys and those who follow him. To develop that, though, would take us a long time, more time than we have today.

10

John Caputo
In Praise of Devilish Hermeneutics

JW: Given your interest in a radical reconceptualization of hermeneutics, and the relation between the inescapability of interpretation and deconstruction as radical affirmation, can you comment on the importance of difference to any such project?

JC: *Difference* has been our word of choice, our favorite child, in academia for the last few decades and I suspect that we are nearing the end of its career. We have worked this marvelous little word very hard and it would be ungrateful of us to expect many more years of service from it. It has earned an emeritus status, and we should be gracious about its retirement and on the watch for another—shall I say— a different motif, a different difference, a difference not only under another name but thought and imagined differently. That being said, let me say why difference has served me so well over the years when it came to articulating the difference between hermeneutics and deconstruction. Hermeneutics has always seemed to me a more moderate and—here is where I have raised the hairs on the back of many a hermeneutic neck—even a more conservative version of deconstruction, where hermeneutics does what deconstruction likewise sets out to do but in a more radical way, the result being what I call a "radical hermeneutics." Gadamer says that hermeneutics is a way of putting one's standpoint into play (*ins Spiel*) and hence of putting it at risk (*aufs Spiel*). That is a brilliant formula that I do not know how to improve upon. Hermeneutics is a way of escaping the circle of the selfsame, a way of breaking the forces by which we are riveted to ourselves. It is the way the different comes along and saves the same from itself. But the question philosophers of the last three decades or so have been asking—this is a simplification, but there is something to it—is whether difference will play a dialectical and oppositional role in relation to the same, in which case you have the "fusion of horizons" that Gadamer advocates, which is a little more reassuring way to deal with difference, or a disseminative role, in which case you have the more radical, open-ended differential difference of deconstruction, in which the hermeneutic desire for difference is radicalized, the result being that things are put a little more in play, made a little riskier. But I repeat, I think that the energy in the concept or quasi-concept of difference is nearly spent, and that we need now to think about how to move on.

JW: In what ways does your pedagogical practice remain attentive to difference? What kinds of readings do attentiveness to difference make possible, and in what ways is it possible to alert students to be sensitive to difference?

JC: The displacement of oppositional difference by means of differential difference has profound social and political consequences. Let us take one of the most pertinent and obvious examples: the patriarchal model. This is an oppositional schema of male and female, a vicious binary and hierarchical schema that denies the fullness of the human to the feminine (the opposed, subordinate term). The feminine was conceived of as passive not active, material not formal, natural not spiritual, able to obey but not to command, and so on—the depth of these oppositions is almost unfathomable. By dropping the oppositional schema we are able to see masculine and feminine as nonhierarchically different without—and here I follow Irigaray—having to give up sexual difference. We are able to imagine the production of what Derrida calls "innumerable" genders, innumerable nuances of the genders, which frees us from the dual prisons of masculine and feminine. That, to take but one example, has to affect all pedagogy. How can one not enter a class of young men and women differently—the institution where I held my first teaching position, in 1965, did not admit women—if one actually understands this? To give a concrete example, as a professor in a Roman Catholic institution, I like to choose readings from feminist theologians and religious authors, readings where God and Christianity are reimagined in nonphallocentric and nonpatriarchical terms. That always produces a positive pedagogic result.

JW: In what ways do you see the institution of education or, if this is the case, the traditional practice of hermeneutics, as being reliant on, and yet inimical to, the work of difference?

JC: As I was just saying, our educational institutions have been deeply modified by the critique of the various "-centrisms," all of which turn on one oppositional schema or the other—West and East, and so on. This transformation has been so extensive that it came under public fire from right-wing theorists like Allan Bloom, William Bennett, and Lynn Chaney for having sacrificed the classical components of the curriculum to political correctness. There is only some truth to that; on the whole, these changes have been extremely liberating and salutary. The real problem facing higher education today is not the challenge posed to the classical humanities by a more radical hermeneutic, but the "managerial" style that is overrunning the university, which turns the students into clients, the professors into midlevel providers of services, and the administration into, well, "administration" in an "administered" social system. That is inimical to learning; things are run in terms of "quality control" and "outcomes." Nothing threatens the humanities more than that.

JW: In what sense would it be possible or even desirable to see the name of God as the articulation of difference generally, or "*différance*" more specifically, in other words?

JC: Mikel Dufrenne objected to Derrida that *différance* sounds like the God of negative theology. Derrida deferred this compliment and insisted that *différance* would make for a strange sort of God, indeed, since *différance* is nothing more than the differential spacing that enters into and constitutes the differential networks we have been discussing. *Différance* is neither divine nor human, theistic nor atheistic, mortal nor immortal, but the condition under which it is possible to speak and think about such things. The better way to think about this, and this is how you put it, is to see that the *name* of God as a name is forged under the conditions of *différance*. I once heard a conservative theologian pound on the desk and repeat several times that God does not depend on *différance*, the pounding and the repetition, I presume, being intended to lend a substance to the argument that it would otherwise lack, as if it became truer with the second repetition and truer still with the third. The point is that while God is in heaven, the *name* of God is inscribed within a terrestrial differential network, as are the Scriptures—*les Saintes Écritures* are *écriture*—and the institutional structures we erect around these sacred names and sacred texts. That does not destroy or level these texts or institutions, but it deprives them of absolute authority. Or rather it disarms those who lay claim to absolutely authority, who authorize themselves absolutely, as interpreters. These people, who confuse themselves with God, indulge in an absolute hermeneutic, a holy (or rather a sanctimonious!) hermeneutic in virtue of which they claim that what they say is absolutely right, the true and holy reading. That, of course, contradicts the very idea of a text and of reading and erases the distinction between the divine and the human. So I see *différance* as playing a very salutary and religiously honorable role in theological discussion, one that warns us to beware of humanly made idols, that reminds us to beware of those who wear long robes. I am interested in fashioning a kind of devilish hermeneutics, a devil's advocate (*advocatus diaboli*) hermeneutics, which displaces the holy hermeneuts who are, to my mind, very dangerous. To take a timely and tragic example, you only pilot a plane into the side of an occupied building if you have signed on to an absolute hermeneutics. The multiple religious wars among the children of Abraham that we are now witnessing, the war of ultraconservative Christians on mainstream liberal democracy in the United States, the war between Arabs and Jews, between Western religions and Islam, turn in no small part on a hermeneutic issue, on the question of how to read a text that has come to be revered as "sacred" and how to run an institution that maintains it has been chartered by God. A theory of *différance* can be very helpful in these matters; it helps to keep our theological feet on the ground.

JW: In your experience, how do students respond to the counterintuitive questioning of theology that the work of Derrida articulates?

JC: They respond marvelously, but that is perhaps because they do not find his questioning counterintuitive, which is perhaps because I do not and because I am the one presenting it to them. Not, at least, if by "counterintuitive" you mean going against the grain of religion. I find the movements and the rhythms of deconstruction, its instincts and desires, to be deeply religious: its identification with the oppressed terms in a hierarchical relationship (the last shall be first), with the "widow, the orphan, and the stranger," its critique of idolatry, its messianic hope for a future to come, its apocalyptic call to "come," the privileging of *doing* the truth over propositional truth, the discourses on the gift, forgiveness, hospitality, friendship, not to mention the autobiographical materials about his circumcision and his white tallith—in a word or two, everything that I have identified under the figure of the "prayers and tears of Jacques Derrida"—all that has a deeply religious tonality and import, one that resonates with, that agrees with rather than running counter to the intuitions of a religious sensibility. *Intuition* is not the right word, because it is too visual, cognitivist, and Greek; let us say instead that these deconstructive motifs resonate with the hopes and desires of a religious sensibility, the desire for messianic peace, for the justice to come. Of course, in Derrida himself, who "quite rightly passes for an atheist," this is a "religion without religion" and an "apocalypse without revelation," that is, a certain structural religion without the texts and traditions of a confessional religion. But the students respond to that, too, and it makes sense to them and they are very interested in seeing what the "difference" is between religion and religion without religion, what difference is made by the "without." At Villanova University, where I teach, we have been conducting a series of conferences under the title of "Religion and Postmodernism," in which Derrida is the main invited speaker. Every time he comes he fills a large auditorium with students and professors who are both deeply interested in religion and fascinated by what he says (although he says this puzzles him). I suppose that what he says is "counterintuitive" in the sense that it brushes against the grain of authoritarian religion and institutionally authorized theology, but it resonates very deeply with a more radically religious heart, with what Augustine calls the "restless heart [*cor inquietum*]," which is in love with love. And God is love. Now that seems like a good point on which to conclude. I cannot think of anything that would improve upon that formula.

11

Gregory L. Ulmer
A-Mail: Differential Imaging

JW: The volume as a whole is oriented toward "thinking difference," an inappropriate, irresponsible, and inaccurate phrase addressing the difference in thinking within the university that the motif of difference has made possible. In the light and the context of the teaching
of "theory," I would like you, on the one hand, to address the experience of teaching in a "theorized" age, teaching within and yet often
against an institution that only barely comprehends the work of so-
called theorizing and, on the other, to consider the various ways in which
personal experience has led to a comprehension of (1) the damping
down of the effects of difference generally; (2) the reduction of difference to just another concept or pedagogical figure within the economy
of what is called "theory"; (3) the subsequent dissemination of difference even on the part of teachers of theory as a result of the specific
Anglo-Americanized reception and translation of continental thought.

GLU: My first response is to say "no thinking difference without
writing difference." Rather than discussing this other writing in the
abstract, I will provide a sample of the notes I have posted to the e-
mail list that I moderate, called "Invent-L." This list began as support for a local project called "creating an electronic community,"
intended to explore the ways new media create virtual relationships
among people across the boundaries of different institutions. It evolved
into something less ambitious, a forum for colleagues and students

interested in grammatology and heuretics. I think of it as a place to test the nature of email as a medium of academic writing. It is a kind of public, collective commonplace book.

Invent-L 1997

EmerAgency

On Thursday, July 10, 1997, C. W. Duff wrote:

> Yes, yes, finally a little politics, a little of the outside reality of poverty and homelessness. Let's not forget that homelessness is deliberately invented by the societies which then deny responsibility for its creation and advent. I know the endless homeless ones who wander the streets and beg. Hunger and humiliation on the street, and the cold, and the indifference and fear (years of it), one encounters in others. Those who are called privileged are just one element in the [. . .]

Now we have a problem on the table, perhaps a disaster, certainly a collective trauma. What is the effect of trauma? Shock. It cannot be assimilated into experience; it remains outside, stuck, repeating itself, returning literally because we cannot figure it.

What action might be taken? The EmerAgency is between the era of belief in progress and the nihilism of "whatever." How to improve the world? You will only make things worse (John Cage). I do not know what to do. At the same time, my discipline offers me a theory. This theory is as alien to my experience as the problem, the homelessness. Except for the trauma of being myself.

Such is the method: homelessness is not something to explain. The EmerAgency does not issue a report with a plan for ending homelessness. Anyway the positivists have published libraries full of such reports. Rather, the disaster in its literalness (being without figure because of its traumatic nature) — since it forecloses representation — is appropriated by the consultant as the vehicle for a metaphor to explore the feeling of how things are with her or him (what has been called "*Stimmung*," attunement).

Art across the disciplines: this is how the new consultancy works. The disaster is not the object of explanation, but the subject. The resulting reconfiguration of the problem is then grounded on a local case. That local instance becomes the scene of change.

Florida Research Ensemble

As we regroup, the Florida Research Ensemble (FRE) retains the principle of the New Consultancy—applying arts practices to community problem solving. We focus by selecting our original "problem"—tourism. You may remember that our original interest in tourism (besides the fact that it is top industry in the Florida economy) had to do with the role tourism has played in the formation of American national identity.

The two examples we gave of this contribution of tourism to the Symbolic dimension of "America" (in our work on electronic monumentality) were Mount Rushmore and the Miss America Pageant—both conceived as ways to attract tourists to South Dakota and the Jersey shore respectively. Now I find another major piece of American Symbolic culture has its origins in tourism. Check out the following, cited from the current issue of *The New Yorker* [July 21, 1997, pp. 4–5]: "Congress designated 'The Star Spangled Banner' our national anthem during the Hoover Administration, when the country's judgment was impaired by clinical depression. The relevant bill—whose sponsor *hoped to promote the tourist trade in his district,* which included Fort McHenry—was rejected three times by the House before it finally passed, on a slow day" (Emphasis in original).

Imaging Florida is the latest version of our effort to add "solonism" to tourism—to make tourism into *theoria*—to include a dimension of reflexivity to the pleasures of sightseeing (as when Solon came back from his trip to Egypt bearing the tale of Atlantis). What the theory suggests we should do is to define the poetics of tourism as a source of national symbology, and then to invent another one. Or even a multitude of such things. Any suggestions?

Free International University

On Thursday, August 7, 1997, Bracha Lichtenberg-Ettinger wrote:

> It will be helpful if you will explain what do you mean by "Emer-Agency as a consulting firm"—is it a university research project? Is it a company that offers consultation in reality? Is it a virtual art project? Is it an educational approach?

Perhaps the best way to explain the status of the EmerAgency as a consulting (in)firm is to report its origins in a visit to the home of Joseph Beuys in Düsseldorf, March of 1980. Having been contacted by one of Beuys's transmitters (in my case it was embodied in a black-and-white illustration of "the Pack," some 2 inches by 3 inches, as part of a book of postwar European art), I had been exhausting the resources of paper communication to reply. Finally I met Ronald Feldman who offered me a kipper eaten by Beuys (head and skeleton). He reported that a visit to Düsseldorf would be welcomed but there was no possibility of determining exactly when the artist would be at home.

Confident that the Pack would not have transmitted for nothing, I chose a time most convenient for my schedule, spring break, 1980, and went to Düsseldorf, sought out the Beuys residence, knocked on the door, which was answered by a man wearing a felt hat and flack jacket. Perversely, pretending not to recognize him, I asked, "Is this the Bueys residence?" We entered the studio at the center of which was a table not much bigger than an American card table. On the table was a pile of mail several feet high, all in a heap, with other heaps on the floor (evidence of mailslides). On one side of the mountain a small clearing had been made, occupied by a notepad and pen. "I am doing my correspondence," said Herr Beuys. "I believe you have several things from me in there somewhere," I replied. He signed all my banknotes. During the conversation Beuys gave me a book, white binding, entitled *Report to the European Economic Community on the Feasibility of Founding a "Free International University for Creativity and Interdisciplinary Research" in Dublin.* This book is the origin of the EmerAgency.

Invent-L 1998

Puncept

Bill Seaman mentioned here or somewhere that he (you) is (are) interested in the "puncept." I just turned up a pretty promising one, and I note it here for those of you who are dabbling with the method. To note that it *is* a method—that I use it to guide or direct research, especially if the puncepts point me to things I wouldn't have thought of otherwise (it is an invention; the results need to be verified).

Just to sketch the process. I am working on Devil's Millhopper Sinkhole as a site for an electronic monument (Florida Rushmore). Part of the "moral" (psychogeography) of the geology of this site is conveyed by linking the site to information about great cities that fell into sinkholes: Atlantis, of course, and the Atlantis of the Sands, Ubar, whose ruins have recently been discovered in Oman (read "omen"). Oh, man! Reading up on Ubar, I learn that it is described in *The Arabian Nights* as a Sodom-and-Gomorrah kind of city, but that it is called "Iram." That's *Iram.*

Then I'm in the library thumbing through various books and come across one that has a chapter (in French) on "the injection of Iram." What could that be? I turn to the chapter, sure, it's still the injection of Iram, but it is a misprint, as you might have guessed, referring to the dream whose interpretation made clear to Freud the nature of his method (the founding dream or the Eureka dream of psychoanalysis): the dream of Irma's (*Irma*, not *Iram*) injection.

Eureka, okay, so the research task now is to fill in the gap set up between Ubar as Iram and Irma, between this city in *The Arabian Nights*, not to mention the city that fell into the sinkhole, that the Challenger Shuttle helped find via remote sensing, before it exploded (watch out, warning, omen), and the specifics of this particular dream.

El Mufarse

I received a notice for a book entitled *Paper Tangos*: "Julie Taylor uses the tango as a window onto Argentine identity and her own experience. They call it *el mufarse*, a particular form of brooding that amounts to a national institution in Argentina, says Ms. Taylor. 'It's a depression, but with a cynicism about the depression itself.' A bitter introspection with a patina of self-indulgence. A mood that relates closely to tango."

El mufarse would be another example, along the lines of *saudade* (samba feeling) or blues, for this state of mind *Stimmung* or attunement that we have been discussing. It may be that music, being so directly related to mood and emotion, that this state of mind question is more easily noticed in such a context. Tango is an interesting case since it seems to travel, historically, more readily than samba. I mean, it is possible to tango.

My project, however, is not to dance (samba or tango). The experiment is to abstract the state of mind from the materiality of the activity, behavior, hypothesizing that electracy is capable of supporting thinking of this sort as "writing," just as alphabetic literacy made it possible to extract concepts from epics, in order to think about "justice" for example without having to go through the Trojan war along with it. In *Heuretics*, I was trying to articulate this process of abstracting embodied states of mind via the mood associated with isolated outposts of the French Foreign Legion, the *cafard*.

Prunious

I just returned from visiting relatives. My uncle, a retired lawyer, was telling me about his difficulties with his daughter-in-law, who is a know-it-all. The difficulty is that she really does seem to know it all, which would be fine except for a certain lack of modesty about it. Uncle, attempting to create some space for himself (in a situation recalling Groucho Marx referring to Harpo as a little bully getting picked on by a big bully) invented during the heat of repartee a new word. He characterized the weather as "prunious," a term he asserted was "common usage." The daughter-in-law challenged him but they did not have an OED handy (life as Scrabble). His question to me was "How do you get a word into the dictionary?" (being a professor of English, perhaps I could use my "contacts" to get "prunious" a hearing so when daughter-in-law checked . . . there it would be). My suggestion was that he get as many people as possible to start using "prunious" in conversations, so that eventually some writer will pick it up, perhaps in a screenplay or editorial, followed eventually by a linguist, and so on.

de Duve Bot

One of the perks of living in Gainesville is that the Harn Museum has a kind of rural theory project in which important contemporary critics and artists come to town. I actually miss many of these events since the museum is over five minutes from my house. Fortunately, Kerry Oliver-Smith, education curator at the Harn, sometimes invites me to have lunch or dinner with the visitors. Such was the case yesterday when we went to Ivey's with Thierry de Duve. I had read *Pictorial Nominalism* and hefted the Kant after Duchamp book several times in the bookstore.

Thierry is great in person as well as in print. However, the point I wanted to make is this. He hates the Internet and the various technologies that support it. We entered into a spirited debate (sorry, Kerry). Inspired by my tenth cup of coffee, I declared that I was going to make a de Duve bot [automated piece of software] in our MOO [MUD (Multiple user dialogue) object oriented] and have it saying all sorts of things. "Over my dead body," said de Duve. Then, to my amazement, he used against the bot effect the same argument against writing stated by "Socrates" in *Phaedrus*. I couldn't believe it. The meaning of the text would escape from its author and the words could be made to mean something else! (for good reason, I won't go into here the Lombardi [former president of the University of Florida] bot that I created a few years back).

The other point that surprised me coming from a theorist of his sophistication was a reification of literate logic as synonymous with "reason."

To be fair, we were talking in shorthand over lunch, and I quite enjoyed the exchange. I mention it just to say: electracy ain't obvious.

Prunious

On Friday, December 11, 1998, Teri Hoskin wrote:

> this Australia thing, with a capital A, is something I do not know. If one could be more specific and say Adelaide . . . then maybe we could begin to talk about a peculiar specificity. Adelaide is one of the only two cities that was not settled as a penal colony. That is, first and foremost a site for disenfranchised (ugly lost thing) dishonoured, undone merchant classes but we'll 'ave a go in the colonies. This town had a tracing made for it before it even had the propensity to consider a map.
>
> Some very dark grieving belongs to this place. Yesterday Andrea said to me; it's almost like there is not enough space here for the anger.

Sorry to delay my response to your introduction to the experience of Adelaide. You are right to reject "Australia" as the category and to insist on Adelaide, on the local setting. The introduction to this list notes its origins in a project addressing specifically Gainesville, Alachua County, Florida. One of the speculations to be tested regarding electracy is that a reasoning from particular to particular is possible, without passing through a universal category; the more local something is, the more generally intelligible it is. Does cyberspace amount to noplace? Not in the sense of Erewhon (utopia). What is the effect of Adelaide-Gainesville gossiping? I'll give one example.

I introduced here recently my uncle's use of the neologism *prunious* (coined in the heat of in-law panic) to describe inclement weather. A couple of days ago, doing a videoconference with London, Craig Freeman and I noted that the students coming into the conference room (as we could see via the ISDN link) were wearing these bulky large outer garments. These garments were wondrous to behold in their padded excess. What use could such items serve? we marveled, becoming self-conscious about our own shirt-sleeved state (contrasting our Florida winter with London's).

Ron Kenley explained by saying that the weather in London was "prunious."

Invent-L 1999

Theoromancy

Ever since the Miami River project started exploring a syncretic form of divination, I have been more sensitive to the world as a forest of symbols. I want to resist this state of mind since the business of reading omens can become obsessive. At times, though, certain phenomena insist, put themselves forward, and "knock on the window" until they are acknowledged.

I was just getting ready to go out late one afternoon recently when Kathy called me into the backyard to see the hawk sitting in a branch of one of our pine trees. She hadn't been able to identify it yet, but it was perched on a fairly low branch. The unusual thing was that it did not fly away when we approached. It craned its head around to stare at us, but it showed no concern otherwise.

Kathy accompanied me back into the house to get the bird guide and I went on to do my errand — picking up some Chinese takeout for dinner. There was quite a bit of traffic so once I had the food I took a different route home. As I pulled up to a traffic light in the left-hand turn lane, I saw a man wearing an old military vest, lots of patches, including a red patch on the shoulder. He was bearded and rough looking, but too young for the Vietnam era. He held a sign saying, "Will work for food." I lowered my window and he turned his head to look at me over one shoulder. He wore mirrored sunglasses.

ME: What's yer war, 'Nam?

VET: No-o-o-o, old timer.

ME: What sort of work can you do?

VET: Yer lookin' at it . . .

ME: You look pretty healthy, though . . .

VET: Got the 'drome bad.

ME: The drome?

VET: The *Syn*-drome, Gulf . . .

ME: Oh, yeah. Okay, I'm an English teacher. I got a quart of sweet 'n' sour chicken here. If you can persuade me as to why you need it more than I do, it's yours.

VET (hesitates): I am bitter, I admit. But if bitterness is guilt, and guilt is remorse, and remorse is chagrin, and chagrin is disappointment, and disappointment is fear, and fear is anger, and anger is passion, and passion is love, then I am in love. This feeling of bitterness-love is sour and sweet, sweet 'n' sour. The funny thing is, despite being in love, I'm hungry.

(Car horn blasts behind me; the light has changed. I hand him the quart container and make my getaway.)

VET (shouting): Parting is such sweet sour!

At home Kathy is in the front yard, talking with the neighbor woman, widowed a couple of years ago, now having a yard sale, everything in the house. A young couple is driving away with a mattress and box springs tied to the roof of their car. "That's the bed Karl died on," the neighbor says.

I tell Kathy I forgot the sweet 'n' sour. She had identified the hawk, which finally flew away. It was the variety called "red-shouldered." After dinner, I wasn't sure that I wanted to open my fortune cookie. Kathy opened it for me: "You will receive important news from an unexpected source."

Disaster

Kathy and I drove to Micanopy last Wednesday, a day of sunshine, light breezes, to have lunch at one of the sandwich shops in this village just outside Gainesville. Crossing Payne's Prairie (a prairie in the French sense Francis Ponge intends in *Le Pré*, not in the sense of "Wagon Train": a wetlands) I notice how high the water is, although the flooding rains that made it rise are a memory that only makes the new threat of brush fires ironic. An egret tries to learn from the ducks in the water too deep for wading. Its name gives me an image for *that feeling*, as if a shore bird's beak knew just the precise moment to thrust and bite the silver thoughts, the regret.

While Kathy is in the antique shops I am free to stand as long as I like in the back room of O. Brisky's used-book store. Mildew, dust, spiders living in the geometries, the histories. Here is something I nearly bought new, but is mine for seven dollars: [Carolyn Forché's collection] *Against Forgetting: Twentieth-Century Poetry of Witness*. A rebuke. The broken spine causes the book to fall open at Paul Celan.

Black milk of daybreak we drink you at night
we drink you at midday Death is a master *aus Deutschland*

we drink you at evening and morning we drink and we drink
this Death is *ein Meister aus Deutschland* his eye it is blue . . .

Thinking as I read: "John Caputo wrote a great chapter, juxta-posing citations and discussions of Adorno et al. with this poem, the Frankfurt School statements about the impossibility of or the obscen-ity of art after Auschwitz . . . refuted by this poem."
Thinking: "I like the way Celan runs on the lines, no punctuation."

he shoots you with shot made of lead shoots you level and true
a man lives in the house your *goldenes Haar* Margarete
he looses his hounds on us grants us a grave in the air
he plays with his vipers and daydreams . . .

Thinking: "The translator does a nice job, leaving the concluding phrases in the original . . ."

. . . der Tod ist ein Meister aus Deutschland
dein goldenes Haar Margarete
dein aschenes Haar Shulamith . . .[1]

While the sunlight only reaches part way into the back room of O. Brisky's, with the dust motes filling the beam. The testimonial witnesses the witnessing even if theoretically there is no witness for the witness.

I am thinking: "This is my job, to stand here and read your golden-haired Marguerite, every word your ashen-haired Shulamith, every word of 'Death Fugue.' The volume is 762 pages, divided into sections begin-ning with "The Armenian Genocide (1909–1918)," concluding with "Revolutions and the Struggle for Democracy in China (1911–1991)." Seven hundred sixty-two pages of poetry against forgetting.

I put the bargain back on the shelf thinking: "The coffee at Mildred's is good black or *au lait*."

A-Mail

In my case, the invent list is a prompt to write things that otherwise I would not write, or maybe even not think. That *flânerie* "idea" for exam-ple (name for a shop specializing in flan). The detritus of thought. Those sparks which fly off the process of my research (reading about "walking"). The "project" in this is "the e-mail experiment": email opens a new dimension of writing. E-mail may replicate, simulate, the func-tions of other media and practices, but it also supports some features specific to itself. What are those?

The kind of writing I have been entering here from time to time is the sort of thing I might put in a journal, daybook . . . for potential reworking, combining into something more substantial later (an essay).

Nutritional analogy: you've seen those reports about how wasteful it is to feed grain to cattle and then have people eat the beef? Better to feed the grain directly to the people and cut out the middle bovine. E-mail is the grain in this story; books are the cattle. The story goes on: feed the grain directly to the people, and then feed the people to the cattle (homage to Stephen King).

Spacing

On Wednesday, January 27, 1999, Mike Montoya wrote:

> Pruinose, or pruinous - adj. - Bot., Zool. covered with a frostlike bloom or powdery secretion, as a plant surface. [Latin pruinos(us) frosty = pruin(a) frost + osus -ose] Random House College Dictionary, 1982.

Here we encounter the problematic of space or layout of letters. Within choral discourse there is no doubt that the position of the *i* is open to permutation hither or yon vis-à-vis the *n*. Should the day come when *prunious* takes its place in the OED, it will find its neighbors to be *pruinous* and *pruniform*, the frostlike bloom and the shape of a plum. The void known as "prunious" may draw nourishment from these neighbors symbiotically, until finally it means on its own.

Montoya went on to ask:

> How does this kind of activity relate to street slang, as in black America? For instance, there is a character (Pootytang?) on Chris Rock's HBO series.

Subcultures have always been major sources of language production and change (Yiddish for a time, and now Ebonics). The Internet could assume this role, in principle. If it does, that will prove it is a community.

Saudade

While we were driving Tyson to the Orlando airport for the first leg of his flight to Osaka, I decided the time was right to explain to him the concept of *saudade*. My example was the film *Central Station*, which I finally "caught up with," as they say. (It was hiding out in the video store, on a shelf organized alphabetically, in a group of films all starting with the letter *C:* no wonder I couldn't find it! Well, there were only two copies fitted in among the walls of blockbusters.)

The protagonist is a woman who has a table at the Central Station in Rio, where she reads and writes letters for illiterate citizens. She has become cynical for various legitimate reasons, so she takes the poor folks' money but doesn't actually mail their letters. She ends up involved with a young boy whose mother was run over by a bus, and helps him find the rest of his family, which requires a trip to the far outer hinterlands of Brazil. At the end she leaves the boy and his family without saying good-bye. In the last scene she is on a bus, writing a letter to the boy, telling him that she "longs for him, and for her own father . . ." They show her face and she is crying and smiling at the same time

Cut to the letter: you see the word *saudade* has been translated as "longing."

What I wanted to explain to Tyson was that if I had not read up on *saudade,* I wouldn't have understood what the actress was doing with her face while she cried (if I hadn't known that *saudade* is a happy sadness, I would have thought she was "grimacing"). And that was just how I felt, too.

Invent-L 2000

Deconstruction

On Wednesday, November 8, 2000, Paul Fishwick wrote:

> called "Chip Detectives." There ensued a 7-step process for "deconstructing a chip." This sort of deconstruction, using the same terminology as in literature, is often referred to as "reverse engineering." Perhaps we can strike up a conversation to explore the differences and similarities behind the two types of deconstruction: one of text versus one of [. . .]

One way to approach an understanding of deconstruction is through the metaphors that Derrida has offered to characterize it. Among these metaphors are at least two based on engineering that I can think of, and both of these involve uses of technology to look for cracks or weaknesses in a foundation or structure. One metaphor played with the term "solicitation" and alluded to bridge design and safety inspection, and the other was seismographic.

Deconstruction belongs to the tradition that views language as fundamentally metaphorical in nature. At the level of logic, the practice of deconstruction resembles the standard procedure by which one refutes an opponent's argument by focusing on any metaphors that may have been used to make a point, and then redirecting the point of the metaphor by picking out some feature of the vehicle that had been suppressed in the original argument, reactivating it to produce a different meaning than the one intended. It is the same sort of technique used in jokes, as in the example of the person who declared his desire to meet a woman who had the ideal beauty of the Venus de Milo, to which the interlocutor replied, "You mean sort of greenish colored and with no arms?"

Deconstruction is in the eye of the beholder, perhaps, but the part that interests me is the appropriative strategy that might be relatable to "reverse engineering." Derrida when writing about another figure in philosophy would not impose a term or concept from outside but would find some term immanent within the object of study, and would then rework that word by means of etymology, homonym, and other linguistic, logical, and poetic means to make the original text say something more, different, other than its stated intention. In this sense it is a critique of intention — the idea that it is important and necessary to control the reception of a text within the limits of what the sender meant to say. Hence Derrida's interest in psychoanalysis, with its experience in dealing with messages that have no senders but only receivers.

My own most extensive experiment with deconstruction as metaphor is in *Heuretics,* in which I (ahem) "deconstruct" the metaphor in "the frontiers of science," and "the adventure of learning." To expose the ideology and cultural specificity of knowledge conducted in the state of mind named by these metaphors I borrow an adventure narrative — *Beau Geste,* specifically the 1939 remake of the film based on the novel, starring Gary Cooper as Beau. My goal was not only critical (in any case, there are plenty of critiques of the scientific world view these days, tracing the destruction of the environment that resulted from science to the Cartesian dualism of mind-body that placed human reality *outside* nature) — but I also attempted to devise an alternative logic — the logic of invention, "heuretics." This logic would save the planet, heal the lame, grow hair and teeth, end obesity, if only it were comprehensible.

Butterflying

To record the event of learning the exact equivalent in nature for the speed at which I bike to school. As it happened, on 8th Avenue, a floodplain heavily wooded on both sides of the street, riding on my Beachcruiser sit up straight large padded seat two-speed (peddle or coast) bicycle a butterfly approached at 9 o'clock in usual erratic pattern of no gyroscope turned in my direction and flattened its line of flight into an absolute due west paralleling me for 40 or 50 feet at my exact speed.

Now if I knew the kilometers per hour speed of this butterfly, I would also know my own rate. For now I can say, "He butterflew to campus."

Zigzag

I have to finish this point about the butterfly that I have been *ponder*ing ever since I first reported the encounter with this critter. I realized later what happened:

I am heading east at a leisurely pace (i.e., as fast as I can go on a Beachcruiser).

The butterfly is fluttering erratically due south.
The butterfly detects my presence as we converge and
attempts to go around me

Problem:

it zigs *left*
but shoulda zagged *right*.

The reason it went into that flat-out straight line of flight that surprised me so and that gave me a measure of my ground speed is that it was trying to get around me and kicked it into high gear when it "realized" that whatever it had encountered was a lot *bigger* than it first thought. Part of my interest in this scene is that I have accepted it as an "emblem" that comments on human effort and falls into the family of wisdom having to do with "moving targets."

FSDD

We were in North Carolina visiting my sister and mother (not the same person). In a Taco Bell. To get one of those Chihuahua toys, part of the successful ad campaign exploiting the image of this so-called dog. We had to get a new one because Kathy discovered I had been using her other one as a voodoo doll. You have to understand that "we" had a Chihuahua for thirteen years. If you have actually lived with one of these midget terrors, you know why in that one installment of the ad the cops call for backup when it looks like the guy is going to drop the *chalupa.* I had placed a few charms strategically on the "doll" to ensure that KoKo (our late pet) could not "return" from you-know-where.

The woman in front of us in line says to the server: "I want one of those little Chi-hooah-hooahs."

The server was just as interesting, and turned out to have a disorder that previously had not been classified: final-syllable-deficit disorder (FSDD). She replied to the ersatz Hawaiian (?): "Oh, you mean the Chihua? We got the one still that says, 'Drop the *chalupa.*'"

I wanted to test to be sure I was hearing right so I asked her, when it was our turn, if Taco Bell might consider producing a pet series, to follow on the success of the Chihua.

"You mean like with poods or cocker spans? Our ads don't have German sheps or Pekins, but just Chihuas, so far, so I don't think so."

Conductive Logic

On Wednesday, November 22, 2000, Adrian Miles wrote:

> the difference between deconstruction and analysis then taking it apart is that in deconstruction there is an assumption that what is being "uncovered" and "taken apart" is something that the argument [. . .]

In the context of grammatology (history and theory of writing), Derrida's project is to locate the limits or boundary of method—analysis and synthesis—within the apparatus of literacy, most explicitly in his work with Hegel and the dialectic. No one can "analyze" Hegel without being or becoming Hegelian. The dialectic invented by the Greeks was just that: analysis and synthesis. A "problem" was a tangle or knot in thought that provoked wonder and curiosity. *Ana-lysis* was the process of untying the knot. Problem began with *aporia*—the dilemma of impasse in reason. *Diaporia* was the recounting of the history of how that dilemma had been treated previously, and *euporia* was providing the new solution, the untying, moving beyond or out of the aporia.

Deconstruction was an introduction of "dream logic" in the dialectic—which is the way I understand the basic linguistic/logical "moves" of deconstructive argument: inversion of the original point, and then its displacement elsewhere. This elsewhere, as I said in an earlier post, was often determined via metaphor or other figurative usage—especially the homonym—that allowed one to jump to an unexpected, surprising semantic domain, discontinuously so to speak. The "secondary elaboration" (dream work) or rhetoric required then was to demonstrate that this jump that at first seemed arbitrary (joke work) was in fact motivated.

In his more recent work Derrida refused the untying procedure altogether, and remained within the dilemma or aporia, bringing forward not some line where the (k)not un(k)notted, but a condition of greatest impossibility. The jump elsewhere is still a part of the aporetic strategy however.

The reverse engineering comparison then would be with a kind of engineering that did not just abductively reproduce the results of the original engineering using a "different" operational language (I'm thinking of Microsoft's method of getting a Mac operating system that avoided patent or copyright lawsuits?), but that produced a different result with added value.

Omens

Working on this hybrid called "critical divination studies." The omen is used now and then as a theme of certain ads. For example, a while back the Florida Lottery introduced a new game, involving three numbers, a scratch-off method as I recall. The ad promoting it showed a person going through the day and these three numbers kept popping up in all kinds of different situations. Unfortunately the person, not being tuned in to omens, being modern and therefore not a magical thinker, did not play the three numbers in the lottery game (and thereby we might conclude, saved some money!).

A current omen-based ad is the AFLAC duck. You've seen the bit with the two men discussing which insurance to buy, and the duck joins them and says, "AFLAC," in response to their questions, but they ignore it. We may infer that the duck is just saying, "Quack-quack," but for the magically abled person who is concerned about insurance, the duck's counsel is recognizable as "AFLAC." The key is *recognition*. The one who is posing a question gets a reply from the world (but the reply is only for that one).

Gall

From my home to [the University of Florida] campus takes about 25 minutes by bicycle. On my one-speed, fat-tired Beachcruiser I push along the sidewalks at a dignified pace, and after the first few minutes time is suspended and I begin to reflect on some work in progress (one theory of creativity, generalizing too easily, no doubt, from Poincaré's insight that came as he stepped onto a bus, claims that bodily movement may be a necessary ingredient in the Eureka experience).

I had been reading Emile Cioran's *All Gall Is Divided*, not only because the mystory told me to look at everything to do with "gall," but also because Cioran is noted for his use of the aphorism, a form that recommends itself again in hypermedia. I was disappointed in the book for the most part, except his proposal for "a general theory of tears." "Gall" appeared in "Derrida at the Little Big Horn" as an emergent name for the humor of modern intellect: yellow bile, the choleric temperament, wormwood, a certain bitterness, that suggested "bitteracy" for digital literacy (bit, byte—biteracy). What was my relationship to this mood?

"Bicycle!"

This word interrupted my reverie. I had just passed the house, now empty, formerly the home of a man arrested for kidnapping a ten-year-old girl (yellow police tape no longer in evidence). An amazing aspect of the case was that the man had two daughters of his own, nearly the same age as the victim. A woman pushing a stroller across my path addressed the child again: "Bicycle!"

The only entities in motion were me and this parent-child battery, with everything else in the background. A special-effects warp instantly and without regard for the ambiguities of ostension flipped the polarity of my position in the scene from subject to object. An image or emblem appeared, metonymy or catachresis perhaps, formed in the child's imagination, of a two-wheeled machine and rider, covered by the sound "bicycle." Didn't the myth of the centaur start this way, with horse and rider being mistaken for a new creature, part human, part beast? Sin tower.

"You cannot protect your solitude if you cannot make yourself odious," Cioran wrote in *All Gall Is Divided* [*Syllogismes d'amertume*].[2] I wonder what he meant by that? The form was clear at least: "You cannot X your Y if you cannot make yourself Z."

I waved at the pair, but their attention was elsewhere. From down the street I could here the didactic tone: "Doggie! Dog-geeeee!" I tried it out for myself. "You cannot abandon your community if you cannot make yourself loved."

Invent-L 2001

Idiomatics

Don't know if telling about how I learned an Italian idiom contributes to this art/drug thread . . . It was a hot day even for Italy in the summer.

I got separated from the group I was with and was a bit uncertain about directions. A group of children had started to follow me, gathering ominously, like Hitchcock's birds. One hand on my wallet, the other on my passport, I was taking no chances, remembering a friend's advice ("If they come around and start patting you, run"). The nearest ones looked at me closely and then one shouted, "Acqua!" (Water!) The others screamed, "Acqua!" and ran ahead, cutting off my progress. I detoured into a nearby park entrance, agreeing with what I took as their diagnosis of my dehydration.

The children fell silent and trailed in after me. At a kiosk I bought a liter bottle of water, "without gas," and sat on a nearby bench to drink. The children did not try to approach, but played nearby, somewhat sullenly. I had been thinking about Antonio Gramsci's *Prison Notebooks*, perhaps prompted by hearing Italian conversation all around me, especially his contempt for Feuerbach's assertion that 'Man is what he eats,' at least taken too literally. "If this were true," Gramsci wrote, perhaps thinking of his own next meal, "then the determining matrix of history would be the kitchen and revolutions would coincide with radical changes in the diet of the masses."[3]

These reflections were interrupted by a flurry among the "birds," whose approach caused me to look up from my notebook in time to notice the woman coming along the path, smartly if lightly dressed, appropriate to the weather, wearing a wide-brimmed hat. As she passed, she lifted her head slightly and we made eye contact for just a moment. "Fuoco!" (Fire!) the children screamed in unison, and flew into a whirl, rushed around the benches and through the chairs arranged around the kiosk. "Fuoco! Fuoco!" they repeated and were still yelling it as they disappeared back in the direction from which we had come when we entered the park. The woman had taken no notice and by this time had reached the entrance herself, where she paused and looked in both directions, as if uncertain about which way to go, or as if waiting a moment.

Theoria

On Thursday, February 8, 2001, John Priestley wrote:

So in addition to the prosthesis of digital technology we need the apparatus of modern Western encoding of images. A cultural [. . .]

The FRE experiments with inventing such a practice of imaging began with the reanimation of the ancient practice of *theoria* that combined in one attitude what later was analyzed out into theory/tourism. In the course of applying the *theoria* to the Miami River, and the encounter with the Haitian trading vessels and their crews there (via Barbara Jo Revelle), we (the letters missing from holism), decided the procedure had to be syncretized. The result was adding divination techniques and forms to the inquiry, so that our consultation was in the sense of "consulting" a diviner. We consulted with the river as divining in the middle voice (Barbara Jo as querent and the rest of the FRE as diviner, with the site being the divination system).

Anyway, the point I wanted to make is that in *Socrates' Ancestor: An Essay on Architectural Beginnings*, by Indra Kagis McEwen, we learn that, "indeed [behold?] the ancient etymologists, from Plutarch onward, usually supposed that the first part of the word 'theoros' was theos, and that a 'theoros' was someone who performed service to, or had care for, a god. . . . The 'caring for a god' aspect of theoria is especially evident when ancient sources use the word 'theoros' to refer to a person who goes to consult an oracle."[4]

Play-Mail

My interest in this e-mail list is that it (e-mail in particular and the Internet in general) opens new institutional apparatus dimensions (electracy). The conventions of writing on Invent-L for me are not defined by university discourse, personal correspondence, art, science . . . To use the querent's division of cognitive/aesthetic that Talan turned into a both-and, I compose my posts in a pluralistic or hybrid spirit of "creativity." One of the most frequent qualifiers used to characterize creative (inventive) thinking and expression is "play." That is an accurate criterion in my experience: often when I post here I do so in a playful frame of mind, but still aiming at the 'work' of electracy. So it is intended neither as art or science, but as invention. Which is not to say that "play" means the same thing to everyone, as the following scene, representing me and my sister playing together in early childhood, may indicate:

BOY: Ouch! Ma-a-a-a-a! Judy pinched me!

GIRL: Did not!

MOM: Hey! Who's been drinking my gin?! (sound of bottles clinking)

BOY: Ow-w-w-w-w-ch!

GIRL: Did not! *Ouch!*

BOY: Did not! *Yow!* Ma-a-a-a!

Parable

Mr. Mentality had been practicing the apotropaic art of indirection and parable that he used to compensate for many sins, so that when his neighbors asked him what was to be done in the most recent crisis he called their attention to the olive orchard.

MR. M.: What do we know about olives?

NEIGHBORS (confer among themselves): That they grow in orchards, and must be harvested by hand, since no machine has been able to get all the olives off the trees!

MR. M.: (pleased): Yes, and how many grades of oil do these olives produce once off the tree?

NEIGHBORS: Extra Vergine, followed by Soprafino, Fino, and Vergine!

MR. M.: So many? Good! And what accounts for the difference in these qualities?

NEIGHBORS (after some hesitation): First there is cold pressing with stones or rollers, to get the best grade. Then this mash is heated and pressed with steel rollers to get the larger quantity of lower grades.

MR. M.: How does one notice which are which?

NEIGHBORS (confused): "Which are which?"

MR. M.: You know, how do you tell, when you are sold Extra Vergine, that you have not been cheated?

NEIGHBORS (confidently): Sweetness. Fruitiness. Flavor. Color.

MR. M.: You really know your olive oils. What then are these oils good for?

NEIGHBORS (smacking their lips): Eating, cooking, dipping, lubricating.

MR. M.: And what else, the olive, anything else you can say about it?

NEIGHBORS (frustrated, going home for dinner): Enough, this isn't helping. We came to talk about the crisis, and you changed the subject, albeit a pleasant one.

MR. M.: "Albeit?"

Mr. Mentality, disappointed that his friends overlooked the theme of the "olive branch," realized he had much to learn about parables. Indirection was good, giving a material basis from which the neighbors could use their common sense to project their understanding onto the unknowns of the problem. But one had to avoid the dangers of cliché and the confusions of multiple associations. His olive story needed more work. The dialogue form was the problem he decided. Better to just tell the story and then let the neighbors fill in the gaps later.

Suddenly, he experienced a strong desire to dip a thick-crusted slice of bread into a dish filled with that green Tuscan oil. While trying to determine which neighbor was most likely to have which oil he could borrow, Mr. Mentality pondered what Eugenio Montale once said, "Something is happening in the Universe / a search for the self / for a reason to start over / and we are in tow, rags / that get tossed out / or fall on their own, one by one."

Choragraphy

A note on Miami Miautre, the FRE experiment in producing a choragraphy of the Miami River. A larger goal of the experiment is to explore the metaphysics of electracy—the category formation specific to imaging—that grows out of the deconstruction of literate metaphysics. One of those happy coincidences appeared in my reading of Aristotle, the sort of supportive context that constitutes *evidence* if not proof. In his effort to define "place" (the "ground" of metaphysics) Aristotle says: "Place is an immobile vessel. Therefore when an enclosed thing moves and changes within something that moves, like a ship in a river, it has the secondary thing serving as a vessel rather than as a place. But place should be immobile. The whole river is rather the place, because the whole is immobile. So the first immobile surface of the surrounding thing, that is place." The connection for Miautre is that Barbara's consultation with the river (in the divining sense) produced as an answer to her question (to the one she asked, to the larger question of *Befindlichkeit*, and to the question she could not think) was the scene of the impounded Haitian vessels, which is a metaphysical scene.

Fuzzy 11–27

I'm working on the electronic monumentality project (9–11) and thinking about how inadequate are my opinions about such important matters as war and peace, death and life, hate and love, despair and hope,
and all the other conceptual pepper and salts. From where I am sitting
in my backyard, I am trying to catch the attention of the hawks or
ospreys circling up high, so they notice the abundance of plump squir-
rels that populate my property. The Chinese would know how to put
into a hexagram the wasps recently congregating around the birdbath.
This immanent passage of experience offers me a better sense of how
things are, what is happening, has happened, and will happen.

Nearby is my temporal calculator, the cat named "Fuzzy"—in his
grave since yesterday—reading "eight years." An underperforming
unit, compared with his predecessors. He is my weeping fractal, since
for him the tears came willy-nilly. The poet Robert Pinsky spoke
well with the image of the door he helped his cat negotiate every day.

> Closed or flung open or ajar, valves
> Of attention. O kitty, if the doors
> Of perception were cleansed
> all things would appear as they are,
>
> Infinite. Come in, darling, drowse
> Comfortably near my feet, I will click
> The barrier closed again behind you, O
> Sister will, fellow-mortal, here we are.[5]

From Fuzzy I may slide up and down the scale: in one direction falls
that yellow leaf; in the other scatters my father's ashes over the Yel-
lowstone River. Is there a continuum from that empty corner of the
couch to the hole in downtown Manhattan? This month of postcard
autumn is a symptom of drought. Those parents whose child was
ridiculed as a dummy when his work was graded by a peer and the
score read aloud in class filed suit in the Supreme Court to challenge
the constitutionality of this pedagogy. The mother said, "I'm not saying it's a big deal for everyone, but isn't every child important?" Something of the appeal of Christianity here: every person, every cat, even
to the very least . . . One man had an intuition when he heard an unexpected sound and stepped into a doorway, from where he saw a giant
ball of flaming jet fuel drop from the sky on the woman waiting the
moment before with him in line for the bus (in Rockaway). Our need

for water soon will exceed the capacities of the Florida aquifer, scientists warned today.

I would not want to be a god, if it were in a cosmogony that included powers of assigning fate—times and places—to my creatures. It is one reason why I am skeptical about religions that speak of love. My appointment with the veterinarian was at 3:30 P.M. EST on Tuesday since there was nothing more to be done except to prevent further suffering. I told Fuzzy everything on the ride over, and apologized on the way back. On Monday, I insisted he still owed me some time for the vet bill I just paid, but Tuesday I agreed we were even for his pedagogy of "The Last Time" (which should also be unconstitutional). As the philosopher said, death is necessary.

The Humane Society has a new policy of "aggressive" promotion of pet adoption, with the goal of eliminating the current euthanasia policy. When I did my Mr. Mentality tape some years ago (the proposal for an electronic monument honoring the sacrifice of millions of cats and dogs annually so that America could fulfill its belief that "a house without a pet is not a home"), the statistics I discovered were stunning (eight million unwanted potential pets euthanized annually). What does that mean? Fuzzy showed me, in his modest, fractal way. And then I scale up from there, from 11–27 to 9–11, and beyond, and I notice my opinions disappearing.

12

J. Hillis Miller
The Degree Zero of Criticism

JW: This collection seeks to address matters concerning what we call "theory" in relation to the practical issues of pedagogy, specifically, the matter of difference within pedagogy and the double question of thinking difference within pedagogy and a different thinking in the institution. How do we address the teaching of the quasi-concept of difference and maintain the radicality of the idea of difference? How do we teach students to address difference and to work with difference?

These questions arise as a response to certain current situations within the university, particularly in the humanities, having to do with the "collapse of difference." At one level, there is a sense that "we" have all agreed on what constitutes difference, what the epistemological identity of difference is, and "we" are all very happy about that, so that "we" can now get on with the institutional aspect of "our" work.

Now, you touch on these issues in your essay "Paul de Man as Allergen" in *Material Events: Paul de Man and the Afterlife of Theory*, in which you discuss the shock or the affront to institutional convention on almost every page of Paul de Man's work, namely, his articulation of a difference within and against the situation of thinking we know what we are supposed to do conventionally when we teach and read. What you identify in de Man's writing is a resistance to common sense, to the ideological work of common sense in an institutional framework, which I read to be at work in your own essays, where you employ the phrases "good reading" or "the good reader" to get at the significance and the difficulties of "thinking difference." Though it appears to be a very general, diffuse idea, "good reading" is in fact extremely specific. By definition, it cannot be defined: it pertains in every example to the singularity of specific texts. So there is always at work a negotiation between the general and the singular that collapses. Given the attention you pay to good reading and the nonidentity of difference that acts of good reading intimate, why is the notion of difference perceived as being so dangerous, and why is there an institutional need to define difference so as to control it?

JHM: The sense of danger stems from the perception of something different about a person or a text, something threatening, more in some persons or texts than in others. We want to control that difference, to understand it, to neutralize it. We identify or prescribe a difference in order to manipulate institutionalized procedures that maintain control by methods of naming and rationalizing. This has a long history. That would be one answer.

Another answer would be a more hypothetical or aggressive one. A community, such as a department of English, operates under a tacit psychological, anthropological, or social law that orders everyone to go on doing "what we do around here," as Stanley Fish puts it. This law is spontaneously and without forethought invoked to expel outsiders or to keep out that which is different from itself so that it can go on functioning. On the one hand, that's a sinister pattern. It can lead, on a larger, national scale, to fascism, for example. On the other hand, it's a normal occurrence. We see it in everyday life. It happens all the time. The old Department of English at Johns Hopkins, of which I was a member for nineteen years (1953–72), was very small, six or seven professors, all men. It was a closely knit community. I found at a certain point that I was caught up in an irresistible scapegoating. The department needed one member that was an outsider. That was the Americanist. The rest of us did European literature. This scapegoating took many forms. When this scholar won the Christian Gauss award, our response to this was to say that we couldn't understand how this could happen. It must have been a mistake. One colleague, a specialist in eighteenth-century and Romantic literature, Earl R. Wasserman, my closest friend in the department for all those years, believed until his dying day that there was no such thing as American literature. Those little things are not *poems*, he said, speaking of Emily Dickinson's work. He needed American (non)literature as the other of real literature, that is, English literature. The scapegoated person in question, a distinguished Americanist named Charles Anderson, was perceived as doing something useless anyway, because he was studying a nonsubject. This attitude, I realized at a certain point, was part of a very powerful psychosocial system, of which we were the unwitting creators and victims. We needed something different from ourselves in order complacently and with a good conscience to be ourselves. What we saw as an identifiable and derisory difference was, however it may be, a haunting by a "wholly other" we were unwilling to acknowledge.

What is peculiar about this kind of social system is that people need that difference and, at the same time, despise it for being from somewhere else. No doubt in many institutions in the United States (and elsewhere) literary theory has played a role something like that played by American literature in the Johns Hopkins English Department of the 1950s and 1960s. While most literature departments recognize the need to have some theorists, or at least one, and therefore support such appointments, conservative departments, or conservative members of departments, depend on having something that at the same time they wish would go away, in this case, theory.

This is a practical, everyday, pedagogical situation. It can, however, be understood in terms of the theoretical distinction to which you were alluding. To put it in Levinasian terms, it is a question of the difference, a difference that can always be brought back to the same, and a radical difference or otherness that cannot be assimilated in a gesture of dialectical sublation. The recuperable notion of otherness is the one we rely on in institutional situations, while the second notion of difference, that of the radical other, what Derrida calls "le tout autre," the wholly or completely other, is, for many people, a difficult notion to accept, or to live with, or to institutionalize, for various reasons. It's hard, for one thing, to distinguish something called "the wholly other" from some kind of quasi-religious transcendence, though Derrida has scrupulously identified that distinction. The idea of the wholly other has become most explicit fairly recently in Derrida, though even his early term *"différance"* is a version of the wholly other. His recent discussions of the "wholly other" radicalize or make more explicit what he means by *"différance"* and the trace.

In the current scene of literary and cultural studies, or in postcolonial studies, the term "other" is appropriated for specific strategic and political moves. The term "other" is used to speak of European and American imperialist attitudes toward non-European cultures and peoples. The notion of nonwhite or non-Western people as "other" is required to the hegemony of Western patriarchy. Such an idea of otherness, in Edward Said's work, for example, depends on a notion of difference in which difference remains within the order of the same. Often what is called for in politicized women's studies or postcolonial studies is a reversal of the power relation between self and other. This presupposes a necessary hierarchy between two groups. One group is on top and subordinates the other. All that can be imagined is the reversal of that, whereby the subordinate or subaltern other now becomes the dominant. That kind of thinking doesn't acknowledge the radical otherness I see as present, not only in the members of other races and cultures, but also in those who are closest to us and most apparently "like us." Our closest neighbor, I claim, is just as other as the most alien person, someone from outside our culture. What we need to imagine, at the horizon of the democracy to come, are communities of dissensus. No doubt it will be difficult to get either dominant or subaltern peoples to work for that.

I'm happy to have literature from non-European cultures taught. I think they should be taught. I'm all for that, especially in English departments these days. English departments should be teaching world Anglophone literatures. Most departments of English in the United States don't teach Canadian literature, South African literature, literature from Australia or New Zealand. Most departments don't teach East Asian or Indian Anglophone literature. An enormous body of Anglophone literature exists which, in its development, is parallel to ours in the United States. It, too, has come or is coming from places that were British colonies. Their literatures in English have developed in response to British models. These literatures seem to me important things to study, a frontier for our discipline, and we're not doing it. In my department [at the University of California, Irvine], for example, nobody, so far as I know, is teaching Australian literature.

Why is this not done? It seems an obvious move to make in an age of globalization. Part of the reason is that all these literatures are considered to be other to British literature and are therefore not part of the business of a department whose main mission is to teach Chaucer, Shakespeare, Samuel Johnson, Dickens, Woolf. Other literatures are "not necessary," and so are left out. American literature used to have that role, as in the example of Johns Hopkins I just gave. World Anglophone literature now has the place that American literature used to have. Wasserman's belief in the nonexistence of American literature is one example, from the 1950s, of the somewhat paranoid structure setting "us" against the denigrated others, but it was not an unusual attitude at that time. Even when American literature came to be more universally accepted as a necessary part of the humanistic curriculum, only a fraction of American literature got canonized, as we now know. That's now rapidly changing, partly through the development of much more inclusive anthologies, including more work by women and "minorities."

Only a few years ago, the primary education in literature in U.S. colleges and universities was by way of English literature, that is, by teaching the literature of a foreign country and, moreover, of a country that we defeated in a war of revolution more than 200 years ago. Yet we went right on acting like a colony. We didn't need to have happen what happened in India or Scotland, that is, the imposition, by imperialist occupiers, of English literature into the school and university curriculum as a means of asserting domination or maintaining it. We did it to ourselves. As you know, English literature as a discipline was invented, not for British youth, who were still being taught almost exclusively Greek and Latin literature right through the nineteenth century and into the twentieth, but in India for the purpose of educating the Indians and in Scotland as a means of putting down the Scots and maintaining rule. The discipline of English literature has always served an imperialist function. What's amazing in the United States is that we bought this without being coerced into it.

That's not to say that Shakespeare and Chaucer are not worth reading. They are intrinsic to the rich heritage of the language that most people speak in the United States. That American universities teach English literature so universally, however, obscures the degree to which English literature is other, in the radical sense of other, to American experience. It takes a while to come to terms with that because it's hidden by the shared language. It's hard for an American to teach English literature because "we all know English." It's our native language, in the version called "American English." An English writer such as Anthony Trollope appears to share the same language and the same assumptions about human life that we Americans have. Significant differences exist, however, and these take some delicate explaining if you are trying to teach English literature.

One difference that impedes our understanding of British writers is that we don't have a class society, or, rather, the U.S. class system is very different from the English one. Just what our class system is would take quite some explaining. My colleague John Rowe has made a beginning with that, in attempt to add the category of "class" in a serious way to the categories of race and gender to cultural studies. In England, in any case, class barriers were, and still are, harder to cross than in the United States. Leonard Bast, in Forster's *Howards End*, is stuck at the border between the working class and the lower middle class, in spite of the efforts he makes to raise himself by self-education. It's hard to explain that to American students. They have, or have been taught to think they have, much more social mobility, especially through education. In the United States, the boundaries between classes are to a considerable degree identified with racial differences, though there is much social mobility even for "minorities" by way of education. Leonard Bast can read John Ruskin until he's blue in the face, but it's not going to make a difference, at least according to Forster, whereas, in the United States, partly through the wider availability of higher education, you can move up, as Fitzgerald's Gatsby is shown to have done, though there are many ironies in Fitzgerald's presentation of Gatsby. I am, it happens, an example of American social mobility, though not of Gatsby's perfidy. You will remember that he got rich partly through "fixing" the World Series. I come from farming families in Virginia. My father was the first person in his family ever to go to college. He became a university president. In just one generation, in the United States, you can move up to the professional classes. I know it's easier now in Britain than it used to be, but it's still not so absolutely taken for granted as a possibility, as in this country.

I find it hard to explain to American students the differences between American and English, at least nineteenth-century English, notions of courtship and marriage. An example is the presupposition of Henry James's *The Awkward Age,* a study of upper-class London life in the late Victorian period. The heroine of that novel, Nanda Brookenham, is unmarriageable, not because she has lost her virtue by having sex before marriage, but just because she knows the facts of sex. Her mother has made the mistake of allowing her too early to listen to adult conversations. It is exceedingly difficult to make that plausible to American students, to say the least.

Another form of difference is the strangeness of literary works, their absolute difference from one another, their radical heterogeneity. Much work teaching literature and writing secondary work about it is devoted, probably unconsciously, to covering up that strangeness by assimilating literary works to preconceived categories. It is extremely difficult to develop strategies of teaching or writing that honor difference in the sense of literary works' strangeness or even uncanniness. Even Anthony Trollope's novels are exceedingly peculiar in their assumptions, if you think objectively about them.

This issue is related to a distinction I would make between theory and reading. Reading encounters that strangeness, willy-nilly, even if efforts are made to suppress it. Theory, on the other hand, as its name suggests (the word *theory* implies clear seeing), has as its goal making universal generalizations. Even theoretical formulations about literature's strangeness, such as I have been making, are not much help in communicating a sense for the singular strangeness of a particular work to students or readers. Insofar as it is the aim of literary theory to make general statements about literature, this goal is incompatible with the experience of reading. If you're a careful reader, if you're what I dare to call a "good reader," that is, a reader open to the otherness of the work, reading never quite fits your theoretical presuppositions. Good readers are readers who see, not what they expected to see, but what is there to "see." Such readers don't say, "I'm going to apply Barthes, Derrida, or whomever, and show that a given 'theory' works." Rather, they recognize through the act of reading that the presupposed theory doesn't work. A discrepancy between assumed theory and the actual experience of reading always exists. It is difficult to this discrepancy, however, because the power of a particular theoretical formulation is such that it can dazzle the discriminating power of reading. The power of theoretical formulation to obliterate difference leads you to say, "Aha! It works," without recognizing that "it" always works if you set aside the singularity of the work that makes it what it is.

I've been reading recently Derrida's *Donner la mort* [*The Gift of Death*]. In the third chapter of that book Derrida reads Kierkegaard's *Fear and Trembling*. That reading is one of the places where Derrida has occasion, apparently casually, to introduce the notion of "le tout autre," the wholly other. The fourth chapter then is a full-scale investigation of the phrase "Tout autre est tout autre." This phrase is more or less impossible to translate because Derrida, in a strategy he frequently employs, takes both words, *tout* and *autre;* and explores the complex and sui generis resonances they have within the confines of the French language. These resonances don't translate without loss into a different language, for example, English. Derrida must have been very happy when he came upon that phrase, "Tout autre est tout autre." He says something like "The phrase just came to me from nowhere."

The chapter about *Fear and Trembling* is fascinating because, for one thing, it's characteristically tricky and unexpected. Derrida performs an active reading. In his case, that's always interesting. Derrida is no doubt a great theorist and philosopher. Almost always, however, he does philosophy theory by way of specific acts of reading.

These recognize, acknowledge, or attempt to come to terms with, the singularity of something textual. In this case, it's Kierkegaard's *Fear and Trembling*. Derrida develops Kierkegaard's distinction between ethical action and speaking. Speaking is necessarily general, according to Kierkegaard. It therefore falsifies the singularity of ethical decision. The latter is incompatible with language. In the account in Genesis, God says, take your beloved son Isaac and sacrifice him. Abraham doesn't say anything to his wife or to anyone else, nor indeed does he say anything to God, the "wholly other," within biblical tradition, after his first response to God's calling of his name, "Abraham," to which Abraham answers, "Behold, here I am." Abraham's decision to obey God is silent, mute, unworded. This is opposed to ethical discourse, which would say something like, "You should always obey God's injunctions, so I shall do that." This, according to Kierkegaard, falsifies decisions that occur in response to absolute demands from the wholly other by reducing them to generalizing language. Of course, the Bible, Kierkegaard, and Derrida, all three, violate this injunction not to speak. All three attempt to speak of Abraham's decision. Both Kierkegaard and Derrida are aware of this paradox or aporia, which is irreducible. The Bible just tells its story. That story is the founding event of the three great religions of the Book — Islam, Judaism, and Christianity — so it's not just any story. When Abraham does speak, Kierkegaard and Derrida aver, he speaks without speaking since what he says is deliberately evasive or misleading. Isaac asks, "My father, . . . where is the lamb for a burnt offering?" Abraham replies, "My son, God will provide himself a lamb for a burnt offering." Abraham says this, and then takes Isaac off to cut his throat. This, Kierkegaard says, ironically voices the truth in a way that obscures it from Isaac and in a way that Abraham himself does not yet understand. You still have to use some language to speak without speaking, as in Abraham's equivocating reply to Isaac. Kierkegaard says Abraham is not telling the truth, but he's not lying either.

Such speaking is a form of silence. What Derrida does with that is extremely interesting. It goes beyond Kierkegaard. It modifies or undermines Kierkegaard's distinction between the ethical and religious dimension of human existence. Derrida does this partly with the help of Husserl. He cannibalizes things he has said in earlier work about Husserl, but puts that to a new use. Derrida says, following what Husserl says in the fifth meditation of the *Cartesian Meditations*, that my neighbor, the other person, the other ego, the alter ego, is unavailable to me through intuition or phenomenological experience. I have no direct access to what the other person is thinking or feeling. I have knowledge of the alter ego only through mediated signs. All we can know of the other person is by way of what Husserl, in a doubly negative phrase, calls "analogical apperception." It's not logical; it's analogical. It's not perception; it's apperception. It's *ana*logical *app*erception, something indirect and highly mediated.

Husserl was, in fact, tormented by the problem of how we can know the other, the alter ego. If the other person is unknowable, then something we know or assume exists escapes phenomenological perception. The phenomenological field would appear to be full of innumerable black holes called "other people." Husserl found this intolerable. He kept searching for a way to reinsert the other person within the phenomenological field of consciousness, to make his or her consciousness something of which I can be directly conscious, not something I know only by way of mediated uncertainties. Apparently, Husserl after his death left a huge number of papers in which he goes on and on trying to solve this problem. It's not quite so simple as to say Husserl thinks there's no direct access to the other. Admitting that is appalling to Husserl because he knows the whole phenomenological project depends on finding some way to affirm direct access to the other. Only that, he thinks, would, for example, permit the establishment of what he considers to be a viable community.

Derrida proposes to explore the consequences of assuming that Husserl's fears are well founded. There are writers, Anthony Trollope, for example, who believe each person has intuitive direct access to the other person's thinking and feeling. Certainly, Trollope's narrators know all the characters intimately, from the inside. His novels depend, for the most part, on the assumption his characters belong to so homogeneous a community that they really do know what the other person is thinking and feeling on a given occasion. It might be a mistake, therefore, to universalize Derrida's assumptions since they would not apply to a writer like Trollope. What Derrida does is to say: if it is the case that my neighbor remains an impenetrable secret, then what Kierkegaard applies only to Abraham's relation to Jehovah also applies to my relationships to other human beings. As a result each of us confronts all the time the absolute demand made on us by each other person. I must take responsibility to respond to the other person's demand. Each of these demands is like the call made on Abraham by God. This demand is irrational in the sense that it can't be generalized in logical or conceptual language. It takes place in the instant and is different every time. It's a momentary experience that cannot be subject to dialectical negation or sublation. Derrida is specific about irrationality. He quotes Kierkegaard as saying, "The instant of decision is a madness." It's a madness because there's no conceptual language that could be adequate to such a moment.

The ethical situation, according to Derrida, is to be forced every moment, every day, to make decisions that sacrifice our responsibilities to all the others for the sake of the one responsibility we decide to fulfill. Derrida has been criticized for one example he gives. He says, "When I feed my cat, I am not feeding all the other thousands of cats all over the world which are starving to death." Derrida has been accused of trivializing the moment of ethical decision when he goes all the way, in a few pages, from Abraham's relation to Jehovah, to the example of "my relation to my cat." I think that's just the point Derrida is making. The demand made on me by any creature is analogous to the demand made on me by God. The multiplicity of creatures, human and animal, makes this universal responsibility, singular in each case, impossible to fulfill and yet absolutely exigent.

This aporetic situation, to return to pedagogy, is related to the sense I have of the absolute otherness and singularity of each and every work of literature. To choose to teach any one of them is not to teach all the others, and yet they all demand to be read and taught. My teaching, moreover, insofar as it's theoretical — and all pedagogy that conceptualizes the results of reading is theoretical — is a falsification of my relation to that given work I have decided to teach. It falls, necessarily, into generalization. That's the double bind of teaching literature. One of the things you are tempted to say about a given literary work to your students is absurd. You want to say, "Wow! This is a wonderful book — I can't tell you, I can't explain to you what a wonderful book this is. It's absolutely unique." You can't go for many seminar hours just saying, "Wow!" You want to say something more. It is your professional obligation to say more. As soon as you start conceptualizing, however, you are falsifying the uniqueness and "unspeakability," as one might barbarously call it, of your reading experience.

This all seems clear enough. The upshot is the conclusion that true ethical decision is silent, but that this causes big problems with certain activities, such as teaching literature. Matters are not quite so simple, however. The notion that silence is an appropriate ethical response is directly contradicted by no less a person than Walter Benjamin in his essay on Goethe's *Elective Affinities* in *Illuminationen,* an essay omitted from the English translation of this book. Hannah Arendt, who supervised the English translation, told me many years ago that the *Elective Affinities* essay was left out because it would not make much sense to Americans, who do not know the German tradition of criticism on that novel. Benjamin's target is Gundolf and other German readers of the *Elective Affinities* in the many decades since it came out. Benjamin raises the question of the ethical character of one of the main personages in Goethe's novel, Ottilie, who makes a silent vow to keep silent, and then silently starves herself to death. Benjamin asks, "Does she have character?" He answers, "No, the opposite is the case." Why? Because her decision to die when she discovers that she has an irresistible passion for Eduard is silent. She never speaks it out, never articulates it. She stops speaking altogether. Benjamin says that because her decision is silent and not shared with the community around her, it's not ethical. Her decision is not a moral decision because all moral decisions have to be expressed through what he calls "Sprachgeist," the spirit of language. Benjamin's word *sittlicher* can be translated either as "ethical" or as "moral," though the nuances of the two words in English are quite different, especially these days. Today "ethical" tends to be used to name a genuine decision, "from the heart," while "moral" tends to be used to define a decision that mechanically obeys an external code of behavior. Benjamin says that not only must a proper moral decision be expressed in language but it also has to be in a language that is shared with others. Here is what Benjamin says in English: "Does she [Ottilie] have character? Is her nature, not so much thanks to openheartedness as through the power of free and decided expression, clear to the eye? She indicates the opposite of all these. . . . No ethical decision can come to life without verbal form, and taken strictly, without having become the object of communication."[1]

This seems to be exactly the opposite of what Kierkegaard and Derrida say. For them, the proper mode of ethical decision is silence. It is silent because it is unspeakable, unspeakably singular. It's a little hard to tell what is at stake in Benjamin's assertions. One might argue or suspect that his use of the terms moral and ethical may perhaps be ironical in the sense that he might be making, in his own way, the Kierkegaardian distinction between the ethical and the religious. Benjamin elsewhere distinguishes between choice (*Wahl*), which for him is mythical, and decision (*Entscheidung*), which is rational, ethical. Ottilie may, in his reading, be making a "choice," not an ethical decision. Benjamin's distinction would then be precisely the one that Kierkegaard makes when he says ethical decision is expressed in general terms, expressible as maxims: you should always tell the truth, you should not steal, and so on, whereas true religious decision, such as Abraham's obedience of God's terrible command, is silent. Ottilie's choice may be a religious or "mythical" rather than ethical one.

Perhaps, then, for Benjamin, too, religious decision is the kind that cannot be expressed and has to be silent. Benjamin's covert point may be that Ottilie is religious but not ethical. Maybe. Perhaps. If so, there would be a deep irony in the passage by Benjamin in his ambiguous use of the term "sittlicher," and in his claim that the ethical does require language and does require to be shared, made overt in the community.

To return to pedagogy, can other than a silent answer be given to the question of why a given teacher decides to teach certain works and not others? Is it a "choice" or a "decision"? These sound like reasonable pedagogical questions. We might refine or make more concrete the questions by asking, in the most immediate and practical way, "Why should we, here, in Southern California, at the University of California, Irvine, teach Yeats's poetry, or the Victorian novel? Why should we ask students to read 'Leda and the Swan' or *Bleak House* or Trollope's *Can You Forgive Her?* or novels by Henry James? What interests other than antiquarian can these works have for us or for our students now?"

Different answers might be given to those questions. One answer might be suggested in Trollope's title for one of his novels, *Can You Forgive Her?* The "you" of the title refers not only to the question of whether Plantagenet Palliser can forgive his wife, Lady Glencora, for almost running away with the dashing and reckless Burgo Fitzgerald, whom she truly loves, nor simply to the question of whether John Gray can forgive Alice Vavasour for saying no so often to his proposals of marriage, and then finally accepting his proposal. The question is also directed to the reader. Can *we* forgive these characters for behaving in the way that they do? Some readers certainly cannot. The novel makes this appeal in three ways, and addresses three issues. First, do you approve of the behavior of the characters or not? This is not an unreasonable question to ask. Do they do the right thing? Second, if you had been in that situation, would you have behaved and decided in the same way? If so, then you can say, "I forgive her. I would have acted in the same way." Third, to put it in Kantian terms, would you be willing to make that form of behavior into a universal maxim or axiom, valid for all time? That's what Kant insists on, that you should always act in such a way that you would be willing to have your behavior made into a universal axiom or a maxim valid for all times and places.

That last question is by no means ever easy to answer. A lot hangs on it, no less than the existence of ethical universals. My inclination, with regard to works of literature, is to resist the demand Kant makes and to say you should not make universal moral generalizations. For example, when Isabel goes back to her bad husband, Gilbert Osmund, in Henry James's *The Portrait of a Lady*, can I say, not only that she does do the right thing, but also that I would have done the same thing in the same circumstances, and I think everyone should always do the same thing in similar circumstances? It's a mistake, I think, however tempting a mistake, to use literature in this way. On the other hand, what you can learn from literature about how to live your life emerges when you pay attention to the singularity of ethical situations and ethical decisions as represented in literature. Characters in great literary works, such as Isabel in *The Portrait of a Lady*, have to decide, but they don't get much help from general axioms. Their stories express the solitude of the ethical decision, the impossibility of deciding according to some kind of grand recipe telling how you should act. This means that you are in difficulties when you try to decide according to abstract calculations whether or not you are doing the right thing. James's novel ends by commenting that Isabel "had not known where to turn; but she knew now. There was a very straight path."[2] She then goes back to Osmund. It evidently appears to her that this is the right thing to do. I think some or many or even most readers may approve of her decision. This is the case even though James leaves the grounds of her decision obscure, partly through giving no explicit reason at all at that ultimate moment in the novel, partly through giving multiple and contradictory, mutually canceling, possible hypothetical proleptic reasons elsewhere earlier in the novel. About her reasons for acting as she does, James, or his narrator, keeps silent. The narrator just tells the reader that now she knew where to turn, that is, away from Caspar Goodwood and back toward Gilbert Osmond.

Reading *The Portrait of a Lady* does not help you all that much in your own life, certainly not by giving you moral maxims, such as "A woman should always be faithful to the husband to whom she is lawfully wedded." The novel does, however teach you that ethical decisions are difficult and that you don't get a lot of easily codifiable help from books, including books on moral philosophy—except to discover that you don't learn a series of infallible moral maxims from literature or from books of moral philosophy. You do learn that, an invaluable lesson, and you do learn that ethical decision is always singular and impossible to justify in general terms. To learn that is to learn a lot from literature. Perhaps it is to learn what it is most essential to know about ethical life.

That's the end of my long answer to your question about "difference" and pedagogy! My answer has made a long zigzag trajectory, but sometimes the longest way round is the shortest way home.

JW: On the matter of the title of Trollope's novel *Can You Forgive Her?:* what struck me as you were speaking was that one of the ways to register the problem of difference and decision is not to follow the Kantian imperative that you were talking about, not to raise the question to the level of generality, but to say that the "you" names every "you" who reads the title as a singularity. It is to understand the implications of that singular reading or response, very much in the way in which you treat the addressee in your essay on Hardy's "The Torn Letter," so that one can at once refer to a certain aspect of generality in the process of speaking about difference and yet address the question of difference itself through singularity.

JHM: So you would say then that the "you" of the title could be in the plural and addressed to all readers, but it could also be stressed in the singular: can *you* forgive her, *you* the singular reader, in the singular act of reading. Yes, I see that.

JW: Which suggests that the reader becomes figured as both the intended recipient and as a kind of revenant haunting every reader and every other reader. I was also struck by your example of Kierkegaard and Derrida's question concerning what takes place "when I feed my cat"[3] from practical, pedagogical experience.

In a seminar on literary theory, about a month ago, a student asked a question on the relevance or importance of Derrida's work. In a 50-minute seminar, I found I gave an answer lasting nearly 40 minutes, and I felt terribly guilty that, even though I had an obligation to these two singularities, to both Derrida and the student, to respond as fully as possible, I also had a responsibility to answer all the other students, something I was not doing. This negotiation and the matter of singularity seem to me to signal an unresolvable, undecidable problem for any moment within teaching, with what the institution every day wants: as you put it, "to get on with things" for the most pragmatic purposes, and so to "damp down" on difference in the most violent way. So there seems to be something of a response here to Frank Kermode's remark that fashionable theory endangers the stability of the institution, and interferes with its "proper, primary work."

JHM: It's hard to know whether Sir Frank said this with any irony. His work is certainly theoretical, and he was one of the first in England to take French theory, for example Roland Barthes, seriously.

JW: Of course, but there seems to be at work, despite the best of intentions in pedagogical practice, some anthropomorphic mimicry in the everyday work of institutions, so that mimicry, having to do with the politics of the self-same, involves a "making over" of difference and singularity in a fairly narcissistic way, in terms of producing a quasi-Arnoldian "best possible image" of itself. And the way this works, if I understand you correctly, is in an act of appropriation and suppression, whereby the erasure of difference takes place through a return to "business as usual." You illustrate this through your examples of the reception of Derrida, Foucault, and others in the Anglo-American university, but I wonder whether you might also address the arrival of cultural studies and other related areas.

JHM: The rapid assimilation of cultural studies by the university, their acceptance by administrators who are scientists, for example, suggests that the university doesn't see cultural studies as all that threatening, however politically motivated cultural studies may sometimes be. Postcolonial and cultural studies are necessary at this time to the development of departments, and I certainly don't oppose them. Nevertheless, cultural studies sometimes involve a return to pretheoretical or precritical assumptions. A symptom of that is the tendency in essays, papers, and books in cultural studies or postcolonial studies to summarize plots or to describe characters as if they were real people, and to let that stand as a reading. I just read a passage by Roland Barthes, where he says a little formalism is an escape from history, while a lot of formalism is a return to history. I like that observation because it displaces the opposition between formalism in the shape of close reading and the serious business of establishing historical context. According to some people in cultural studies, you don't want to do close reading any more because it's old fashioned, it's ahistorical, it's sequestered from reality, it's conservative or reactionary. These put-downs are used as a justification for not looking closely at the texts discussed. The return to talking about characters in novels as though they were real people, based closely on the authors themselves or on historical personages, along with a summary of plot action, is of course the most traditional and unreflective form of criticism you could possibly imagine. There's quite a bit of that in cultural studies essays. It is as though the lessons of structuralism and poststructuralism, to say nothing of the New Criticism, had been forgotten almost overnight. So we seem to be back in the 1920s and 1930s, with a not very sophisticated methodology. When what is done in cultural studies is compared to the strategies of anthropological research, the procedures of the former don't appear to be all that sophisticated in technique. I consider cultural studies to be, to a considerable degree, a form of social science. Those who practice cultural studies have much to learn from the protocols and institutional rigors of, for example, anthropology. I know many in cultural studies would say anthropology is tainted by having been to some degree an arm of Western imperialism, but anthropologists have been very much aware of that issue for decades and have debated it in sophisticated ways. I would like to see people who do cultural studies have a real training in sociology and anthropology. A whole new pedagogy and curriculum needs to be developed, quite different from traditional training in literary history and literary criticism. To some degree that is already taking place, but, insofar as cultural studies are done within English departments, that will mean revolutionary changes in the curricula of those departments.

How do we come to terms with the pedagogical problems you describe? I think it's true that teaching one work rather than others or singling out one student to help rather than others is like feeding your own cat and not feeding the others. There's no way we can be simultaneously helpful to all the students in a given class. In a class discussion, one or two people will often dominate the conversation. Sometimes they're smart, and sometimes they're not; sometimes helpful to the others, and sometimes not. We've all had the experience of teaching a class in which a given student doesn't say anything, just sits there like a log—and then turns in a paper that's terrific. You realize that this person about whom you knew almost nothing is actually extremely intelligent. A student of mine at Yale in an undergraduate class on poetry sat and said nothing, He then turned in a paper on William Carlos Williams that was wonderful. I didn't know him at all, except as a name, Roger Gilbert. I then said something condescending when I returned the paper, like "This is terrific; where did you learn this stuff?" It turned out he was Sandra Gilbert's son. So there was an answer to my query, not just that he was Sandra Gilbert's son, but that his intrinsic gifts had been added to a helpful household environment for learning how to read. I don't think he had much to learn from me. You're absolutely right about this dilemma of being forced to give uneven attention to different students, feeding one cat to the exclusion of others. I don't see any way out of this, although the possibility in American institutions for "independent reading courses" can help. These are not like universal tutorials, as in British universities, but an option that enterprising students can talk professors into doing. So there are ways around the problem you mention.

I want to say just a little more about pedagogy: In my judgment, the best way to teach good reading is not through presenting, for example, a theory of the aporia, though there might be a place for this, but by the empirical act of reading some text. The place to begin is with the (apparently) naive act of reading, without theoretical presuppositions (impossible of course), some literary text or other. This might lead to an experience of what aporia means. In reading, you might vicariously or in imagination live with an aporia.

Dickens's *Bleak House*, for example, presents two kinds of decision as expressed in two kinds of speech acts. One is the public, institutional kind involving legal writing, documents. This is opposed to private or silent decisions, such as Esther Summerson's inward decision to accept her situation as the illegitimate daughter of Lady Dedlock. She silently resolves to do her best to be helpful to those around her and not to damage Lady Dedlock's reputation by revealing what she knows. Documents, signed affidavits, and so on, as in the law case in Chancery of Jarndyce and Jarndyce, constitute not a way to "do things with words," in J. L. Austin's phrase, but a way to use words not to do things, except to prolong an institutionalized running in place. Of course the reader is given knowledge of Esther's silent resolve. I don't see any way you can get around the following contradiction: The novel constitutes a document, whereas the book itself shows documents to be of no use. Silence is better. How can we know that, however, unless the silence is worded, any more than we can know of Abraham's silent acceptance of God's command, except through the telling of the story in Genesis? This is an aporia, a possible impossibility. I don't think you can get beyond it. Students might perhaps better learn what an aporia is through a thoughtful reading of *Bleak House* than by having the meaning of *aporia* explained to them abstractly. Literature proves such things on the readers' pulses, as John Keats put it.

There are, by the way, documents in *Bleak House* that *are* efficacious speech acts. Sir Leicester, Lady Dedlock's husband, after he's had his stroke and can no longer speak, painfully scribbles a note to Inspector Bucket: "Full forgiveness. Find —." Bucket stops him there because he understands the rest.[4] Lady Dedlock's final note just before she dies is another such "felicitous" speech act, a request for forgiveness. It ends: "Farewell. Forgive." It is "felicitous" because it works. It puts its readers — Esther, for example — in the situation of needing to choose whether or not to forgive. That takes us back to Trollope's title, *Can You Forgive Her?* The request for forgiveness and the granting of forgiveness are particular kinds of speech acts, with special rules. As Derrida has argued in his seminars on pardon and perjury, the only thing that requires pardon is the unpardonable, such as Lady Dedlock's guilty act. If Sir Leicester and Esther can forgive her, can we? The novel, however, ends with a return to Esther's silence: "[T]hey can very well do without much beauty in me — even supposing —."

13

Werner Hamacher
To Leave the Word to Someone Else

JW: This project concerns questions of difference, difference within pedagogical processes and institutional structures, and whether change within the educational process can be effected through reading, writing, and teaching students to be attentive to difference and alterity.[1]

I want to situate the first question concerning difference, at least initially, to comments from two essays of yours that address, at least implicitly, the matter of difference, and which — as I read them — articulate in their contours, if not actually performing, the movement of difference, of which your writing is acutely aware. The first comes from your essay on Jean-Luc Nancy, "Où, séance, touche de Nancy." The opening of the essay focuses on the continuity inscribed in the remarking of the "here," a continuity that, as your essay makes clear, is also a discontinuity, or, as you put it, "between the repetition and its interruption, between the connexion and its break."[2] Thus each "here" effects both a rhythm and a *punctum* and the performance of the "here" is dependent on the simultaneous effect of difference and what perhaps might be described as a "momentary blindness to difference" that allows the expression of every "here" as the acknowledgment and experience of the present *as such*.

Now to another commentary, from *Pleroma*, which concerns a matter of reading and temporality: reading, you contend, is "not yet the immanent movement of self-reproduction which it already is."[3] This formula points to an experience of the impossible. It addresses a spacing as well as a displacing, a reading of simultaneity and yet also of the opening to reading of a temporality, as well as a spatial relationship dependent on an awareness of difference.

Between the two citations, we can read another figure of the "between," one by which we begin to come to terms with difference, without being able to control it. This is the tracing of difference between the remark (*hic et nunc*) and the event of reading. This "between" is what interests us as critics and teachers, and indeed, in our acts of reading and writing, it is what places us, in the very figure of *inter-est*, as subject to difference, in the place and the taking place of the "between." Tracing such a figuration involves a comprehension, as you show, of spatiotemporal relationships irreducible to the hermeneutic simplicity of either a final meaning or an absolute structure. If this is the case, how do we bring this to bear not only in our analyses but also in the pedagogical process, in the face of structural, institutional imposition? How do we maintain difference in the process of teaching students to be attentive to the effects of thinking otherwise as they take place in the pedagogical encounter?

WH: The "between" in the remarks that you quote is, strictly speaking, a misnomer — an imprecise, ambiguous, misleading term and a term that, even when applied there, is not only inaccurate [*verfehlt*], but also a nonentity [*fehlt*]. "Between" here thus falls short of the mark because it promotes the misunderstanding that this "between" would lie "between" imposed points in time and space, or "between" already constituted subjects, or "between" one process and another. However, the "between" mentioned here is not a between of this kind, which would to a certain extent be added additionally or belatedly to already imposed entities and which would lead to a relation or to the temporal space necessary for a relation between them. The "between" mentioned here does not lend itself to being dated, it cannot be located, it cannot be fixed and neither lies between points nor between subjects and other subjects, nor between subjects and objects, and therefore neither between objects and other objects. In fact, it does not lie in general, it does not lie still, but it moves. It does not move on a prescribed track, but moves where tracks do not yet exist, where they are being created step by step — this "between" proceeds always in that place where neither objects nor subjects, nor their spatiotemporal determinants are given, it proceeds to a nowhere and a never, and amounts occasionally only then to such subjects and objects. What we call "subjects" and what we call "objects" are only the resultants of relations —

they amount to the between, this between does not result from them. Our concept of being is formed from the essence [*Seinsart*] of the objective present, or from the subjective forms within which this present is encompassed; therefore, it cannot be understood as the between, which we are talking of here, as this concept of being in the present, the between *preceding* subjects and *preceding* objects, the between that proceeds in a nowhere and a never, because it is not preceded by any space or time coordinates by which it could orient itself.

Between *is* not. Or, rather, between "is" nothing. It "is" — above all — nothing of which one could talk without it not already participating [*mitreden*]. And, participating in this way, it would pull all talk inside itself and its nothingness and would unspeak it [*entreden*]. This nothing of our imaginations, of our names, concepts, and our language — this between that cannot be grasped — plays around [*umspielen*] and surrounds everything we can possibly imagine, name, or comprehend. It plays with and *re*interprets everything in another sense (another direction and another field), for from this nothing everything gets another determination than the one that is usually meant — and possibly none. What is determined can only be determined in such a way that it is codetermined by this nothingness — or by this nothing. Everything that is determined is determined with reference to another that differs from it, and which is separated by a "between"; it is then determined only by virtue of the passage through this between, and the passage through this nothing. Therefore it counts: each determination is codetermined by a nothing and is therefore "in-determined." One can only determine in this way, which leaves a determination *open* to further determinations, at the point where those determinations break or are erased. And this also counts, this particularly counts first and foremost for the word *between* — it names a field, definitely, that spans "between" the one and the other (field, element, mark, entity, and so on); but it labels it in such a way that this area can extend further than its manifest determination reaches, and so this area can also slide itself inside elements, marks, entities, undefining its definition and implanting itself in each demarcation.

A between can exist, for instance, between two points, but a between can also split a point off from itself. Even if I define a point A as itself, and I write A = A, the identity [*Selbigkeit*] is dependent on the intervening relation (=), which has to be passed through by A, so that it can itself constitute itself as A. A = A, the sentence of identity, may present itself as the destruction of the difference of the A to itself, but its self-equality [*Sich-selbst-Gleichheit*] is impossible without this difference, without the between that separates A from A, and which, only through this separation, unites them. Every synthesis, even the most primitive, is dependent on a nonsynthesis or even on a nonthesis, in order to be a synthesis. No identity without a between. This between does not actually precede the identity, it does not follow it, it is neither inherent in it nor is it external to it — all these relations are dependent on predications, which again require an "is" or an "is equal to," and on which the play of the between repeats itself. The between is impredicative [*imprädikabel*]. It is neither possible to dispute the identity or the being, nor to concede it to it, it is not an element of an affirmative or of a privative, but of an infinite determination.

One could now suppose that the being of the between is an entirely uncanny mode of being, which is best characterized as "interbeing [*Zwischensein*]," as it moves between one being and another. Since it is obvious, however, that between is no proper and somehow autonomous field, yet it constitutes itself only from its extremes as an independent field of movement. These extremes, however, are included in its movement, and this between has to be characterized both as a movement of extremization and as a movement of indefinition — therefore of ex-tremization — but still as a movement of the infinitive nature of the nothing, which constitutes this between. One can hardly claim therefore that the relation between two elements is at the same time a relation of these elements to their relation; rather: each relation between two is a relation to the nothing of this relation. When I refer to "an other," I do not refer to a fixed, determined, secured, rigid relation, which would stand like a table between us, but, rather, to the flexible possibilities of this other, to which the latter relation is also part of in extremis, which I attribute to its "not-being [*Nichtsein*]," and to which, therefore, the latter relation is in extremis part of, so that such a relation does not exist at all. Such a relation — which by no means stops being a relation — is the relation to the nonrelation; and more specifically, it is relation *out of* nonrelation, relation *out of* withdrawal, *relatio ex nihilo*. When we think of "between" and "relation" otherwise than as coming from nothingness, we think of them as a subsequent result [*Konvenienz*] between two given entities, and, therefore, we do not think of this "between" at all, because we think of it according to a model of an already constituted object. Moreover, we do not think of the object out of its constitution because we think of it as an already constituted, established, and installed object; and we do not think of the given because we do not think of it out of the movement of its giving [*Gebung*], but as something present.

Relatio ex nihilo — I do not speak of *creatio* — this means also that each relation between a two is first of all a relation out of this nothing and on this nothing. The pedagogical processes you are asking about are such relations between two at least. In fact, they are *never* relations between *only* a two — there is always at least a third involved in them: language, and with this language an infinity of medial, institutional, situational, social, political, historical instances, which intervene from one to the other, both as joints and gaps, between this two at least, although the fundamental structure of this third instance and of the infinity attached to it is already charted in the relation between the two, therefore I can neglect it here for the time being. This pedagogical binary relationship [*Zweierbeziehung*] starts (looking at it closely) exactly with that nothing — for I cannot, strictly speaking, rely on anything, back on anything, take anything as given, when I start teaching somebody (and this includes myself) something. Whenever I presuppose something as known or as fixable, I will have to notice sooner or later that what I said could not be understood, accepted, or approved, precisely because I made that presumption of consensus, or at least of the possibility of consensus. In this premise lies the difficulty. Obviously, I am not talking here about pedagogical operations on the basis of axioms; these also have their difficulties, but they are difficulties that are resolved by way of the axioms themselves. Mathematical axioms are *the* learnable; but they are only learnable because they are sets [*Setzungen*] of ideal relations between ideal constructions; they are simply learnable because they can only be learned *by heart*. The difficulties with sets of such axioms are not then considered at all, and can in fact be disregarded for millennia — until, as demonstrated through Riemann, Cantor, and Russell, the excluded sets break out at the end and shake the entire axiomatic system. Set against this learning one commences with this shaking [*Erschütterung*] — with the solicitation of fixed data, of ideal languages, of valid conventions, and of their consequences — and only in this shaking does learning remain possible.

Learning has only, therefore, to an extent — a variable extent — to do with the handing down of a fixed stock of knowledge, with the passing on of collections of findings [*Erkenntnis-Sammlungen*] and with the transmission of data. These belong to the assumptions that one makes and has to make because they are already made, whether or not one wants this, whether for good or bad. The insight that they are indeed made, these assumptions, can only be reached by those who have obtained distance from them, and thus have already taken a step back from them. Each historical progression of findings, obtained through learning, is in reality a step back from the assumptions thus recognized. When I hear the sentence "Muse, name me the man . . . [Nenne mir Muse den Mann, . . .]"—and I do not find anything surprising in the fact that a Muse is being addressed and asked to name someone or other—then I live in the world of an addressable Muse, who is expected to name someone or other, and so on. But only when I do not take it for granted [*selbstverständlich*], when I find it incomprehensible [*unverständlich*] that a Muse—whatever that may be—is being addressed; when the name "Muse," her address, and her naming do not mean anything to me, only then, in this sheer incomprehension, or at least in this conceptual confusion [*Begriffsstutzigkeit*], can it dawn on me what a "Muse" and what her naming could be. The "Muse" starts to speak out of nothingness—out of the nonknown, nonrecognized, nonunderstood, always out of a nothing that is a nothing of theory, as well as a nothing of technology and a nothing of practice—a noncapacity, nonability, nondone. And thus learning: it always starts with this nothingness, with this unearthed action and knowledge gap, this slope on the edge of the firm knowledge and action. I suppose, therefore, that good teachers are those who lead their students—and first of all themselves—to such borders, and always to ever more borders, and who make clearer and clearer that the safe ground of knowledge under their feet offers just as much support as a straw to a drowning person. And good students? Perhaps those who ask for the motives for these earth and water metaphors and who notice that in this definition of good teachers findings are defined as a threat of heart and soul, as a revelation *à corps perdu*, as Hegel says, and who continue to ask what then learning has to do with living and surviving, why it should have to do with a loss rather than a gain.

Our task, so it seems to me, is the renewed, circumspect, persistent, flexible, rational and passionate exploration of the nothingness, of the nothings, of nothings of all kinds and relations and of all times and places. And this, of course, not only in matters of pedagogy and of institutions of knowledge. Therefore, we have to continue to think through this again and again, that which for Plato and Aristotle was the *thaumazein,* we have to work further through what was for Maimonides and the Kalam and Hermann Cohen the "infinite judgment [*unendliche Urteil*]," we have to think further about the question of Leibniz and Benjamin and Heidegger, "why there is something rather than nothing." But with regard to what concerns pedagogy, this *agoge* of the *pais,* we do well to respect the handed-down conviction, which consists of the construction and expansion of knowledge, but to complete this conviction through the revelation that no such construction and no expansion is possible without the dismantling, without the constantly executed reduction of knowledge to its beginning out of nothing. Learning starts with unlearning [*Entlernen*]. We gather "around" the suspension and *in* the suspension of all knowledge, ability and action. It is only this suspension which is "between" us, and *out of* which we become we. And this suspension, is also the "between" of the *inter*view.

JW: The attempt to think difference would seem to have provoked an overhasty reading or response of what takes place in the university in the name of "theory," "poststructuralism," "deconstruction," all of which is alleged to have created a crisis. Yet the question of thinking difference also concerns the response and responsibility of deciding, of coming to terms with the undecidable in order to acknowledge the work of difference within and possibly at the very limits of the institutional framework, within the politics of pedagogy conventionally assumed. Is this decision making not perhaps the confrontation with the modern and the opening to difference to itself in the context of the so-called modern university? Is it perhaps the case that, far from instituting the crisis in question, whatever is called "poststructuralism," "theory," "deconstruction," has instead addressed that matter of difference that we name "modernity," which is precisely the difference the university chooses not to acknowledge, chooses not to make a decision about, and instead displaces in the name of the atemporal quasi-transcendental or quasi-universal phenomenon of "the university today"?

WH: I am not quite sure that I grasp your question, its implications, and its scope in their entirety. Perhaps the best I can do is to address some of the topics you touch upon, and say quite up front and even in a somewhat apodictic style what comes to my mind concerning some of the notions, turns of phrase, and ideas you have used in your question.

What I meant to say is simply — all too simply — that we have to start from scratch in whatever situation we find ourselves, be it coded "pedagogical" or "political," "theoretical," "institutional," or "intimate." While I doubt that those terms and codings are pertinent beyond the limits of a very restricted social and experiental area, I assume that a response to any situation, however it may be termed or encoded, is never a response to this particular "situation" alone, it is never an answer to a well-posed and reposed question, nor is it fully determined by the elements of this "situation" itself since each situation is already a situation in another situation or with another situation that, in turn, is not entirely governed by its "own" elements. Descartes's idea that there is something mightier than the I in the I that doubts its existence, this idea of the infinite is indeed inherent in every "situation" of which we can think, imagine, dream up, theorize, or experience. Perhaps it is not necessary to draw the Cartesian conclusion and claim the existence of God, but it is hardly deniable that this idea of the infinite never stops deranging and widening the circle of "situations," in which we can possibly find ourselves. And this derangement and widening can occur both vertically and horizontally, turning each "situation"—infinitely—into a "parasituation." Thinking "difference," therefore, is, strictly speaking, a redundant formula. Thinking is thinking difference. And there is no conceivable response in an emphatic or not so emphatic sense of the term, there is no responsible response to anything, be it "question," "situation," "problem," "demand," or "desire." There is no response whatever if it is not a response to something lacking in the question, situation, demand, or desire, something lacking in determination, contour, profile, shape, and form. Accordingly, there is no way of coming "to terms" with the undecidable. Responding, however circumspect, careful, and responsible as it could afford to be, is never responding exclusively. Responding cannot avoid beginning anew. It must, of necessity, be a beginning, and a beginning where the demand, the situation, lacks, is at fault, deficient, or overcomplex, contradictory, or confused. The burden—and it is a terrible burden—of responsibility lies not so much in responding to the coded and determined requirements of an institution, a discipline, or a field, nor even in responding to the perceptible demands of a student—that may be difficult, but it is hardly a challenge. The real burden of the response—and often, at least for me, a terrifying burden—is the necessity to invent the question. Responsibility strikes me as an initiative, but—and there's the rub—it is an initiative in a matter that is already very sensibly, sometimes pressingly and even hauntingly there, and yet which lacks determination, address, or form. To take responsibility, therefore, seems to mean to take the initiative for something both undeniably existent and at the same time lacking, very pronounced and yet mumbled, pressing and still undirected—and, accordingly, to take the initiative from where I am not, and certainly am not the first. However, it is an initiative, an initiative in crisis, and indeed the hyperbolic crisis of a decision that needs to be taken without anybody being already available and prepared to take it.

No, I am not adverse to the notion of crisis, but I believe, rather, that it needs to be rearticulated, refined, and resharpened—or reinvented—with a careful eye toward the all too nostalgic and often downright reactionary use the theorists made of it, particularly those of the 1920s, since it was during the first three decades of the last century that this notion most widely flourished. But the "crisis of the university"? Quite frankly, I assume that there has always been a crisis of the university, in the university, between the university and the other institutions of social reproduction, of learning, of archival and inventive research, of techno-scientific and of speculative exploration, and always a crisis of the so called autonomy and *in* the very call for the autonomy of the university. What has become very dramatic during the last quarter of a century, however, are two tendencies in Europe and the Americas—and probably not only there—that very urgently require a careful response. The first is the diminution of budgets and, accordingly, of academic positions in the humanities—or rather the shifting of budgets and positions from the humanities to the sciences and the bureaucracy—accompanied by an increase of pressure exercised by politicians and administrators on the humanities to do immediately useful work measured by standards proper to the sciences, to administration and industry, and accompanied by a scientistic and administrational turn in the mentality of humanities' faculties. The universities are turning into centers for the administration of administration, with a massive political neutralization as a consequence. The second tendency with a rather dramatic impact on academic work results from the international migrations that more and more—and not only in the United States but also throughout Europe and Asia as well—change the traditional student populations and require a careful transformation in the topics of study. The university is, in this regard, turning into a migrating university. If the turn to an administrational infrastructure and mentality brings about a dimming of the political sense, there is at least some hope that the changes introduced in academia by the pressure of international migrations will be able to counter political neutralization (which is particularly ominous in continental Europe at this time). But while there is not too much cause for optimism in this regard either, I think it imperative to relaunch again and again the problem of the political, of the necessities and the risks of both politicization and depoliticization, to address the increasing threat to theoretical *and* political work through the aggressive impact of administration, organization, and bureaucracy, of everything that enforces and narrows regulations and norms, and to engage in particular—and, if at all possible, not only thematically, "in theory," but practically, in the development of alternative ways—with the transformation of work: since it is work—and work of all kind, from soul work to exploited labor to the belligerent or silent work of capital—that causes our pains and offers some promise of change.

We have no chance of dealing with these massive contradictions, tensions, ambiguities, or rifts—which are, incidentally, always asynchronies—if we don't realize that they pass through us, and that we *are* those rifts, those tensions, and ambiguities; and that we belong, each of us in a different way, to different tendencies (to "administration" and "migration" for example), to different movements, to different ages "at a time." Much would be gained in our institutions of learning, *for* and *against* them, if we would come to acknowledge that *nostra res agitur*—that it is always *about* us that we are talking, always *to* us, *for* us and *against* us, and that it is always *us* that we are talking, whenever we talk. Whenever we teach, explore, theorize, formalize, act, we teach *us*—we are the topic, we the addressee, we the professors—we explore *us*, also when we explore the mechanics of administration and the ways of migration, we formalize *us*, even when we encounter an absolute resistance against formalization in the splits we keep reintroducing in us, the administrators, the migrants, the administrators torn apart by migration. And whenever we act, we act *us*, truly *à corps perdu*, and *à raison perdue*, since we act someone and as someone who isn't there yet, condemning us to *act* acting, and to quote "ourselves" in every now from the future.

There is not much point in calling the developments to which I have alluded either "modern" or "postmodern"—I have the impression that both concepts are utterly used up, void, without analytical force. Modern—in contradistinction to what? And as for "postmodernism," it may well be the sterile branch of a certain romanticism. But under, or for, whatever denomination "theory" has worked, in particular in the United States, I think it has conducted and provoked remarkable work as long as it hasn't chosen to bury itself in parochialism, as long as it has kept migrating, wandering and wondering. And indeed, one of the forms of avoiding to move—but to move, in every sense of the word, is what we are bound to do—one of the forms of stalling is certainly to take refuge in normative concepts, in universals, in the notion, for example, of "the university" or "the university today." But, then again, we cannot do without using those concepts. Even the seemingly least universal shift—"this," "here," "today"—is already a universal. I am not going to elaborate on the vertiginous arguments Hegel has provided for the analysis of the "here" and "now." We cannot jump over the ambiguities of our linguistic means, we *are*, in a sense, our linguistic means and *are* their ambiguities. The refuge taken in the so-called universals is an untenable immediatism, with often disastrous moral and political effects, if it is not honestly taken as what indeed it is, a refuge, an asylum on the way to another one. We cannot jump into the "thing in itself," any more than we can jump into the future. The jump is always in the here and now — and *this* jump is "the thing itself," if there ever *is* such a thing. It is in the "universal" and in "the university now," between the contradictory tendencies, for example, that I have, all too roughly, characterized as "administrational" and "migrational," between the pressure for immediate profit and the infinite patience of research, between strict regulations and their suspension. We have to use this jump, and use it as a chance to keep jumping.

On one point, perhaps two, I hesitate to agree with you. The notion of the "quasi-transcendental" has not been introduced to characterize anything "atemporal." I remember having encountered this notion for the first time during the mid-seventies in writings of some Protestant theologians, who were drawing, not without some critical edge, on the Heidegger of *Being and Time* and trying to articulate some of the consequences for the structure of the temporal self. The notion of the "quasi-transcendental" has experienced a certain revival in the meantime, but I must confess that I am still rather unhappy with this terminological choice and the accent it confers to analytical work. That a structure is "like" or "somehow like" a transcendental gives an indication concerning its status and functioning, it wards off in particular a number of empiricist misunderstandings, and stresses a shift in the workings of formative concepts that allow for cognition of objects, relations, events. It points out — or I understand it to point out — an intrinsic deficiency in concepts, but also in attitudes, attentions, forms of action and interaction, that disclose a world and contribute to changing it. In this regard, the notion of the "quasi-transcendental" takes into account the (rather devastating) experience of a faltering or failing of transcendental concepts, that is of a detranscendentalization, in particular of notions as "the true," "the good," "the beautiful," an experience that has been belabored and advanced, in very different ways with very different outcomes, by Hegel and Nietzsche. In the notion "quasi-transcendental," the horizon of transcendentality, however, remains the line of reference, the standard, and model for conceptual work, it remains, in a way, the ideal against which conceptual movements are measured. Without denying the decisive gains that have been brought about by the transcendental question, in particular in Kant, but also in the critical, the speculative, and the phenomenological traditions after him, and indeed because of them, we need to shift the accent of our inquiry toward the question, what allows for transcendental forms to occur, without ever attaining the status and the function of such forms? The Kantian question concerned the possibility of concepts providing access to the cognition of objects; our question should be, must not any such possibility be accompanied by an insurmountable resistance against its realization? What grants such a possibility? What is the possibility of this possibility? Does it indeed result from the work of productive imagination? And from it alone? Or from any other faculty, capability, potentiality, and their synthesis? Doesn't it rather require *also* the lack of some faculty, some inability, the vacation of potentiality? For anything, even a possibility, to occur, it needs a free space, an unoccupied realm in the conceptual and the sensible territory, it needs an opening even in the topographies of time and space, if they are considered as belonging to the transcendental conditions of our experience. It needs an opening of the transcendental horizon altogether, and even an opening in our notions of the opening. It is not some thing, yet there is no thing without it — there is no thing without this "without a thing." This vacancy, for want of a better word, but to indicate at least its impact on the formative activity exercised by concepts and practices on our world and on ourselves, could be called "adtranscendental" and "atranscendental" and, with a fitting condensation, "attranscendental." It doesn't designate anything that is "like" the transcendental, since nothing — and that is what we are talking about — doesn't resemble any thing (and yet, of course, the borders between them are porous). It approaches, lingers around, haunts, and unsettles all the forms we are able to create and produce, displaces and shifts even our time forms, and therefore, without being relinquished from time, is also atemporal in the sense of achronic.

Wherever an intervention, be it pedagogical, political, artistic, or theoretical, occurs, it occurs at the undefined — or overdetermined — borders of established forms, *at* those forms, *in* their interstices, and pores, *between* conflicting parties, tendencies, times and, if that can be said in English, *at* them. There are the zones of an "ad-vent" of what is "today," and of what allows and invites us to keep it coming.

JW: To come back to the "between" and the matter of pedagogy, the between that you situate clearly has radical implications with regard to the thinking of any ontico-ontological "category," "concept," or "identity," which, in turn and as you imply, is irreducible to any simple manifestation in dialectical opposition or negative theology. Would it be possible or even desirable to think the between in relation both to the event and the motif of *khora?* What are the implications for reading, for critical exegesis, in coming to terms with the radicality of the between? And finally, what are the implications of comprehending this "figure without figure" in the praxis of your pedagogy?

WH: I don't want to give the impression that I am an aficionado of the in-between — I don't feel sufficiently well "rounded" to invest too much in this notion — but I have used it to try and clarify the movement of a certain point addressed in our conversation. (We need to admit, however, that the notion of the between doesn't indicate much of a movement.) On the other hand, I have felt very often, if not always, to be between — "between two stools," between literature and philosophy, between contradictory or different interests, impulses, wishes, between languages and families, between commitments and continents, between ages — without hardly ever really feeling at ease in this awkward and sometimes messy zone. One of the effects of this feeling of being unsettled was to take this experience as seriously as possible, while conceding that it has already been elaborated in ways that don't need much more assistance. If I were to give a very rapid bibliographical survey, I would refer to Augustine's remark "inter urinas et faeces nascimur," to Lawrence Sterne, and to Jean Paul, to Hölderlin's poetry of the between, to Hegel's — if I remember correctly, quite dismissive — remarks on the *Zwischen* somewhere in his *Encyclopaedia* and to Kierkegaard's explorations of "interest" as *inter-esse,* to Heidegger's brief but decisive passage in *Being and Time* on the in-between "between" birth and death as not being an *après-coup* relation between already established *relata,* but rather the happening of a relation that first allows those extremes, its poles, to occur, to Merleau-Ponty's and Hannah Arendt's remarks on natality and mortality (evidently closely connected with Heidegger) and, of course, I would refer to Derrida's admirable treatment of Mallarmé's "entre" in his "La double séance" ["The Double Session"]. All of these texts — and they could be multiplied without much effort — amount to an "entropology" of sorts. There is hardly anything I could possibly add to them — except, perhaps, the weird word *entropology,* which I just made up to gather some of the implications and point to some consequences of this time, this space, this speaking in between, that all these texts talk about and from which they talk.

One could call the exploration of the between — of *any* between — entropology, not so much to stress a distinction from *anthropology* and its subdisciplines (psychology, sociology, historiography, and so on) but rather so as to expose the structural features of what anthropology is concerned with, and to readdress, rethink, and analyze those features and their premises further. What needs to be reworked and worked through is indeed the whole tradition of the determinations of the human being's position between what is called, on the one hand, "animal" or "machine" and, on the other, "god," between past and future, between sensuality and reason, birth and death, norm and liberty, culture and anarchy, and so on. All those "betweens" have given rise to dualisms and decisionisms, synthetisms and fusionisms, to the ideas of transcendence and of immanence, to countless concepts of mediation, translation, signification and so forth.

Painfully and luckily, what is human is difficult to define; but it is, in particular, difficult to define as the carrier of a human substance, or of an essence, that remains unaffected by its very definition, that is, by the linguistic predicament. The human being, the entity in-between, is, in that sense, a tropological entity, which at the same time is set off from any thoroughgoing determination through linguistic figures, since the field of language is not entirely covered by tropes, and the notion of the human is not saturated by language. In between tropes, and in the pores of the tropes, in their voids, faults, or crevasses, in the "inter-tropes," if one may say so, between figures of speech, figures of thought, figures of action, we can discover the field that first allows those figures to occur, allows them to enter into conflict, to overlap, to reinforce or to suspend each other. It is not a tropological field, rather an "an-tropological" expanse that, however, is not defined negatively and once and for all through the exclusion of tropes since it is in principle infinitely open to figuration, and only by this very openness permits the motility of tropes and figures—very much like the empty space of the Greek and Latin atomists that allows the elements, the *stoichai,* the letters, to move according to their clinamen. While allowing figurations to occur, this "entropological" or "an-tropological" area can never itself be an object of thematization, figuration, or conceptualization without at once withdrawing from any shape given to it.

What has to concern us most, then, is the relation between figuration and what withdraws from it. The notorious rhetorical concepts to designate those complex liminal relations—allegory and irony—are quite inadequately and misleadingly called "master tropes" since both, and both differently, block the very possibility to identify them. Irony is the figure about which nobody can be sure that it truly is the figure of irony, allegory, by saying something other than what it manifestly says,

says its own muteness. Both are figures of the voiding of figuration, both perform their exposition to a semantic and pragmatic void. While in information theory, the lack of information, and a certain chaos that goes with it, is claimed to be measurable —and measurable in terms of *entropy* — the lack of information in fact cannot be but incalculable, immeasurable, infinite, if any one information needs at least a minimal difference from another one to be constituted as such. There is no metalanguage in a strict sense, no possibility to define thoroughly a closed system that, as such, could relate to its surrounding, no metafigure, no "master" or "*mater* trope" that would allow the formalization the possibilities of signifying, of referential, or constitutive relations. These relations —the in-between of the entities defined by our sciences and our practices —are events, whenever they are nonformalizable, incalculable, unforeseeable, and as such, if you want, chaotic or "khoratic." To consider relations as events and to stress their "evential" trait was certainly one of the merits of Gadamer, who recently died at a formidable 102 years of age. The anthropology that he, with many others of his and the following generations, cherished need not be given up; but it should be enriched, complicated, and pushed to the point where, as entropology, it opens itself to the possibility of encountering no object, of being guided by no subject, and of corresponding to no logos.

I need to insist here on saying "the *possibility* of encountering no object . . ." since what we keep meeting are in fact, I am tempted to say, most often "objects," and hardly ever what doesn't correspond to their conceptual frame —objects as resistance to what we mean to do or mean to mean, objects in the form of objections, objects as refutation of our intentions, as obstacle in our way, as hindrance to our ideas, handicap to our abilities. There is something quite marvelous about objects. We should write, we should live a great, magnificent apology of objects. They are very much down to earth, stubborn, insistent, patient, some are useful, some useless, some dreadfully indifferent, some unimaginably delicate, and they have —up to a point—one inestimable advantage. They are not we, not ourselves. And yet, despite these lovable characters, they are, whenever they are objects, *our* objects. Our relation to them is *our* relation, they are our relatives. What interests me most intensely, however, is that dimension of objects or what is in them that doesn't belong to me or to us, that doesn't regard me, concern me and doesn't relate to me. It would be hard to tell, if this kind of interest —which I believe to be the only productive one —springs from the acceptance of an incest taboo or from its transgression, since it is directed toward what is not related to me, toward the nonrelatives, but at once toward what is interdicted, prohibited, and thus still in relation to me.) In all the lovable objects, I relate to something that is not an object, may never become one, and may not even be a "thing." I relate to "something" that doesn't allow for, that doesn't submit, that doesn't subject itself to a relation. This relation to an unrelatable, this irrelation, is the truly "objective" one, and no object could possibly appear without its absolute objection to becoming merely an object *for* someone.

The relation we have talked about earlier, the relation that is the in-between, becomes an event only insofar as it is a relation to "something" that refutes any relationship. It is this refutation or this absolute objection that should become palpable in any analysis of an "object," be it a text, a social or political phenomenon, a philosophical issue; it is this infinite objection that should become discernable in our dealings with art and literature as well as in our daily affairs. This refutation or this objection is, I think, the area into which and from which we talk, the area of a kind of justice and possibly of a kind of happiness. It may be a rather mournful one, even a deeply distressed one, but we wouldn't even have a chance of talking in terms of justice and happiness, if we wouldn't be talking toward that objection that keeps, in one way or another, in all kinds of idiolects, saying, "Alles ist anders" (Everything is other—than you say it is). Touching this area, is teaching.

Teaching, however easy it may be sometimes, is structurally one of the most *difficult* practices anybody can engage in. It is "difficult" in the sense that it doesn't correspond to any particular faculty we could claim to muster, and "difficult" in the sense that it resists being done (*facere*). Strictly speaking, it cannot be *done* at all. The Enlightenment definition urges one to teach self-reliance and even autonomy—yet it is evident that those who tell you to listen only to yourself either cancel their own instruction or put you under an irresolvable double bind. The dilemma doesn't diminish in the least if we claim to address in teaching an instance that is said not to concern us. "Concern yourself with something that doesn't concern you" would mean "Don't concern yourself," "Don't listen to me," and even "You don't hear anything," "I don't say anything." Such a teaching, very close to whatever you can read in Zen anecdotes, is a disaster of undoing rather that the epitome of instruction. The discourses these injunctions or performances combine are accompanied, however, by a third—one that is neither injunction nor performance—but wholly dependent on a virtual scale of tonalities or "pragmatic" gestures running from mute depression through hysterical gaiety, from sarcasm through irony and humor. It is this third, this open, in-determined, flexible tonality, which upsets the double bind, it is this tone (not a voice) which rises from its split and allows it to move, to change, to alter itself and to "speak." While the situation of teaching is bound in a theatrical setting, that paralyzes each and every thought by prohibiting it to leave the theater of didactic operations, or, rather, like a theater of war, spreads and infects all surrounding areas, the tone in which this double bind is propounded, this tone or this gesture alone remains—though not by necessity—quite heterogeneous to the scene. It is able to transport a different, a third, fourth, fifth message, to suspend the contradictions, or to expose them, to stress their theatricality, and to prepare a tabula rasa for those who are addressed in this double discourse: a forum for the listeners to speak. Teaching is all too often thought of as one (teacher) speaking to another (pupil) who listens and then repeats whatever he or she has heard. It should be rather thought of and practiced as a discourse to incite and to excite another discourse that is not programmed by the first and that does not repeat it. Only under this condition has teaching a chance to become something other than show business that in turn engenders show business. Only then it has a chance not to be a prohibition of talking ("Don't listen to me," "You don't hear anything"). Indeed, one of the greatest challenges to the autism of show teaching and its prohibition of speech ("I only act as if I am teaching, in fact I am performing a show, I myself am mute"), one of the greatest incitements for speech is silence. The silence of listening. Silence can be applied in teaching very much as it can in analysis. It lets speak and invites speech. It is not a performative speech act—many of the so-called acts are silencing acts—it is an admission of an event. And there are many silences. Many admissions.

Whatever we teach—and whatever we teach to our students and colleagues, but also to ourselves—ought to be talking. But to teach talking, we need to listen, and we need to talk in such a way that we listen—to others, to ourselves—and, while still speaking, leave the word to someone else. To someone outside the theater of teaching, to someone out of class.

Contributors

Derek Attridge teaches in the English Department at the University of York, England. He is the author and editor of a number of books, including *Peculiar Language: Literature as Difference from the Renaissance to James Joyce* (1988), a selection of Derrida's essays entitled *Acts of Literature* (1992), *Joyce Effects: On Language, Theory, and History* (2000), and *The Singularity of Literature* (forthcoming).

John D. Caputo is David R. Cook Professor of Philosophy at Villanova University, where he has taught since 1968. His most recent works include *Deconstruction in a Nutshell: A Conversation with Jacques Derrida* (1997), *The Prayers and Tears of Jacques Derrida* (1997), and *On Religion* (2001). He is currently at work on a study of deconstruction and the scriptural notion of the "kingdom of God," entitled *Sacred Anarchy.*

Mary Ann Caws is Distinguished Professor of English, French, and Comparative Literature at the Graduate Center of the City University of New York. She has written widely on the interactions of art and literature, and has translated numerous volumes of poetry and criticism. She is the author of *Picasso's Weeping Woman: The Life and Art of Dora Maar* (2000), and a brief biography of Virginia Woolf for the Penguin U.K. series Illustrated Lives (published by Overlook Press in the United States); the editor and cotranslator of *Manifesto: A Century of Isms* (2001), *Surrealist Painters and Poets* (2001), *Mallarmé in Prose* (2001), *Surrealist Love Poems* (2002), and *Vita Sackville-West: Selected Writings* (2002); and the translator of Louis-René des Forets, *Ostinato* (2002). She is currently at work preparing the *Yale Book of Twentieth-Century French Poetry.*

Jonathan Culler is Senior Associate Dean of Arts and Sciences at Cornell University, where he has served as Professor of English and Comparative Literature, Director of the Society for the Humanities, and Chair of the Department of Comparative Literature and of the Department of English, having taught at Cambridge University, Oxford University, and Yale University before coming to Cornell in 1977. Recipient of the James Russell Lowell Prize from the Modern Language Association of America and of fellowships from the John Simon Guggenheim Memorial Foundation and the National Endowment for the Humanities, and a past president of the American Comparative Literature Association, he is the author of several seminal texts in his field, including *On Deconstruction: Theory and Criticism after Structuralism* (1982), *Framing the Sign: Criticism and Its Institutions* (1992), and *Literary Theory: A Very Short Introduction* (1997). His books have been translated into more than a dozen languages.

Werner Hamacher is Director of the Institute for Comparative Literature at the Goethe University, Frankfurt am Main, having taught at the Free University, Berlin, and The Johns Hopkins University, and held visiting appointments at Yale University, the École Normale Supérieure in Paris, and New York University. His publications include *Premises: Studies in Philosophy and Literature from Kant to Celan* (1996), *Maser* (1998), and *Pleroma: Reading in Hegel* (1998). He is editor of the Stanford University Press series Meridian: Crossing Aesthetics.

Kevin Hart is Professor of English at the University of Notre Dame. His books include *The Trespass of the Sign* (1991), *A. D. Hope* (1992), and *Samuel Johnson and the Culture of Property* (1999). He has translated *The Buried Harbour: Selected Poems of Giuseppe Ungaretti* (1988) and edited *The Oxford Book of Australian Religious Verse* (1994). His most recent collection of poetry is *Flame Tree: Selected Poems* (2002). He has recently completed *The Dark Gaze: Maurice Blanchot and the Sacred* and, with Geoffrey Hartman, *Maurice Blanchot: The Power of Contestation*.

Peggy Kamuf is Marion Frances Chevalier Professor in French and Comparative Literature at the University of Southern California. Her books include *Fictions of Feminine Desire* (1982), *Signature Pieces: On the Institution of Authorship* (1988), and *The Division of Literature: or, The University in Deconstruction* (1997). She has edited *A Derrida Reader: Between the Blinds* (1991); has translated numerous texts by Jacques Derrida, including *Points . . . : Interviews, 1974–1994* (1995), *Resistances of Psychoanalysis* (1998); and has edited, translated, and introduced his *Without Alibi* (2002).

John P. Leavey, Jr., is Professor and Chair of the Department of English at the University of Florida. The author of *Glassary* (1986) and the translator of numerous texts of Jacques Derrida, including *Glas* (1986), he continues his work in translating and translation theory.

J. Hillis Miller is Distinguished Professor of English and Comparative Literature at the University of California, Irvine, having taught for many years at The Johns Hopkins University and Yale University. He is the author of many books and articles about nineteenth- and twentieth-century literature and literary theory, most recently, *Black Holes* (1999), *Speech Acts in Literature* (2001), *Others* (2001), and *On Literature* (2002). He is at work on *Speech Acts in Henry James*.

Arkady Plotnitsky is Professor of English and University Faculty Scholar at Purdue University, where he is also Director of the Theory and Cultural Studies Program. He is the author of several books and many articles on critical and cultural theory, continental philosophy, British and European Romanticism, and the relationships among literature, philosophy, and science, most recently *The Knowable and the Unknowable: Modern Science, Nonclassical Thought, and "The Two Cultures"* (2002).

Avital Ronell is Professor of German, English, and Comparative Literature at New York University, where she is Chair of the German Studies Department. She also teaches philosophy at the European Graduate School in Switzerland and has appeared in a number of films and videos. A translator of some of his early works, Avital Ronell teaches a yearly seminar with Jacques Derrida in New York. Her works include *Dictations: On Haunted Writing* (1986), *The Telephone Book* (1989), *Crack Wars: Literature, Addiction, Mania* (1992), and *Stupidity* (2002). Her forthcoming book *The Test Drive*, to be published by University of Illinois Press, explores the figure of testing in traditional and contemporary discursive formations.

Nicholas Royle is Professor of English at the University of Sussex. His books include: *Telepathy and Literature* (1991); *After Derrida* (1995); with Andrew Bennett, *An Introduction to Literature, Criticism and Theory* (2d ed., 1999); and *The Uncanny* (2002). He is coeditor of the *Oxford Literary Review*.

Gregory L. Ulmer is Professor of English and Media Studies at the University of Florida. He also teaches in the Media and Communications Program of the European Graduate School, Saas-Fee, Switzerland, and in the Networked Writing Environment (NWE), which features web design as the medium of learning. He is the author of *Applied Grammatology: Post (e)-Pedagogy from Jacques Derrida to Joseph Beuys* (1985), *Teletheory: Grammatology in the Age of Video* (1989), and *Heuretics: The Logic of Invention* (1994), two other monographs, a textbook for writing about literature, and some fifty articles and chapters exploring the shift in the apparatus of language from literacy to electracy. He has addressed international media arts conferences in Helsinki, Sydney, Hamburg, Halifax, Nottingham, and throughout the United States. His current projects include two forthcoming book-length studies: *Miami Miautre: Mapping the Virtual City* (coauthored with the Florida Research Ensemble*)*, and *Internet Invention: From Literacy to Electracy*.

Julian Wolfreys is Professor of English at the University of Florida. He is the author of numerous articles and books, including, most recently, *Victorian Hauntings: Spectrality, Gothic, the Uncanny and Literature* (2001). He has also edited and coedited several volumes, including *The Edinburgh Encyclopaedia of Modern Criticism and Theory* (2002) and *Glossalalia* (2003), and he is general editor of the Palgrave series Transitions. He has recently completed *Occasional Deconstructions,* to be published by the State University of New York Press.

Notes

Introduction

    1. Anidjar, *"Our Place in al-Andalus,"* 3.

    2. The idea of the interview appears to have a particular national history, at least as far as the *Oxford English Dictionary* is concerned. Recent use of the term, signifying a discussion between a member of the press and a prominent public figure, develops in the mid-nineteenth century and appears to be a phenomenon of North American political journalism. In 1897, the *Westminster Gazette* claimed that one Joseph M'Cullagh, from Saint Louis, was the inventor of the modern newspaper interview. Although the *Pall Mall Gazette* had recognized the advent of the interview as a "permanent gain" to journalism, the BBC was still to maintain by the mid-twentieth century that official policy was to prefer talks to interviews, lectures being apt to be more carefully thought through.

    3. Derrida, *Who's Afraid of Philosophy?*, 69. Emphasis added.

    4. Ibid., 73.

    5. Derrida, *Dissemination*, 5.

    6. See, for example, Derrida, "The University without Condition," 202–37.

    7. Ibid., 206.

    8. Ibid., 208.

    9. Weber, "Introduction: Upside-Down Writing," 1–4; 3.

1: Nicholas Royle

    1. See Simmons and Worth, *Derrida Downunder;* see also Cohen, *Jacques Derrida and the Humanities.*

2. Derrida, "The Future of the Profession," 259.

3. Ibid., 237.

4. Derrida, *Of Grammatology*, 18.

5. Foucault, "The Order of Discourse," 69.

6. See Derrida, "Outwork," 5.

7. Derrida, "Biodegradables," 812–73.

8. Jay, *Cultural Semantics*, 84.

3: Peggy Kamuf

1. de Man, "The Return to Philology," 24.

2. Ibid., 23.

3. As Rodolphe Gasché has recently argued, very probingly, in *The Wild Card of Reading* (see esp. chap. 4).

4. Would you mind it if I cited a long passage here from Derrida, which recurred to me as I thought about all this? It's from one of his first published interviews, "*Ja*, or the *faux-bond* II," 49–51, and it reflects on the interview "symptom," although it does not use that term:

> What is important here is the improvisation — contrived like all so-called free association — well anyway, what is called improvisation. It is never absolute, it never has the purity of what one thinks one can require of a forced improvisation: the surprise of the person interrogated, the absolutely spontaneous, instantaneous, almost simultaneous response. . . . A battery of anticipatory and delaying devices, of slowing-down procedures are already in place as soon as one opens one's mouth — even if there is no microphone or electric typewriter present — in order to protect against improvised exposition. And yet, even if it always already does this, it never succeeds. . . . The use one may make of all these apotropaic machines will always end up forming a place that is exposed, vulnerable, and invisible to whoever tries out all the clever ruses; it is a blind spot. . . . There always remains improvisation, and that is what counts here. . . . Someone is interrogated who has taken, who thinks he has taken (up to a certain point) the time to write and to elaborate coded, supercoded machines, and so forth. . . . Then he is asked some questions. These are of a kind that, in any case, he will not be able to answer at leisure and in a manner as closely controlled as in a published text where he can correct galleys and page proofs. The interesting thing, then, or at least the pertinent thing is not *what* he says . . . but what he selects, what selects . . . itself in the rush as he clips out clichés from the more or less informed mass of possible discourses, letting himself be restricted by the situation, the interlocutors. This is what will betray his defenses in the end. . . . It is another way of remaining an exhibitionist around the edges. But whoever decided that all of this deserved to be published or that anything deserved to be published . . .?

4: Avital Ronell

1. This interview, updated and expanded for this collection, originally appeared in *JAC* [Journal of advanced composition] 20, no. 2 (2000): 243–81.

5: Arkady Plotnitsky

1. Derrida, *Positions*, 42–43.
2. Nietzsche, *Thus Spoke Zarathustra*, 195.
3. Derrida, *Of Grammatology*, 85. Emphasis original.
4. See de Man, *Blindness and Insight*.
5. de Man, *The Rhetoric of Romanticism*, 122.
6. Ibid., 122–23.
7. Derrida, *Of Grammatology*, 26.
8. de Man, *Aesthetic Ideology*, 132–37.
9. de Man, *Rhetoric of Romanticism*, 289.
10. de Man, *Aesthetic Ideology*, 70–73.
11. Nietzsche, *The Gay Science*, 356. Translation modified.
12. Nietzsche, *Thus Spoke Zarathustra*, 78.
13. Hamacher, *Pleroma*, 3.
14. Derrida, "Différance," in *Margins of Philosophy*, 5–6.
15. Nietzsche, *Gay Science*, 32.

6: John P. Leavey, Jr.

1. Kafka, *The Trial*, 154, 150, 224, respectively.

8: Jonathan Culler

1. Barthes, *S/Z*, 3.
2. Johnson, *The Critical Difference*, 3–12.
3. Saussure, *Course in General Linguistics*, 120.

11: Gregory L. Ulmer

1. Celan, "Death Fugue," 63.
2. Cioran, "The Circus of Solitude," in *All Gall Is Divided*, 69.
3. Gramsci, *Prison Notebooks*, 354.
4. McEwen, *Socrates' Ancestor*, 21.
5. Pinsky, "Door," 64.

12: J. Hillis Miller

1. In the original German: "Hat sie Charakter? Ist ihre Natur, nicht so dank eigener Offenherzigkeit als kraft des freien und erschlossenen Ausdrucks, klar vor Augen? Das Gegenteil von dem all bezeichnet sie. . . . Kein sittlicher Entschluss kann ohne sprachliche Gestalt, und streng genommen, ohne darin Gegenstand der Mitteilung geworden zu sein, ins Leben treten." Benjamin, *Illuminationen*, 121, 122. Translation mine.

2. James, *The Portrait of a Lady*, 644.

3. Derrida, in *The Gift of Death*, 70–71, goes on to say:

> I can respond only to the one (or to the One), that is, to the other, by sacrificing that one to the other. I am responsible to any one (that is to say to any other) only by failing in my responsibility to all the others, to the ethical or political generality. And I can never justify this sacrifice, I must always hold my peace about it. Whether I want to or not, I can never justify the fact that I prefer or sacrifice any one (any other) to the other. . . . What binds me to singularities, to this one or that one . . . remains finally undecidable . . . as unjustifiable as the infinite sacrifice I make at each moment. These singularities represent others, a wholly other form of alterity: one other or some other persons, but also places, animals, languages. How would you ever justify the fact that you sacrifice all the cats in the world to the cat that you feed at home every morning for years, whereas other cats die of hunger at every instant?

4. Dickens, *Bleak House*, 859.

13: Werner Hamacher

1. This interview was translated into English by Ariane Reichle and Julian Wolfreys.

2. Hamacher, "Où, séance, touche de Nancy," 216.

3. Hamacher, *Pleroma*, 3.

Works Cited

Anidjar, Gil. *"Our Place in al-Andalus": Kabbalah, Philosophy, Literature in Arab-Jewish Letters.* Stanford: Stanford University Press, 2002.

Antelme, Robert. *L'espèce humaine.* Paris: Gallimard, 1957.

Barthes, Roland. *S/Z.* Translated by Richard Miller. New York: Hill and Wang, 1974.

Benjamin, Walter. *Illuminationen.* Frankfurt am Main: Suhrkamp, 1969.

Caws, Mary Ann, ed. *City Images: Perspectives from Literature, Philosophy, and Film.* Amsterdam: Gordon and Breach, 1991.

Celan, Paul. "Death Fugue." In Carolyn Forché, ed., *Against Forgetting: Twentieth-Century Poetry of Witness,* 61–63. New York: Norton, 1993.

Cioran, Emile M. *All Gall Is Divided: Gnomes and Apothegms.* Translated by Richard Howard. New York: Arcade, 1999.

Cohen, Tom, ed. *Jacques Derrida and the Humanities.* Cambridge: Cambridge University Press, 2001.

Culler, Jonathan. *Literary Theory: A Very Short Introduction.* Oxford: Oxford University Press, 2000.

Deleuze, Gilles. *Difference and Repetition.* Translated by Paul Patton. London: Athlone Press, 1994.

de Lubac, Henri. *Surnaturel: Études historiques.* Paris: Desclée de Brouwer, 1991.

de Man, Paul. *Aesthetic Ideology.* Edited with an introduction by Andrzej Warminski. Minneapolis: University of Minnesota Press, 1996.

_____. *Blindness and Insight: Essays in the Rhetoric of Contemporary Criticism.* Minneapolis: University of Minnesota Press, 1983.

_____. "The Return to Philology." In *The Resistance to Theory*, 21–26. Minneapolis: University of Minnesota Press, 1986.

_____. *The Rhetoric of Romanticism*. New York: Columbia University Press, 1984.

Deleuze, Gilles, and Félix Guattari. *What is Philosophy?* Translated by Graham Burchell and Hugh Tomlinson. London: Verso, 1994.

Derrida, Jacques. *Acts of Literature.* Edited by Derek Attridge. New York: Routledge, 1992.

_____. "Biodegradables: Seven Diary Fragments." Translated by Peggy Kamuf. *Critical Inquiry*, 15:4 (1989): 812–73.

_____. *Dissemination.* Translated by Barbara Johnson. Chicago: University of Chicago Press, 1981.

_____. "The Double Session." In *Dissemination*, translated by Barbara Johnson, 173–286. Chicago: University of Chicago Press, 1981.

_____. "The Future of the Profession; or, The Unconditional University." In *Derrida Downunder: Deconstructing (in) the Antipodes*, edited by Laurence Simmons and Heather Worth, 233–247. Palmerston, New Zealand: Dunmore Press, 2001.

_____. *The Gift of Death.* Translated by David Wills. Chicago: University of Chicago Press, 1995.

_____. *Glas.* Translated by John P. Leavey Jr. and Richard Rend. Lincoln: University of Nebraska Press.

_____. "*Ja,* or, the *faux-bond* II." In *Points . . . : Interviews, 1974–1994,* translated by Peggy Kamuf et al., 30–77. Edited by Elizabeth Weber. Stanford: Stanford University Press, 1995.

_____. *Margins of Philosophy.* Translated by Alan Bass. Chicago: University of Chicago Press, 1982.

_____. *Monolingualism of the Other; or, The Prosthesis of Origin.* Translated by Patrick Mensah. Stanford: Stanford University Press, 1998.

_____. *Of Grammatology.* Translated by Gayatri Chakravorty Spivak. Baltimore: The Johns Hopkins University Press, 1975.

_____. *On the Name.* Edited by Thomas Dutoit. Stanford: Stanford University Press, 1995.

_____. *The Other Heading: Reflections on Today's Europe.* Translated by Pascale-Anne Brault and Michael B. Naas. Introduction by Michael B. Naas. Bloomington: University of Indiana Press, 1992.

_____. "Outwork: Prefacing." In *Dissemination*, translated by Barbara Johnson, 1–59. Chicago: University of Chicago Press, 1981.

_____. *Points . . . : Interviews, 1974–1994.* Translated by Peggy Kamuf et al. Edited by Elizabeth Weber. Stanford: Stanford University Press, 1995.

_____. *Positions.* Translated by Alan Bass. Chicago: University of Chicago Press, 1981.

_____. *The Post Card: From Socrates to Freud and Beyond.* Translated by Alan Bass. Chicago: University of Chicago Press, 1987.

_____. "Two Words for Joyce." Translated by Geoff Bennington. In *Post-Structuralist Joyce: Essays from the French,* edited by Derek Attridge and Daniel Ferrer, 145–61. Cambridge: Cambridge University Press, 1984.

_____. "The University without Condition." In *Without Alibi,* translated, edited, and introduced by Peggy Kamuf, 202–37. Stanford: Stanford University Press, 2002.

_____. *Who's Afraid of Philosophy? Right to Philosophy I.* Translated by Jan Plug. Stanford: Stanford University Press, 2002.

Dickens, Charles. *Bleak House.* Edited with an introduction by Nicola Bradbury. London: Penguin, 1996.

Duras, Marguerite. *La douleur.* Paris: Gallimard, 1993.

Forché, Carolyn, ed. *Against Forgetting: Twentieth-Century Poetry of Witness.* New York: Norton, 1993.

Foucault, Michel. "The Order of Discourse." Translated by Ian McLeod. In *Untying the Text: A Post-Structuralist Reader,* edited by Robert Young, 51–78. London: Routledge and Kegan Paul, 1981.

Gasché, Rodolphe. *The Wild Card of Reading: On Paul de Man.* Cambridge, Mass.: Harvard University Press, 1998.

Gramsci, Antonio. *Prison Notebooks.* 2 vols. Translated by Joseph A. Buttigieg and Antonio Callari. Edited with introduction by Joseph A. Buttigieg. European Perspectives. New York: Columbia University Press, 1992.

Hamacher, Werner. "Où, séance, touche de Nancy." Translated by Ian H. Mageden. *Paragraph* 7, no. 2 (July 1994): 103–19.

_____. *Pleroma: Reading in Hegel.* Translated by David Walker and Simon Jarvis. Stanford: Stanford University Press, 1998.

Hart, Kevin. *The Trespass of the Sign: Deconstruction, Theology, and Philosophy.* Cambridge: Cambridge University Press, 1989.

James, Henry. *The Portrait of a Lady.* Introduction by Graham Greene. Oxford: Oxford University Press, 1981.

Jay, Martin. *Cultural Semantics.* London: Athlone Press, 1997.

Johnson, Barbara. *The Critical Difference: Essays in the Contemporary Rhetoric of Reading.* Baltimore: The Johns Hopkins University Press, 1985.

Kafka, Franz. *The Trial.* Translated by Breon Mitchell. New York: Schocken Books, 1998.

Miller, J. Hillis. "Paul de Man as Allergen." *In Material Events: Paul de Man and the Afterlife of Theory,* edited by Tom Cohen et al., 183–204. Minneapolis: University of Minnesota Press, 2001.

Nancy, Jean-Luc. *Birth to Presence.* Translated by Brian Holmes et al. Stanford: Stanford University Press, 1993.

Nietzsche, Friedrich. *The Gay Science.* Translated by Walter Kaufmann. New York: Vintage, 1974.

_____. *Thus Spoke Zarathustra.* Translated by Walter Kaufmann. New York: Penguin, 1976.

Pinsky, Robert. "Door." *New Yorker,* April 2, 2001, p. 64.

Plotnitsky, Arkady. *The Knowable and the Unknowable: Modern Science, Nonclassical Thought, and the "Two Cultures."* Ann Arbor: University of Michigan Press, 2002.

———. "Reading Bohr: Complementarity, Epistemology, Entanglement, and Decoherence." In *Decoherence and Its Implications in Quantum Computation and Information Transfer,* edited by Tony Gonis and Patrice E. A. Turchi. n.p. NATO Science Series. Amsterdam: IOS Press, 1991.

Readings, Bill. *The University in Ruins.* Cambridge, Mass.: Harvard University Press, 1996.

Ronell, Avital. *Crack Wars: Literature, Addiction, Mania.* Lincoln: University of Nebraska Press, 1992.

———. *Dictations: On Haunted Writing.* Lincoln: University of Nebraska Press, 1986.

———. *Finitude's Score: Essays for the End of the Millennium.* Lincoln: University of Nebraska Press, 1994.

———. *Stupidity.* Urbana: University of Illinois Press, 2002.

———. *The Telephone Book: Technology, Schizophrenia, Electric Speech.* Lincoln: University of Nebraska Press, 1989.

Royle, Nicholas. "Night Writing: Deconstruction Reading Politics." In *The Uncanny,* 112–32. New York: Manchester University Press, 2003.

———. *Telepathy and Literature: Essays on the Reading Mind.* Oxford: Blackwell, 1990.

———. *The Uncanny.* New York: Manchester University Press, 2002.

———. "The Uncanny: An Introduction." In *The Uncanny,* 1–38. New York: Manchester University Press, 2002.

Saussure, Ferdinand de. *Course in General Linguistics.* Int. Jonathan Culler. Trans. Wade Baskin. Ed. Charles Bally and Albert Sechehaye, in collaboration with Albert Reidlinger. London: Fontana/Collins, 1981.

Schlegel, Friedrich von. *Lucinda and the Fragments.* Translated by Peter Firchow. Minneapolis: University of Minnesota Press, 1971.

Simmons, Laurence, and Heather Worth, eds. *Derrida Downunder: Deconstructing (in) the Antipodes.* Palmerston, New Zealand: Dunmore Press, 2001.

Weber, Elizabeth. "Introduction: Upside-Down Writing." In Jacques Derrida, *Points . . . : Interviews, 1974–1994,* translated by Peggy Kamuf et al., 1–4. Edited by Elizabeth Weber. Stanford: Stanford University Press, 1995.

Index

Guattari, Félix, 75, 76–77, 82, 85. *See also* Gilles Deleuze
What is Philosophy? 85
Gulf War, the, 45, 55, 66

Hall, Stuart, 105
Hamacher, Werner, 65, 84
Haunting, 1, 10, 46–47, 48, 64–65, 172, 176
H.D., 107
Hegel, G. W. F., 35, 60, 73, 77, 79, 82, 138, 170, 174, 175
The Phenomenology of Spirit, 77
Heidegger, Martin, 10, 28, 37, 38–39, 46, 49, 53, 55, 64, 73, 77, 114, 116, 170, 175, 177
Being and Time, 175, 177
Heisenberg, Werner, 71, 83, 87
Heraclitus, 77
Hermeneutics, 119–20, 121, 122, 166
Heuretics, 125
Heuretics (Gregory W. Ulmer, 136)
HIV/AIDS, 66
Hölderlin, Friedrich, 41, 48, 73, 177
Homer, 77
Homoeroticism, 17
Homosexuality, 16–17
Human, the, 11–12, 17, 45, 120, 178
Humanism, 44–45, 46, 56, 151
Humanities, the, 11, 20, 23, 24, 68, 70, 71, 72, 74, 78, 81, 82, 104, 106, 121
Husserl, Edmund, 154–55
Hypertext, 43–44

Internet, the, 22, 24, 26, 129
Interview, the, 25–26, 27, 30, 91, 92, 171
Iraq, 36
Irigaray, Luce, 71, 76, 120
Irvine, University of California, 150
Islam, 122, 154
Iterability, 23–24, 82

James, Henry, 49, 152, 158, 159
The Awkward Age, 152
The Portrait of a Lady, 159
Jameson, Fredric, 53
Jay, Martin, 10

Johns Hopkins University, 148, 149, 150
Johnson, Barbara, 107, 109
Johnson, Samuel, 116, 150
Joyce, James, 7, 53
Judaism, 154
Juno, Andrea, 34, 35, 58
Justice, xx

Kafka, Franz, 9, 33, 82, 98
The Penal Colony, 98
The Trial, 98
Kamuf, Peggy, 1, 3, 4, 9
Kant, Immanuel, 50, 73, 77, 79, 81, 82, 114, 158, 175–76
Keats, John, 163
Kermode, Frank, 160, 161
Kierkegaard, Søren, 35, 153–54, 157, 160, 177
Fear and Trembling, 153–54
Kleist, Heinrich von, 34, 79, 82
Knowable and the Unknowable, the, 71
Kristeva, Julia, 10
Kuhn, Thomas S., 72

Lacan, Jacques, 10, 62, 64, 71, 72, 73, 87, 107
Landow, George, 43
Laurence, Andrew, 42
Law, xx, 56
Leibniz, Gottfried Wilhelm, 77, 170
Levinas, Emmanuel, 13, 16, 21, 56, 71, 87
Literary Theory (Jonathan Culler), 106, 107
Lyotard, Jean–François, 54, 63, 71, 73
Différend, the, 63

Mallarmé, Stéphane, 69, 177
Marx, Karl, 49
McEwan, Indra Kagis, 142
Mealworm, Stephanie, 69
Merleau-Ponty, Maurice, 177
MFA (Master of Fine Arts), 74
Miller, J. Hillis, 1; "Paul de Man as Allergen," 147
MLA (Modern Language Association), 4–5

Perspectives in Continental Philosophy
John D. Caputo, series editor